How Health Care Can Be Cost-Effective and Fair

POPULATION-LEVEL BIOETHICS
Ethics and the Public's Health

Series Editors
Rutgers School of Public Health
Daniel, Harvard School of Public Health

Editorial Board
Dan Brock, Harvard University
John Broome, Oxford University
Norman Daniels, Harvard University
Marc Fleurbaey, Princeton University
Julio Frenk, Harvard University
Daniel M. Hausman, Rutgers University
Frances Kamm, Rutgers University
Michael Marmot, University College, London
Christopher Murray, Institute for Health Metrics and Evaluation,
University of Washington
Amartya Sen, Harvard University

VOLUMES IN THE SERIES

Inequalities in Health: Concepts, Measures, and Ethics
Edited by Nir Eyal, Samia A. Hurst, Ole F. Norheim, and Dan Wikler

Valuing Health: Well-Being, Freedom, and Suffering
Daniel M. Hausman

Identified Versus Statistical Lives: An Interdisciplinary Perspective
Edited by I. Glenn Cohen, Norman Daniels, and Nir Eyal

Saving People from the Harm of Death
Edited by Espen Gamlund and Carl Tollef Solberg
Foreword by Jeff McMahan

Measuring the Global Burden of Disease
Edited by Nir Eyal, Samia A. Hurst, Christopher J. L. Murray, S. Andrew Schroeder,
and Daniel Wikler

How Health Care Can Be Cost-Effective and Fair
Daniel M. Hausman

How Health Care Can Be Cost-Effective and Fair

DANIEL M. HAUSMAN

Center for Population-Level Bioethics

Rutgers University

OXFORD
UNIVERSITY PRESS

Oxford University Press is a department of the University of Oxford. It furthers the University's objective of excellence in research, scholarship, and education by publishing worldwide. Oxford is a registered trade mark of Oxford University Press in the UK and certain other countries.

Published in the United States of America by Oxford University Press
198 Madison Avenue, New York, NY 10016, United States of America.

© Oxford University Press 2023

All rights reserved. No part of this publication may be reproduced, stored in a retrieval system, or transmitted, in any form or by any means, without the prior permission in writing of Oxford University Press, or as expressly permitted by law, by license, or under terms agreed with the appropriate reproduction rights organization. Inquiries concerning reproduction outside the scope of the above should be sent to the Rights Department, Oxford University Press, at the address above.

You must not circulate this work in any other form
and you must impose this same condition on any acquirer.

Library of Congress Cataloging-in-Publication Data
Names: Hausman, Daniel M., 1947– author.
Title: How health care can be cost-effective and fair / Daniel M. Hausman.
Other titles: Population level bioethics series.
Description: New York, NY : Oxford University Press, [2023] |
Series: Population level bioethics |
Includes bibliographical references and index.
Identifiers: LCCN 2022034997 (print) | LCCN 2022034998 (ebook) |
ISBN 9780197656969 (hardback) | ISBN 9780197656983 (epub) |
ISBN 9780197656990 (online)
Subjects: MESH: Health Resources | Cost-Benefit Analysis | Health Care Rationing
Classification: LCC RA410.5 (print) | LCC RA410.5 (ebook) | NLM W 74.1 |
DDC 362.1068/1—dc23/eng/20220919
LC record available at https://lccn.loc.gov/2022034997
LC ebook record available at https://lccn.loc.gov/2022034998

DOI: 10.1093/oso/9780197656969.001.0001

This material is not intended to be, and should not be considered, a substitute for medical or other professional advice. Treatment for the conditions described in this material is highly dependent on the individual circumstances. And, while this material is designed to offer accurate information with respect to the subject matter covered and to be current as of the time it was written, research and knowledge about medical and health issues is constantly evolving and dose schedules for medications are being revised continually, with new side effects recognized and accounted for regularly. Readers must therefore always check the product information and clinical procedures with the most up-to-date published product information and data sheets provided by the manufacturers and the most recent codes of conduct and safety regulation. The publisher and the authors make no representations or warranties to readers, express or implied, as to the accuracy or completeness of this material. Without limiting the foregoing, the publisher and the authors make no representations or warranties as to the accuracy or efficacy of the drug dosages mentioned in the material. The authors and the publisher do not accept, and expressly disclaim, any responsibility for any liability, loss, or risk that may be claimed or incurred as a consequence of the use and/ or application of any of the contents of this material.

1 3 5 7 9 8 6 4 2
Printed by Integrated Books International, United States of America

Contents

Introduction ... 1

1. Measuring Health and the "Effectiveness" of Health Care ... 9
   1.1 The Need for Health Care Policy ... 9
   1.2 What Is "Health"? ... 12
   1.3 Health Comparisons ... 15
   1.4 Generic Health Measurement and the EQ-5D ... 17
   1.5 Problems with Quality Weights ... 19
   1.6 Why Measure the Value of Health States? ... 21
   1.7 Conclusion ... 23

2. Cost-Effectiveness, Well-Being, and Freedom ... 24
   2.1 C-E Allocation: Why Do It? ... 24
   2.2 Cost-Effectiveness: A First Look ... 25
   2.3 Cost-Effectiveness and Opportunity Cost ... 28
   2.4 Incremental Cost-Effectiveness and Opportunity Cost ... 30
   2.5 Conclusion: The Attractions of Cost-Effectiveness ... 33

3. Conceptual, Technical, and Ethical Problems with Cost-Effectiveness ... 35
   3.1 Personal and Public Values ... 35
   3.2 Social Values of Health Improvements ... 41
   3.3 Discounting ... 46
   3.4 Age Weighting ... 50
   3.5 Is Allocation by Cost-Effectiveness Fair? ... 51
       3.5.1 How Might C-E Allocation Be Unfair? Discrimination ... 53
       3.5.2 How Might C-E Allocation Be Unfair? The "Fair Chances" Complaint ... 53
       3.5.3 How Might C-E Allocation Be Unfair? The Severity Complaint ... 56
       3.5.4 How Might C-E Allocation Be Unfair? Against Additive Aggregation ... 57
       3.5.5 Summary: The Fairness Challenges to C-E Allocation ... 59
   3.6 Conclusion and Additional Qualms About the Fairness of C-E Allocation ... 60

4. Theories of Fair Distribution ... 62
   4.1 Suggestive Visions of Fairness ... 64
   4.2 Problems of Fair Distribution ... 67

- 4.3 Assigning Distributive Shares — 69
  - 4.3.1 Cooperative Game Theory and Fairness: The Nucleolus — 70
  - 4.3.2 Fairness and Cooperative Game Theory: The Shapley Value — 72
- 4.4 Broome's Theory: Divisible Goods — 75
- 4.5 Broome's Theory: Indivisible Goods — 78
- 4.6 Challenges to Broome's Theory — 84
- 4.7 Fairness When Claims Differ Both in Size and in Strength — 88
- 4.8 Other Theories of Fair Distribution — 91
  - 4.8.1 Larry Temkin: Fairness, Desert, and Equality — 91
  - 4.8.2 Matthew Adler: Fairness and Social Welfare Functions — 93
- 4.9 Conclusion — 96

5. What Is a Fair Allocation of Health Care? — 98
   - 5.1 Claims to Health Care — 98
   - 5.2 Satisfying Health Care Claims Proportionately — 101
   - 5.3 Fairness and Equal Access — 105
   - 5.4 Fairness and Costs — 106
   - 5.5 Access and Heterogeneity — 108
   - 5.6 Conclusion — 109

6. Fair Chances — 111
   - 6.1 Formulating the Fair Chances Objection — 111
   - 6.2 Another View of Fairness — 112
   - 6.3 Epidemic — 114
   - 6.4 The Lottery Backstory — 116
   - 6.5 Satisfying Procedural Claims — 119
   - 6.6 "Natural Lotteries" and Fair Chances — 122
   - 6.7 Is It Fair to Give M Only to Those Who Need Only One Dose? — 125
   - 6.8 Conclusion — 126

7. Does Cost-Effectiveness Fail to Give Sufficient Priority to Severity? — 131
   - 7.1 Measuring Severity: Who Is Worse Off? — 132
   - 7.2 Survey Results: Priority to Those Who Are More Severely Ill — 135
   - 7.3 Implementing Priority for Severity — 140
   - 7.4 Chronic Severity, Prioritarianism, and Egalitarianism — 144
   - 7.5 Compassion, Solidarity, and Severity — 150
   - 7.6 Conclusion — 151

8. To Aggregate or Not to Aggregate — 154
   - 8.1 Why Not Aggregate? — 156
   - 8.2 Partial Aggregation — 159
   - 8.3 Some Surmountable Challenges for Partial Aggregation — 164
   - 8.4 Against Partial Aggregation of Health Care: All Claims to Health Care Are Relevant — 167
     - 8.4.1 Small Probabilities of Large Benefits — 168

   8.4.2 Small Benefits and Risks of Major Harms   173
   8.4.3 Implausible Implications for Health Care   174
 8.5 Aggregation Without Aggravation   175
 8.6 Conclusion   177

9. Discrimination   178
 9.1 C-E Allocation and Three Kinds of Objectionable Discrimination   178
 9.2 When Is Discrimination Wrong?   181
 9.3 Valuing Life Extension   184
 9.4 Avoiding Wrongful Discrimination   189
 9.5 Conclusion   191

10. Health Care: Respectful, Cost-Effective, and Fair   193
 10.1 The Structure of the Health Care System: Universal Health Care   193
 10.2 Health Care and Health Insurance: Problems with Markets   196
 10.3 What Principles Should Determine Which Treatments Universal Health Care Covers?   204
 10.4 Is C-E Allocation Unfair?   206
   10.4.1 Fair Chances   209
   10.4.2 Severity   209
   10.4.3 Aggregation   210
   10.4.4 Discrimination   210
   10.4.5 Other Qualms about Cost-Effectiveness   212
 10.5 Conclusions on Fairness in Health Care   213
 10.6 Concluding Words   215

Acknowledgments and Sources   217
References   221
Index   237

Introduction

The provision of health care has always been an important part of human communities because it is a central part of the caring for one another that makes us a social species. Through most of human history, health care has been little more than providing comfort and acceptance to the ailing, and that comfort and acceptance are not to be despised. One of the horrors of dying from COVID-19 has been the isolation of the gravely ill from their closest relations.

Nowadays, health care, even in the poorest nations, has far more to offer the ill than a hug, a prayer, and a receptive ear, but this efficacy comes at a high cost—more than 10% of the national income in most affluent societies. Both the efficacy of health care and its cost make it very important that its provision be efficient and just. Health care contributes not only to health but also to prosperity, social solidarity, individual dignity, autonomy, and financial security.

Because modern health care experts such an important influence on what people can do and whether they will flourish or suffer, it is crucial that it be distributed in an ethically acceptable way. Getting the distribution of health care wrong may impoverish, humiliate, torment, and kill people. In order to assess the distribution of health care, policymakers need to know how health care systems function, and they need theories predicting the consequences of as yet untried policies. Economic analysis is crucial to moral appraisal: As such a large part of the economy, health care needs to be efficient. To make health care efficient, many economists have argued for relying on cost-effectiveness information to allocate health-related resources among alternative uses. On the other hand, many critics have argued that it is unfair to allow considerations of cost-effectiveness to guide allocation.

How should health-related resources be distributed? What principles should govern at a macro level a health care system or health care *policies*? This book offers a partial answer to this large and difficult question. By a health care system, I mean the policies and institutions that determine access to health care. I am not concerned in this book with micro-level "bedside" ethical questions concerning the application of health care policies to individuals. For example, this book is concerned with principles that determine whether and on what terms a health care system makes heart bypass surgery available, not whether a particular patient is eligible. One might think of this book as a foray into "administrative ethics"—that is, the principles that should govern the decision-making of legislators and administrators and their interactions with the people whom they represent and serve. In their dealings with one another, individuals encounter different constraints on their moral deliberations. Individuals can sometimes favor friends and relatives in a way that would be clearly impermissible for administrators. On the other hand, individuals often must abide by rules that administrators can change. Administrators will often have better knowledge of the social consequences of social practices, whereas individuals have far more detailed information concerning particular people and their circumstances. The actions of individuals, unlike those of administrators, may be private and without wider consequences. One should not be surprised to discover that somewhat different principles apply to individuals than to administrators, such as those responsible for constructing and regulating a health care system.

Much of what I shall say can be applied more generally to public health policies and institutions (Dawson 2011). However, in focusing only on health care, this book is already long and intricate, and the "care" of individuals in "health care" matters to its argument. For the purposes of compact expression, I often refer to health care as "treatment," but I do not mean to exclude prevention, protection, informing, and giving comfort, which are essential aspects of health care. Substituting "treatment, prevention, informing, and caring" for "treatment" would have made the discussion tedious.

Just about everyone agrees that health care should be compassionate, respectful, and fair to individuals. It should be responsive to their values and choices, and it should allocate resources in a way that makes people better off and better able to guide their own lives. However, agreement at this level of abstraction masks underlying disagreements. For example, consider a decision in a middle-income country whether to use a portion of the health budget to pay for dialysis for individuals whose kidney function is below a certain level. Is doing so required by benevolence? Is it unfair to say "no"? Does saying "no" properly respect the values of individuals? Does providing dialysis produce more good than using the resources in other ways? Would it be unfair not to provide dialysis? Because there are disagreements about relevant ethical criteria such as compassion, fairness, choice, and benevolence, it is not surprising that their applications to health care are contested, too.

One might hope to find in this book an algorithm that incorporates most of the relevant ethical considerations and thus can output an ethically acceptable policy choice for any specification of the relevant facts about any given society. This algorithmic aspiration is untenable. Even if it were possible to make each of the relevant ethical considerations precise, there is no plausible general specification of the trade-offs between them (Bognar and Hirose 2014). For example, coping with the COVID-19 pandemic by writing off the lives of the elderly and otherwise vulnerable would be very "efficient": It would ultimately result in a healthier population and much less economic disruption than the steps employed to slow the disease's spread. Such a policy, which I am certainly not endorsing, would be egregiously unfair. In this case, fairness trumps efficiency at promoting health and well-being.

Fairness is not always trumps. It is not the ultimate value. If there is not enough of a life-saving medicine to treat everyone who needs it, it might be fairest not to give it to anyone, but that would be out of the question. Efficiency sometimes outweighs fairness. Compassion may sometimes outweigh both efficiency and fairness. Rather than arguing for some algorithm that properly prioritizes each of the relevant ethical considerations that ought to govern a health care system, I argue that several different principles, which may conflict with one another, should govern policies. I defend a large role for "consequentialist" considerations—that is, judging policies by their aggregate consequences—but I do not think that these considerations always take precedence. If only one standard is applicable or there is a clear priority among the relevant considerations, then the principles pick out the best policy. Unfortunately, there will be many cases in which standards conflict and there are no clear priorities. In those cases, the best fallback is to rely on appropriately structured representative political processes to decide (Daniels and Sabin 2002).

Although the book focuses on the moral principles that should govern the allocation of health care, I briefly discuss in Chapter 10 the policies and institutions that conform to those principles. The principles do not pick out any single best implementation, and this book offers no detailed blueprint for an ethically ideal health care system. Although there are decisive arguments against relying on unregulated health insurance and health care markets, heavily regulated markets are one attractive way to implement an ethically acceptable health care system. Until Chapter 10, I shall for simplicity treat the allocation of health care as if it were determined by the provision of a state-run non-market universal health care system. However, nothing in this book rules out private insurance and medical practice.

How the nation's income is allocated bears heavily on people's well-being and opportunity, and expenditures by many different branches of government as well as by individuals influence population health. The amount devoted to health care can simply fall out of other choices such as whether to build a new bomb, new schools, or expand a hospital. Alternatively, it would be possible, although arbitrary, to allow some prespecified cost-effectiveness threshold to determine the health care budget. However, I suppose that the health care budget is set by a separate adjudication of the claims of the many branches of government. The "effectiveness" in "cost-effectiveness" is a measure exclusively of improvement in health or health-related well-being and hence not a measure that compares the benefits of health to the benefits of education, housing, or the air force. An ideal determination of the health care budget weighs the possible benefits of alternative allocations of national income among all the private and public uses of that income in terms of all relevant ethical criteria. Even the mere specification of the task is enormously complicated.

In reality, shares of the resources available for government allocation are determined by a political struggle among advocates for different uses, and total allocations are also affected by people's consumption choices. These choices can be shaped by taxes, subsidies, and many means of persuasion, but policymakers are often happy to leave the choice with individuals. Doing so often enhances both efficiency and freedom, but individual choice is no panacea. Chapter 10 explains the drawbacks of allowing individual health insurance purchases to determine the allocation of health care. Leaving many of these complexities in the background, I take the health care budget to be predetermined. The question this book is concerned with is how to distribute this budget among alternative treatments in the ethically best way, and in particular it is a defense of cost-effectiveness as one very useful guide to the allocation of health-related resources. By a guide, I mean one relevant ethical consideration among several. I do not mean and do not believe that cost-effectiveness should be the only consideration guiding the distribution of health care. The ethical best distribution will instead be a compromise among different values. Although it takes the health care budget as given, this book's ambitions are still large. It defends relying heavily on cost-effectiveness to allocate health care while at the same time this book is critical of its measures of effectiveness.

Health care is important to individuals in two main ways: It helps people avoid pain and distress, and it helps them make choices and carry out the actions they choose. It does most of these things by its contribution to health, which is both good in itself and instrumental to most of the objectives of individuals. Health makes choice both possible and effective, and it frees us from health-related pain and anguish. Health does not free us from distress caused by the failure of plans, the ending of friendships, disappointments in love, or the death of those whom we care about, but it enables the healing of the distress that is present within even the best lives. Due to the importance of health, several ethical considerations are relevant to its allocation. Two of these—well-being and "choice" (i.e., freedom, opportunity, and autonomy or self-determination)—encompass most of the ways in which health care directly benefits individuals.

Health care is not just a matter of preventing and treating disease. We do that for cattle and chickens, too. How we organize health care reflects and partly constitutes the character of social relations in our societies. Concerns about justice, human dignity, and the respect we owe to others and ourselves place constraints on how a health care system promotes the interests and the freedoms of individuals. If one aspires, as I do, to a society of equals, a society without second-class citizens, it is of great importance that health care manifest respect and concern for everyone.

It is nevertheless helpful to distinguish between the goals of health care—what we want health care to do for us—and the ethical considerations that should guide the pursuit of those goals. Although being treated unfairly is harmful to those who get the short end of the stick, treating people fairly is not one of the purposes of health care. A health care system should manifest the virtues of justice, fairness, and respect while promoting its goals of protecting choice and making people better off.

One of the central goals of health care is the protection and enhancement of individual flourishing. Health care enhances individual well-being by alleviating fear, pain, and other distress; by bolstering abilities; and by facilitating actions and relations that make people's lives worth living. It saves lives and enables individuals to address their needs and desires and the needs and desires of others. The benevolent intentions of health care are manifested both in the care it provides and, more painfully, in refusals to provide care so as to husband resources for more urgent needs. When economists and others speak about the efficiency of a health care policy or institution, they are thinking about whether it is contributing as much as it can to the well-being of individuals with the resources it has at its disposal. The general value of benevolence thus maps on to the specific values of compassion and efficiency with respect to making people better off.

The protection and enhancement of freedom or choice—that is, individuals' abilities to direct their lives—is a second objective of health care that may not always be distinguished from the first. Health care can expand choice by increasing opportunity; by loosening constraints; and by enhancing, protecting, or restoring abilities to make choices and to carry out what one has chosen to do. Whether or not restoring an injured veteran's ability to walk makes the veteran better off, it expands the range of activities among which the veteran can choose. Who knows how rich a life the veteran would have if their ability to walk were never restored? There is no need to answer or even to raise that question to know that there are a wider range of pursuits open to those who can walk. Improving health thus promotes choice as well as well-being. *How* health care is provided also affects freedom: If health care is cheaper, individuals can choose to work less. If it is provided to all, more individuals can take greater risks. The libertarian and the utilitarian both want greater efficiency in health care—one to expand freedom, the other to enhance well-being.

One might question whether there are two aims here. Isn't expanding choice simply one way of enhancing well-being? If one regards whatever is in any way beneficial to an individual as enhancing the individual's well-being, then unless expanding choice is not good for people, it enhances well-being. So, one might argue, one leaves nothing out by maintaining that the benefits of health care lie exclusively in enhancing well-being.

This conclusion is misleading. Of course, choice or justice typically contribute to well-being and are valuable because of that contribution. But does their contribution to well-being exhaust their value? Is it possible that freedom and well-being might compete? These are substantive questions, which are not settled by stipulating that well-being comprises whatever is good for an individual. On any account of well-being that gives it specific content, such as the view that well-being is happiness, choice (or justice or equality) may have value other than via its contribution to well-being.

It is possible to think of justice, fairness, and showing respect as additional objectives for a health system, but they are not individual benefits of health care on a par with improvements in well-being or expansions of freedom. The aim of health care is to make people better off and to expand what they can do, not to enhance justice and show respect. In the course of enhancing well-being and freedom, we want health care to be just, respectful, compassionate, and fair—just as we want education and the legal system to be fair, just, and respectful. Fairness is not what we have health care *for*. Health care arrangements affect the texture of a society, the extent to which individuals identify with one another, and the extent to which the institutions of a society manifest an equal concern with the fates of all those who reside within it. Justice in health care is thus both an indication of overall justice and a contribution to it.[1] Justice also bears crucially on *how fairly* a health care system goes about enhancing opportunity and promoting health and well-being, and it is in that regard that I mainly assess the justice of health care.

The relevant concerns about justice in the promotion of flourishing and freedom by means of health care are in part concerns about fairness. A segregated health care system that limits African Americans to substandard segregated hospitals is unjust and, intuitively, *unfair*. On the other hand, a doctor who indiscriminately does unnecessary blood tests on her patients for her own profit intentionally violates her patients' rights to bodily integrity and behaves unjustly, but if she treats all her patients in the same way, then, arguably, she does not treat her patients unfairly.[2] I focus on matters of *comparative* justice, which are also matters of fairness. It is more natural to consider the importance of fairness to lie in *how* the health care system distributes the benefits (to well-being and choice)

---

[1] One might also regard some illnesses as unjust inflictions on innocent individuals that health care alleviates. But it is questionable whether there is anything *unjust* about becoming ill, and in any case, health care is not conditional on appraisals of the justice or injustice of different afflictions.

[2] When my dissertation advisor, Sydney Morgenbesser, was called for jury duty in a police brutality case, he was asked whether he had ever been treated unfairly by the police. He answered that during demonstrations at Columbia University, he was hit over the head, but that it was perfectly fair because the police were hitting everyone over the head.

that health improvements bring rather than an as additional good that health care brings. Fairness is a matter of how the goods of health care are distributed. There are many putative cases in which an allocation of health care may be unfair even though it succeeds in enhancing well-being or freedom. Much of this book is concerned with diagnosing, dispelling, and resolving conflicts between fairness, on the one hand, and expanding welfare and freedom, on the other hand.

Although there are well-defined ways in which the allocation of health care may be unfair, such as providing substandard care to racial minorities, the many insights philosophers have had concerning fairness and especially unfairness do not boil down to a systematic theory of fair health care. A perusal of the literature finds no satisfactory specification of what constitutes fair health care (Pereira 1993). For example, Anthony Culyer (2001) maintains that the distribution of health care is fully equitable if and only if it equalizes health. This claim links the ethical appraisal of the allocation of health care to the resulting distribution of health, because the main (but not the sole) point of health care is protecting and improving health. But Culyer's view provides little guidance without some specification of what it is for the members of a population to be equally healthy, when some are older than others, enjoy different diets, engage in different activities, live in different environments, suffer different injuries, and so forth. Moreover, it is doubtful whether equality in health should be an objective for health policy. Suppose that (contrary to fact) the poor and socially excluded were healthier, perhaps because they are unable to afford the excess calories that have made the rich obese and sickly, despite their access to better health care. In that state of affairs, shifting additional health care resources to the rich would not make health care more equitable (Hausman 2007; Temkin 2016, pp. 284–285).

In their intricate and insightful essay, "Equity in Health and Health Care", Marc Fleurbaey and Erik Schokkaert (2012) tackle the problem of specifying what constitutes fair health care by formulating measures of equity in health and in health care that depend on the source of inequalities. First, they set aside inequalities that cannot be addressed by policies, such as inequalities due to age or incurable disease. Among remediable health deficiencies, they regard inequalities that derive from genuinely free choice as fair, whereas inequalities in health that are due to factors such as race, religion, or social status are typically unfair. In Fleurbaey and Schokkaert's view, *health care* (as opposed to health) is allocated fairly when all differences in its consumption derive from differences in needs for health care and free choices (p. 1035).

Julian Le Grand (1987) allows irremediable health deficiencies to count as fair or unfair, but his view is otherwise similar, "if an individual's ill health results from factors beyond his or her control then the situation is inequitable; if it results from factors within his or her control then it is equitable" (p. 267). Positively, Le Grand thinks that justice requires that health depend on choice. Negatively,

Le Grand maintains that factors beyond an individual's control should have no effect on health. Note that Le Grand's account, like that of Fleurbaey and Schokkaert (2012), says nothing about the fair way to allow costs to influence access to health care. Neither account considers explicitly when it is fair to refuse to provide care, owing to its expense, even if the care addresses urgent and important needs.

Another view of fair health care relies on cost-effectiveness. I know of no one who has made this suggestion explicitly, and it might seem ironic, given how often reliance on cost-effectiveness has been condemned as unfair. Nevertheless, one way to articulate a notion of equal treatment of individuals with wildly different and changing needs, which compete for resources, would be to maintain that individuals should have equal access to all treatments that respond to their needs that are at least as cost-effective as some threshold value. This conception of fair health care is explored in Chapter 5.

Alternatively, one can conclude correctly that whether health care is fair depends on how well its allocation responds to health care needs, on whether it is appropriately sensitive to costs, and on whether it is insensitive to factors that ought to be irrelevant. Although in my view correct, this generalization is disappointingly vague. Allocating health care by its cost-effectiveness appears to conform to it, but the devil is in the details that the chapters of this book examine.

1
Measuring Health and the "Effectiveness" of Health Care

This chapter lays the groundwork for the discussion in Chapter 2 of how cost-effectiveness information can be used to guide the allocation of health resources.[1] Accordingly, this chapter aims to accomplish the following:

1. Provide a rationale for health care policy that focuses mainly on improving health
2. Explain what a *health improvement* is and how health improvements can be measured
3. Raise questions about the accuracy and precision of measurements of health improvements

Because the cost-effectiveness of health care policies presupposes measurement of the health improvements resulting from those policies, it is critical to comprehending and appraising allocation by cost-effectiveness that one grasp how health improvements are conceptualized and measured. This chapter aims to provide that grasp.

1.1 The Need for Health Care Policy

Progress in medical science has made health care virtually indispensable to living well. Although there are lucky individuals who are never ill and die peacefully in their sleep, they benefit from the dramatic decline in infectious diseases that

---

[1] What I am calling "cost-effectiveness analysis" is sometimes called instead "cost-value analysis" or "cost-utility analysis" by those who want to use the cost-effectiveness terminology for comparisons of treatments of the same specific health problems. For example, Pinkerton et al. write, "Analyses that use QALYs [quality-adjusted life years] to quantify effectiveness are known as cost-utility analyses" (2002, p. 75). When health policies address different health problems, some commentators would prefer to ask which of the policies has the best cost/value ratio rather than asking whether one health policy is more cost-effective than another. These verbal complications are aggravated by Erik Nord's (1999) very reasonable proposal to use the language of "cost-value analysis" to refer to evaluations of alternative policies with respect to the ratio of cost to the "social value" (as opposed to the individual benefit) of the health care policy. In Nord's terminology, the social value depends on both individual benefit and considerations of fairness.

medicine and public health measures have engineered. Access to health care is a modern necessity, but much of it is too expensive for individuals to provide for themselves. Affluent countries devote 10% or more of gross domestic product to health care (nearly 20% in the United States).[2] Because the need for health care is sometimes not only expensive to satisfy but also urgent and unpredictable, individuals need health insurance. However, unregulated insurance markets cannot meet the need for health care. The poor cannot afford the premiums; neither can those with preexisting conditions. If individuals are free to purchase insurance or remain uninsured as they choose, what happens when the uninsured have a heart attack or are injured in an automobile accident and arrive unconscious in the emergency room? As I argue at greater length in Chapter 10, relying on unregulated health insurance and health care markets is ruled out by benevolence and by concerns about opportunity and fairness. If, as I assume, one is committed to these values and insists that everyone should have access to a wide range of health care, then there is no way to avoid having to choose among health care policies. An ethical choice should promote health and well-being and enhance freedom, and it should do so fairly. Government must concern itself with access to health care.

Public policy is concerned with many things other than health, such as education, transportation, sanitation, and housing. The resources the state acquires through taxation are used to address many social concerns in addition to health care. Although one can sort state action into separate domains—departments or ministries of health, education, transportation, housing, child protection, defense, and so forth—policies concerning one domain typically have consequences for several domains. Health care policies have implications for education, whereas educational policies (like sanitation, child protection, transportation, housing, and pollution control) have implications for health. Indeed, population health may be more sensitive to education, housing, sanitation, and environmental protection than it is to health care. Moreover, private choices influence many of these outcomes, including the allocation of health care. Individual choices can be effective ways of implementing state policies, or, on the other hand, ways of resisting them.

Because of the interdependencies among policies in separate domains of government and of individual choices, these policies should ideally be addressed simultaneously. The best way to address some specific health problem might well lie in a change in housing or sanitation, not in health care. Lead poisoning is better dealt with by renovating older dwellings than by medical treatment. Similarly, educational deficiencies might be better addressed by nutrition or

---

[2] World Bank, "Current Health Expenditure" (https://data.worldbank.org/indicator/SH.XPD.CHEX.GD.ZS).

dentistry than by an improvement in instruction. An ideal would be to construct a model of the interactions among policies and their consequences that will guide legislators and regulators in their efforts to enhance well-being, freedom, and justice. Unfortunately, a unified model of government policy is a very tall order. It is enormously challenging even to list the most important interdependencies, and when one considers the political context in which policy and funding decisions are made, the proposal for unified policy development and evaluation appears utopian.

A more reasonable possibility than amalgamating all the departments and ministries within government into a single unified "department of social policy" would be to maintain separate budgets for separate departments of health, education, housing, etc. However, rather than using their budgets to promote only their distinctive aims, the departments would share the aim of promoting the overall good and differ only in the instruments at their disposal to promote that aim. Rather than using the health budget exclusively to promote health, the health department would direct health care and public health measures to foster the overall good. The broader and narrower aims will often justify the same policies because the best way for the health department to increase the overall good is often to improve health as much as possible. But the implications of health policies for education, economic growth, income security, and the distribution of income would not be ignored. Moreover, the non-health consequences of health care, like the consequences of other social policies for health, would influence how the overall budget should be divided among the different departments of government.

This idea, which owes a great deal to a proposal by John Broome (2002b) and to arguments of Erik Schokkaert (2020), is sensible, and its advantages are evident. It would be absurd to ignore the non-health consequences of health policies. For example (as James Wilson pointed out to me), because universal health care prevents many health-related bankruptcies, it may be superior to alternative ways of distributing health care, even if it were to offer no better health outcomes. Especially in less affluent countries, differences in the consequences of health policies for education, economic productivity, and democratic governance are often as important as their consequences for health. It is a good thing if the right hand knows what the left hand is doing and that education, housing, and health policy work toward the same ends rather than undermining one another.

However, there are practical objections to the proposal that the divisions of government all pursue the same ends. The common end (a "better society") is more contested and less clearly delineated than the narrower objectives of specific departments of government. The data, tools, and culture of policy analysts in the divisions of government differ. Enormous intellectual resources are needed to estimate the overall consequences of the policies of particular departments of government. For example, determining the consequences for employment, travel delays, or housing values of amalgamating small hospitals into regional health centers requires different analytical tools, models, and data than comparing the costs and efficacy of competing chemotherapy drugs.

The solution to this conundrum that I favor is a compromise between narrowing the goals of health care policy to the promotion of health and asking the health system to promote the general betterment of society. The shrewd response to the impracticality of calculating and appraising the overall consequences of health policies is to operationalize these objectives of health policy. A good approximation of a health care policy that aims for the overall best for the society is a health care policy that aims to improve population health as much as it can while considering on a case-by-case basis important non-health causes and consequences of health policies when these become evident. One way to devise health policy, and specifically a health care policy that will have the best overall consequences, is to select those policies that bring about the greatest improvement in health and then make adjustments when significant non-medical causes and consequences become evident.

To devise policies that bring about the greatest improvement in health, one needs some way of measuring health improvements. Will additional blood pressure screening contribute more to population health and ultimately to a better society than a program to reduce smoking and alcohol consumption among pregnant women? Measuring health improvements is a complicated matter, which I have discussed at length in *Valuing Health: Well-Being, Freedom, and Suffering* (Hausman 2015). Elaboration and further defense of the claims I make in the rest of this chapter concerning the conceptualization and measurement of health improvements can be found there.

1.2 What Is "Health"?

To understand how to appraise or measure health improvements, one should start with an account of health. The account that I find most cogent largely follows Christopher Boorse's position (1977, 1987, 1997). He regards both organisms as a whole and the parts or processes within organisms as goal-directed systems. Although his account applies to plants and animals as well as humans, I am concerned here exclusively with human health. Parts of people such as their stomachs or ears have specific functions. For example, one of the kidney's jobs is to remove impurities from the blood. The specific functions of parts contribute to the highest level goals of the organism, which are survival and, for a portion of the life span, reproduction.

The parts of humans may carry out their functions well or badly—that is, at different levels of "functional efficiency." One organism is healthier than another or healthier at one time than at another if its parts are operating with greater functional efficiency. To say that people are healthy (and not just that they are healthier than others) is to say that the efficiency with which their parts are functioning is not too much worse (with respect to its consequences for survival and reproduction) than the median level of functioning in the relevant reference class of humans of the same sex and age. This physiological conception of health is one of many notions of health. For example, from a diagnostic perspective, someone may count as fully healthy, even though a physiologist can identify various pathologies.

This sketch leaves out important details. For example, whether some part is doing its job depends on the environment as well as the capacity of the part. Many parts are active intermittently, and their functional efficiency lies in their readiness to act when they are needed. The sketch here provides only enough background to clarify what the measurement of health improvements involves. For that purpose, we can withhold judgment concerning the most controversial aspect of Boorse's view, which is his claim that health consists in functional efficiency that is not too much worse than the median level. Let us consider instead only what his analysis implies for the comparative notion of a part being healthier—that is, having a greater functional efficiency—than another (Hausman 2014; Schroeder 2013). On Boorse's view, other things being equal, one person, Peter, is healthier now than he was last month if some organ system in Peter is functioning more efficiently than last month and none is functioning less efficiently. Similarly, other things being equal, Peter is healthier than Paul if some organ, such as his heart, is functioning more efficiently than Paul's, and none is functioning less efficiently.[3]

Although this comparative notion of health avoids the controversies concerning whether health is statistically normal functional efficiency, it is still controversial because it evaluates the functioning of a part in terms of its contribution to survival and reproduction rather than in terms of its contribution to some normative objective, such as happiness, freedom, or preference satisfaction. This account of what it is to be healthier contains a largely uncontroversial core, consisting of four claims:

1. The human body and mind contain parts that have functions.
2. These parts and processes carry out their functions with different degrees of adequacy. (Their functional efficiency varies.)

---

[3] Although this is a sufficient condition, for Peter's health being better than Paul's, it is not always the case that improving the functioning of the part of Paul that is performing badly will make Paul healthier. It might instead cause some other part of Paul to break down.

3. Parts are healthier when they carry out their functions more adequately (when they are functioning more efficiently).
4. Individuals are healthier when their parts are healthier.

With respect to the first claim, there is no disagreement in the literature that parts of our bodies have functions, but there is considerable disagreement concerning what constitutes a function (Ariew 2002). Like Boorse, I favor a "goal contribution" view of functions. Pumping blood is a function of the heart because pumping blood contributes to the continuation of the life of a human. The alternative "etiological" view maintains that what makes pumping blood a function of the heart rather than just something that the heart does (however advantageous its working may be) is evolutionary history. Pumping blood is a function of the heart because the fitness advantage of circulating blood explains why selection favored organisms with pumping hearts (Wright 1973). Defenders of a goal-contribution view can agree with those holding an etiological view concerning the evolutionary *explanation* for why humans have an organ that pumps blood, but they distinguish an ascription of a function to some part of an organism, which they take to depend on what a part does now, from the evolutionary explanation of its presence and properties. Although I shall take for granted a goal-contribution view, my argument does not depend on which view of functions one favors.

The second and third statements are uncontroversial—at least until one gets specific about the criteria of "successful" functioning. There are obviously differences in how well parts of our bodies function, which can be described as differences in the health of those parts. Boorse spells out the adequacy or efficiency of functioning in terms of survival and reproduction. Someone who holds an evaluative view might instead regard functioning as adequate or efficient to the extent to which it contributes to well-being or valued capabilities.

So long as the fourth claim, that individuals are healthier when their parts are healthier, is left vague about *how* the health comparisons between people are related to the health comparisons between their parts, the fourth claim is also uncontroversial. Moreover, one can say that if no part of Peter is less healthy than the corresponding part of Paul, then Peter is no less healthy than Paul. If, in addition, some part of Peter is healthier than the corresponding part in Paul, and no part in Peter is less healthy than the corresponding part in Paul, then Peter is healthier than Paul. But this connection between health comparisons among parts and health comparisons among people does not get one far because it is so often the case that some parts of Peter are healthier than the corresponding parts of Paul while other parts of Paul are healthier than parts of Peter. From a physiological perspective, there is, in fact, no need to define relations *between organisms* of "healthier than" and "at least as healthy as," and Boorse never defines these relations. However, if one wants to measure the losses of health brought on by injuries and illnesses or the contributions to health that result from medical or public health interventions, then one needs to be able to compare changes in overall health and not just changes in the health of individual organs or systems.

1.3 Health Comparisons

Although designers of a health care system apparently need to make "generic" or overall health comparisons, I do not think that it is possible to do so, apart from the special case in which the parts of one human at a time are functioning with at least the same efficiency of the parts of another or of the same person at a different time. To the question, "Is Peter with his bad back healthier than Paul with his severe dementia?" the correct answer is to deny that it is possible to compare quantities or magnitudes of health. Obviously, Paul's health is much *worse* than Peter's; and if one interprets the question "Who is healthier?" as "Whose health is *better*?" then the health comparison may be easy. Severe dementia is worse than a bad back. What makes the comparison possible is that one is comparing how good or bad the health states are, not who is healthier.

I suggest that there are no quantities or magnitudes of health to compare or measure. Consider the analogous question whether one bundle of commodities and services is larger than another. Just as there are no truth conditions for the claim that in 2016 Queen Elizabeth consumed more goods and services than Barack Obama, so there are no truth conditions for the claim that in 2016 Obama was healthier than Elizabeth. Obama consumed more almonds than Elizabeth, whereas she drank more tea. Counting numbers of items of different kinds would make the comparison arbitrarily depend on how one individuates items of consumption. To ask who consumed more is to misunderstand consumption. One can compare the quantities of particular goods they consumed or the total *value* of their consumption, but not the overall sizes of their consumption bundles. Similarly, unless every one of Obama's parts was functioning in 2016 at least as efficiently as every one of Elizabeth's parts, which is impossible because they do not have all the same organs, there is no way to compare how much health each possessed. One can compare their kidney or lung function, but the only way to compare their overall health is by how good it is.

As mentioned in the Introduction, health has both instrumental and noninstrumental value. Feeling well and possessing the full panoply of normal physical and mental capacities are important parts of well-being, in addition to enabling people to carry out those activities and form those relations that constitute other elements of well-being. Those who hold an evaluative view of health (Reznek 1987, Engelhardt 1997, Cooper 2002), in which it is a conceptual truth that greater health is better for people, might propose that the value of health constitutes a measure of the quantity of health when so understood. They might propose that we define what it is for Peter to be healthier than Paul as "Peter is healthier than Paul if and only if Peter's health *is better than* Paul's." But such a view is not tenable. Consider again the analogy with the size and value of a commodity bundle. It is obfuscating to say that Obama's consumption is larger than Elizabeth's if and only if his consumption has a greater value, because the relative value of their respective consumption bundles may change due to a change in prices without any change in the composition of the bundles.

The same problem defeats the definition of being healthier as being in better health. How healthy people are depends on what is "within the skin," whereas how good their health is depends in addition on the geographical, technological, and cultural environment and their wants and objectives. Computer programs that read text out loud do not improve vision, but they make being blind less disabling. Blindness was a worse health state before such devices were available. For this reason, one cannot take comparisons of the value of health to be comparisons of quantities or magnitudes of health. Just as one cannot measure the size of a commodity bundle by its cost, because the cost depends both on the constituents of the bundle and on their price, so one cannot compare the quantity of health by how good or bad people's health is, because the value of their health depends on their environment and people's interests as well as on the functioning of their parts.

Recognizing that the value of health, unlike health itself, depends on the environment and on the interests and objectives of individuals refutes the simple view that Peter is healthier than Paul if and only if Peter's health *is better than* Paul's. One needs to distinguish health from its context-dependent value. Only the latter is measurable. To define measures of the value of health, evaluative conceptions of health would have to draw an awkward contrast between the context-independent value that supposedly partly constitutes health and the actual values of health in different contexts.[4]

If, as I have argued, health states can only be compared in magnitude or quantity in the special case in which one health state dominates another, then the objective of enhancing health cannot be construed as maximizing the quantity or magnitude of health. This impossibility is not, however, a problem, if health care aims to *improve* rather than to *increase* health. What is important in devising a

---

[4] One might identify the context-independent value that defines health as the non-instrumental value of health. Instead of maintaining that Peter is healthier than Paul if and only if Peter's health is better, one might assert that Peter is healthier than Paul if and only if Peter's health is non-instrumentally better than Paul's. This offers a possible response to my assertion that "healthier than" is only defined in cases of dominance. However, I deny that health is partly constituted by its non-instrumental value.

health care system is reducing the harms of ill health, not increasing some quantity or magnitude called "health." Lasik eye surgery improves the functional efficiency of the eyes, whereas corrective lenses in eyeglasses do not. But what matters with respect to the allocation of health care is whether either enables individuals to see better, at what costs and with what side effects. Rather than measures of health and changes in its quantity or magnitude, what is wanted is a measure[5] of the *impacts* of diminished health states and improvements or declines in health.

To appraise the harm that diminished health does, one needs to understand those harms as well as the benefits successful health care may provide. As suggested in the Introduction, the harms fall under two general headings: losses of well-being—especially pain and distress—and losses of opportunity and self-determination. What one needs is a classification of health states in terms of these aspects and then an assignment of values to those health states.

1.4 Generic Health Measurement and the EQ-5D

The health measurement schemes that health economists have devised—as admirable as they are in many ways—are, in my view, faulty. There are several systems designed to measure "generic health," including the impact of illness and of the improvements health care may provide.[6] I focus on one of these, the EuroQol 5-Dimensions questionnaire (EQ-5D), which is used in several countries, most prominently in England by the National Institute for Health and Care Excellence. It consists of a classification of *health states* and an assignment of "quality weights" to health states. The health of individuals is measured by the time individuals spend in health states weighted by the qualities of those health states.[7]

The EQ-5D classifies health states along five dimensions: mobility, self-care, usual activities, pain/distress, and anxiety/depression. These dimensions are either aspects of health (mobility, pain, and anxiety) or causal consequences of aspects of health (self-care and usual activities). Along each of the dimensions, the EQ-5D recognizes three levels: no problem, moderate problem, and severe

---

[5] Or measures. I argue in Chapter 3 that the measure of the personal value of health—its value from the perspective of individuals with their desires and objectives—may differ from the measure of the public value of health that ought to govern the allocation of health care.

[6] For useful overviews, see Drummond et al. (1997), Chatterji et al. (2002), Brazier et al. (2007), and Cookson and Culyer 2010.

[7] The EQ-5D is designed to define and value the health states of adults, and comparatively little work has been done to categorize the health states of children and to assign quantitative values to their qualities that are comparable to the values assigned to adults' health states. See Kind et al. (2015) and Lipman et al. (2021). I shall unfortunately have nothing more to say in this book about the valuation of children's health.

problem. The classification thus distinguishes 3^5 or 243 health states in addition to unconscious and dead. A five-level version, which I shall not discuss, distinguishes 5^5 or 3,125 health states. The EQ-5D provides a coarse classification of health states, lumping together very different health conditions. But even this coarse classification generates hundreds of health states. The Health Utilities Index Mark 3 (HUI3), a Canadian health classification system, has eight dimensions and distinguishes five or six levels on each dimension for a total of 972,000 health states.

What distinguishes health states from one another are their current characteristics, not their history or prognosis. Someone with a symptomless fatal cancer could be in the best health state, with no problems on any of the five dimensions. How *healthy someone is* cannot be read off their *health state* at a moment in time. How good or bad Zelda's *health* (as opposed to her *health state*) is depends on the trajectory of health states through which she has passed and will pass. This feature of health states, which may seem odd, just takes some getting used to. A more problematic aspect of health states is that their values are independent of how long individuals are in them and of the values of the health states that precede and succeed them. The distress and limitations from being unable to see for a day are not 1/30th the distress and limitations of being unable to see for a month, but health measurement systems assume that they are the same. If the quality of a health state were not treated as independent of its duration and of the health states adjacent to it, it would be necessary to describe people's health by an unworkably large number of sequences of health statuses (Mehrez and Gafni 1989, 1993).

Having classified every health circumstance as falling into one of the 243 cells in the health state classification, economists then seek to determine the health-related quality of life (HRQoL) that characterizes that health state. "Full health"—that is, no problems on any of the EQ-5D's dimensions—is assigned the quality weight of 1; death gets the quality weight of 0. Negative weights are assigned to health states that are worse than death. The value assigned to Ann's overall health consists of the sum of the quality-weighted years she experiences. Suppose that Ann is now 30 years old and that the quality weight of each of her first 20 years were 1, whereas the quality weight of the past 10 years of her life has been 0.8. In that case, she has so far enjoyed 28 quality-adjusted life years (QALYs).

Rather than considering separately the consequences of health states for well-being and for choice, and then considering how the health care system bears on the well-being, freedom, and justice of the society (which I think better responds to the ethical objectives of health care), the EQ-5D relies on a single dimension of health-state evaluation, HRQoL, which in principle captures the bearing of health on both well-being and choice. In practice, without commenting on what HRQoL could be, health economists move quickly on to measure it by eliciting preferences among health states from members of the population with whom the health care system is concerned (Hausman 2012c). Respondents are sometimes asked simply to locate health states on a scale from 0 to 100, which is useful mainly as indicating preference ordering. To get numbers with an interval or ratio significance,[8] survey respondents are asked to make a "time trade-off"—that is, to express their preferences between a longer life in a diminished health state and a shorter life in full health. For example, if an individual is indifferent between 10 years in some diminished health state H and 8 years in full health, then the value of H is $10 \times V(H) = 8 \times 1$, or $V(H) = 0.8$.

1.5 Problems with Quality Weights

The reliance on preferences to assign quality weights to health states is not surprising because economists regularly take preference satisfaction to indicate or constitute well-being. However, eliciting preferences in order to assign values to health states is questionable. When individuals are asked to compare familiar alternatives that they fully understand, one can expect the preferences individuals express to be reasonably reliable indicators of the values people attribute to those alternatives. But with unfamiliar and complicated comparisons, there is little reason to be confident that the quality weights one elicits from survey responders reflect their considered assessment of the alternatives.

Among the many problems with the procedures for eliciting preferences and with the quality weights they imply, consider six. First, the quality weights derived from a representative sample from the population differ significantly and systematically from the quality weights implicit in the preferences of those who have experienced different health problems.[9] What reason do we have to rely on the numbers derived from the population survey? Second, respondents who are asked to express preferences among health states are not given clearly specified alternatives to compare. What is a "moderate" problem with usual activities? Is needing a wheelchair a moderate or a severe problem with mobility? Are "usual activities" those that are usual for paraplegics, 80-year-olds, or healthy young adults? Third, comparing health states is difficult. If one faced an actual choice between a shorter life in full health and a longer life in a diminished health state,

---

[8] In an interval scale, such as everyday temperature scales, only the choices of a zero and the unit interval are arbitrary, which means that a measurement on one interval scale will be a positive linear transformation of a measurement on any other interval scale. If there is an objectively fixed zero point, then one has a ratio scale. Measurements of ratios of quantities such as length will be the same on all ratio scales.

[9] For some of the evidence, see Patrick et al. (1982), Balaban et al. (1986), Revicki et al. (1996), Bennett et al. (1997), Boyd et al. (1990), Dolan (1999), Nord (1999, pp. 84–88), Wu (2001), Ubel et al. (2003), Smith et al. (2006), Sackett and Torrance (1978), and Slevin et al. (1990).

one would want to think hard about which one prefers. Respondents answer rapidly with little difficulty, which should make one suspect that they are answering some easier question rather than grappling with the time trade-off.

Fourth, data concerning the consistency of people's choices and the effects of different methods of eliciting preferences are disquieting. The HUI3 assigns a quality weight to complete deafness of 0.465, whereas the Institute for Health Metrics and Evaluation in two large-scale surveys found values corresponding to quality weights for "profound hearing loss" of 0.969 (Salomon et al. 2012, p. 22) and 0.739 (Global Burden of Disease Collaborative Network 2017).[10] Asked twice to judge which of two individuals in a variety of different health states is healthier, with just a few minutes in between, respondents gave the same answer only 70% of the time. Moreover, respondents sometimes judged those in strictly dominated health states to be healthier. Although this last flaw may simply indicate inattention or carelessness, these answers were not removed from the sample.

A fifth problem follows from the fact that many health states have different values in different environments. Those health states have no single value. In order to generate a single quality weight from the many different values elicited from respondents, health economists average their responses. Is it legitimate to do so? Averaging is a way of getting rid of noise, but it also hides differences in value in different contexts and in the attitudes of different groups within the society. One can lessen the variance by specifying a standard context with respect to which health problems are to be compared, but the value in that context (the "standard value") may be irrelevant to many members of the society.

Sixth, one might wonder whether the whole endeavor to value health states by eliciting people's attitudes toward them is well conceived. Does it evade the task of evaluating health states rather than addressing it? In eliciting preferences, it seems that health economists are delegating the difficult problem of assigning values to health states to survey respondents rather than addressing it head on. Members of the population at large know much less than sociologists and health professionals about how health states bear on opportunities and on well-being. Why rely on judges who are not well informed and whose off-the-cuff answers show little willingness to grapple with the difficult task of evaluating health states?[11]

---

[10] The Institute for Health Metrics and Evaluation found "disability weights" of 0.031 and 0.261 on a scale from 0 (no health loss) to 1 (as bad as death). Given differences in measurement methods, one might not be able to measure directly the quality weights in the text, but these complications are not germane.

[11] Some of these problems can be diminished by relying instead on deliberative groups, but these pose their own problems of expense and representativeness (Dolan, Cookson, and Ferguson 1999).

There is more to be said about these six criticisms, but cumulatively they should make one suspicious of the quality weights health measurement systems assign to health states. It is questionable whether the values of health states should be conceptualized as quality weights and whether they should be inferred from preferences. Even if this is the correct way to value health states, preference surveys are, as shown previously, not well-conceived and not reliable. Furthermore, even if the quality weights one can infer from preference surveys were accurate, they are highly imprecise. In the case of the EQ-5D, the quality weights are reported to three significant digits, but that much precision is not justified by the data, which are very noisy. Why assign a quality weight with three significant digits to the value of deafness when different surveys, using similar methods, do not agree in even a single significant digit. Moreover, because of the expense and difficulty of eliciting preferences among health states directly from survey respondents, preferences were elicited only with respect to 42 of the EQ-5D's 243 health states, and the quality weights for the other 201 health states are inferred from the directly calculated values coupled with assumptions about how values among health states depend on values attached to "steps" along the different dimensions. The fact that most of the values of health states are imputed from preferences among other health states further diminishes the precision of the quality weights.

1.6 Why Measure the Value of Health States?

There are many reasons why individuals and policy analysts might want a measure of overall health. Policymakers and philanthropists want to know where health is particularly good or bad to investigate what factors are most responsible for differences in health. A second reason for measuring the value of health states is that individuals may want to know not just how effective treatments are and what are their main side effects but also how much better or worse one's HRQoL will be with one treatment rather than another. Individuals facing the possibility of not being able to walk might want to know what it would be like, and the average HRQoL of those confined to a wheelchair provides important information. That average reflects the preferences individuals express in surveys, which in turn presumably depend on what respondents know of the discomfort individuals feel and also how significantly the inability to walk limits their activities. The discomfort (as opposed to the emotional reaction to the change) probably varies little from individual to individual, whereas the importance of the activity

Reliance on a representative sample of the population is particularly problematic with respect to assigning values to the health states of children.

limitations will vary, depending on the environment individuals find themselves in and especially on their differing objectives and differing abilities to adapt. An inability to walk has a very different significance for differing careers and recreations. For those who can adapt easily and who live in a wheelchair-friendly environment, there may be little loss, unlike those who have difficulty giving up aspirations rendered infeasible by the inability to walk. The quality weights attached to health states are averages over the different values individuals would attach to health states in different environments, and those weights may vary with changes in the distribution of individual interests. Call these quality weights the (average) private values of health states.

Average private values provide individuals with useful information. They indicate how strongly survey respondents prefer not to lose the use of their legs. But this book is a study of a third use of health state values: to determine priorities for the allocations of health care. One might think that private values would serve to establish priorities as well as to inform individual clinical choices. After all, one might argue that just as individuals are concerned to protect and improve their own QALYs, so the state ought to allocate health care to enlarge the sum of individuals' QALYs. Why shouldn't the same measure serve both purposes?

This line of thought is mistaken. The question "What priority for treatment should a health state have?" should be distinguished from "How much does a health state on average diminish individuals' expected QALYs?" Giving the same answer to both questions is often counterintuitive. For example, according to the EQ-5D, a loss of mobility, such as needing a cane or walker, coupled with no other health deficiencies, has a HRQoL of approximately 7/8 (Dolan 1997, p. 1105). In time trade-offs, individuals would give up approximately 1/8 of their remaining life to be able to walk unassisted. But establishing this personal value of mobility does not imply that saving a life should have the same priority as enabling eight individuals to jettison their walkers.

In Chapter 3, I give a more theoretical argument that the values of health states that should guide the allocation of health care differ from the personal values that reflect individual preferences among health states. Macro-level allocation needs a measure of what I call the "public" value rather than the personal value of health states. What distinguishes the two, I argue, is that the private value of an activity limitation, unlike the public value, depends in large part on individual objectives. The loss of a finger of very little importance to a radio announcer may be a horrible tragedy for a musician. Its public value, in contrast, depends instead on the variety and scope of the activity limitations it imposes. The significance of the constraints health states impose on the variety and scope of activities that are available to individuals will in turn depend to some extent on evaluations of human possibilities that are shared within a national community.

1.7 Conclusion

Governments cannot avoid formulating health care policies, even if legislators hope to rely heavily on private insurance and care. Health policies aim mainly to improve health, but policymakers must be alert to the consequences of health policy on other aspects of society—and reciprocally, the effects of non-health policies on health. Health is a matter of how well the parts and processes within the body and mind are functioning with respect to securing the individual's continued life and reproduction, but there are no truth conditions for the claim that one person is healthier than another, except in the unusual case in which the functioning of every one of the parts and processes within one person is at least as efficient as the corresponding part or process in the other person. To compare health states with and without health care, policymakers fortunately do not need to compare quantities or magnitudes of health. They need instead some way of measuring how much better or worse some health states are than others.

As argued in the Introduction, well-being and opportunity are the dimensions along which health states should be evaluated, but in this chapter, I noted an ambiguity in assessing how health constrains activities. Current schemes for evaluating health states, such as the EQ-5D, consist of a classification of health states and an assignment of quality weights to health states that are determined by a representative sample's preferences among health states. This method of assigning values to health states is questionable, and there are reasons to doubt its results. This conclusion is a serious matter because the use of cost-effectiveness information to allocate health-related resources presupposes reliable and reasonably precise measurement of the improvements in health that various health care policies can be expected to have. We pursue these issues further in Chapter 10.

2
Cost-Effectiveness, Well-Being, and Freedom

In this chapter, I explain what allocation via cost-effectiveness (which I call "c-e allocation") involves in theory and, to some extent, in practice, and I assess how successfully c-e allocation furthers the task of designing a health care system that promotes the fundamental values of making people better off and expanding their opportunities. Questions about the justice and fairness of c-e allocation will wait until Chapter 3.

2.1 C-E Allocation: Why Do It?

Suppose, quite realistically, that the health care budget either for a universal health care system or for a private health insurance company is not sufficient to provide all the health care to the insured that is expected to be beneficial. If the budget cannot be enlarged, and the prices of health care procedures cannot be reduced, then policymakers have to decide which procedures to provide and which not to provide. That decision will be complicated for private insurance companies by marketing considerations. Let us abstract from these and suppose that the goal is to reimburse the insured for those procedures that bring about the greatest improvements in health and well-being.

Cost–benefit analysis, which is a general method of assessing the improvements in well-being that policies can be expected to provide, measures how much the "winners" from alternative policies would be willing to pay and subtracts from that amount the compensation "losers" would require. Adding "distributional weights" to counteract the effect of differences in wealth among the members of the population, policy analysts can then compare the policies by their "net benefit." Because cost–benefit analysis measures the benefits and costs of transportation or housing policies in the same way that it assesses health policies, in principle it offers guidance about how to allocate resources among policies of all kinds, not just among health policies.[1]

---

[1] For an introduction to cost–benefit analysis, see Mishan (1971, 1981), Layard and Glaister 1994, Boadway (2016), and as applied to health care, see Fleurbaey et al. (2013).

Health economists have usually shied away from using cost–benefit analysis because they have been reluctant to place monetary values on life-saving and health improvement and because they have been concerned that cost–benefit analysis implies that treatments of the rich turn out to be more valuable than treatments of the poor. Whether health economists have been wise to eschew cost–benefit analysis is a subject for another inquiry. In defending the use of cost-effectiveness information to guide the allocation of health care, I do not argue that cost-effectiveness is a better way to assess health care policies than cost–benefit analyses. I instead assess criticisms that apply to the use of both cost–benefit and cost-effectiveness analyses. So, if one chooses, one can read this book as a hesitant defense of both cost–benefit and cost-effectiveness analysis. Matters are complicated enough if we stick to cost-effectiveness.

To determine which array of health care can be expected to bring about the greatest health improvement, one needs some method of measuring health improvements with respect to both mortality and morbidity. As documented in Chapter 1, methods of measuring health are faulty, but let us temporarily set aside qualms about their accuracy and precision. In addition, policymakers need to take account of the costs of treatments. At the same time that treatments convey health benefits, with a fixed budget, their costs make other treatments unavailable. In selecting a set of procedures for which insurance will provide reimbursement, policymakers need to attend to both the benefits and the costs of treatments. If the treatments selected improve health per unit of cost more than any of the treatments that are not selected, then those treatments provide the greatest improvement of health that can be generated from that fixed budget. One aim of health policy analysis is to find the most "cost-effective" treatments—that is, the treatments with the smallest cost to effectiveness ratio. There may be competing objectives, which for now we set aside.

2.2 Cost-Effectiveness: A First Look

As explained in Chapter 1, Section 1.1, there are powerful practical reasons why, when deciding among specific health care policies such as whether to provide heart bypass surgeries, health policymakers take the health care budget for granted rather than, for example, considering the possibilities of reducing health expenditures in order to lower taxes or provide better lunches to elementary school children. Supposing that the health care budget has somehow or other been determined, health economists face the problem of determining how it should be spent. Cost-effectiveness reasoning offers a solution.[2]

---

[2] For detailed presentations, see Drummond et al. (1997); Hutubessy et al. 2002. Edejer et al. (2003); Neumann et al. (2017); Cookson et al. (2021); and Lauer, Morton, and Bertram (2020). For a recent reconsideration of cost-effectiveness, see Norheim, Emanuel, and Millum (2020).

This chapter describes how cost-effectiveness bears on which treatments to provide.

A naive presentation of cost-effectiveness analysis notes that each health care intervention uses resources that have a given cost and each has a certain "effectiveness," by which is meant it provides a health benefit whose value is determined by some generic health measurement system such as the EQ-5D. Each health care intervention will have a cost-effectiveness ratio: the cost in the relevant currency, whether it be dollars, rupees, or pesos, divided by the effectiveness measured in quality-adjusted life years (QALYs) or some other measure of the value of health. One can then adopt health interventions one-by-one, starting with the most cost-effective—that is, the intervention with the *smallest* cost-effectiveness ratio—until one has exhausted the health budget. In that way, one will have maximized the health improvement—the number of QALYs—that the health budget can provide.

Anthony Culyer (2016) offers the following useful analogy. Think about arranging books along a shelf in order of height, with the tallest book on the left, as shown in Figure 2.1. The height of a book corresponds to the QALYs per dollar that a treatment provides (the reciprocal of the treatment's cost-effectiveness), and the thickness of the book corresponds to the total cost of providing the treatment. The area of its spine (the height times the thickness of the book [(QALYs/dollar).(dollars)]) is a measure of the total QALYs the treatment provides. Starting at the left, health care policymakers acquire books (treatments) until

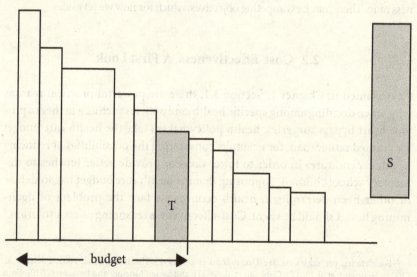

Figure 2.1 The well-ordered bookshelf.

they have used up the budget, which corresponds to some distance from the left edge of the shelf. Increasing or decreasing the budget shifts the dividing line or threshold between the to-be-purchased books on the left and unpurchased books to the right.

Consider the QALY per dollar ratio of the least cost-effective treatment—that is, the right-most book that is purchased ("the threshold book," which is marked with a T in Figure 2.1). With the purchase of T, the budget is exhausted. That effectiveness/cost ratio (the height of T) constitutes the threshold beyond which treatments are not worth providing, given the current budget. If one of the less cost-effective treatments to the right of the budget's limit were switched with one of the "taller" treatments to the left of the budget cutoff, the health care system would produce fewer QALYs. Replacing some treatment on the left-hand portion with a taller treatment such as S in Figure 2.1 will increase the area to the left of the budget limit, which is covered by the book spines—that is, it will increase the QALYs that can be obtained with this budget.

This picture of cost-effectiveness analysis is too simple because it is not feasible (or cost-effective) to calculate the cost-effectiveness of every currently employed treatment. Moreover, the cost-effectiveness of a treatment is not independent of what other treatments are in use.[3] Policymakers are not starting from scratch: There is already a set of accepted clinical strategies on which the budget is spent, whose cost-effectiveness is in many cases unknown. Rather than adding treatments for conditions that were previously completely untreated, medical research usually makes it possible to substitute new treatments for existing treatments. In addition, the costs and effectiveness of treatments are not constants. Drugs may become cheaper in larger quantities. Some interventions, such as vaccination, increase in effectiveness as more individuals are treated and then diminish after herd immunity has been achieved. Other treatments become less effective when they are more widely used by less well-trained doctors or on patients who may have more comorbidities. Rather than looking at the average cost-effectiveness of some treatment, economists do and should focus on the marginal cost-effectiveness. A more sophisticated presentation of cost-effectiveness reasoning must take all this into account.

---

[3] Here is an example, adapted from Ubel (2000, p. 6). Suppose one is assessing a screening test, T^* that costs $20. When given to 100,000 people (for a cost of $2,000,000), it saves 100 lives. One might conclude that its cost-effectiveness (with effectiveness understood here simply as lives saved) is $20,000/life. But if one already has another test T' that costs $10 and saves 99 lives when administered to 100,000 people, the incremental cost-effectiveness of T^* is $1,000,000 per additional life saved.

2.3 Cost-Effectiveness and Opportunity Cost

Culyer's (2016) bookshelf analogy is not just a device to help grasp the naive view of cost-effectiveness. It is also helpful in clarifying what is involved in the actual implementation of c-e allocation, where the cost-effectiveness of many of the treatments that are currently in use is not known.

To model how cost-effectiveness determines whether to provide some new treatment, when the budget is already devoted to a set of treatments, whose cost-effectiveness is in many cases not known, suppose that the book arranger is blind and knows the exact height only of those books whose heights have been measured and marked in braille on their spines.[4] By reading the braille markings and roughly by touch, the arranger knows that the books on the shelf are not arrayed strictly in order of height. For the most part, taller books tend to be toward the left end of the shelf and shorter books to the right. But, as shown in Figure 2.2, there are some short books to the left of the budget cutoff point and some tall books to the right. When publishers send new books on inspection, they are required to mark the height in braille on the book's spine. The book arranger, who is trying to get the greatest total area of book spines to the left of the threshold (the most QALYs), need not be particularly concerned with how books are arranged within either the area to the left or the area to the right of the threshold. What is important is that books to the left of the threshold be taller than the

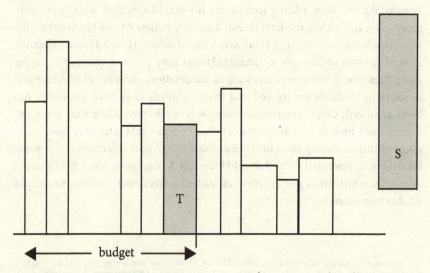

Figure 2.2 A less orderly bookshelf.

---

[4] This is an addition of mine, not to be found in Culyer's (2016) essay.

books on the right. Not knowing all the heights of the books, a practical test is to compare the cost-effectiveness of new treatments with the threshold level.

However, because the books are not in strict order by height, the threshold book—the right-most book in the portion of the shelf covered by the budget—need not be the shortest book in that portion of the shelf nor need be taller than every book to its right. If the criterion determining whether a book should be moved between the regions or where a new book should go is comparison of its height to the threshold book, then if the threshold book is too tall (the threshold dollar/QALY ratio too small), some of the books that are placed to the right of the threshold will be quite cost-effective. If the threshold is too short (the dollar/QALY ratio too large), then some treatments that are placed to the left of the threshold are not sufficiently cost-effective. If the threshold is mistaken, either the budget is spent in part on treatments that are not cost-effective or cost-effective treatments that could have been afforded are not provided.[5] Claxton et al. (2015a, 2015b) argue that the threshold value for the cost-effectiveness of new treatments used in England by the National Institute for Health and Care Excellence (NICE) is in fact too high (or, in other words, that the threshold QALY/£ ratio is too low). Consequently, there are budget shortfalls, and existing cost-effective treatments are unsystematically cut back.

The bookshelf analogy is especially helpful in conceptualizing *opportunity cost*, which is one of the simplest and most important insights of economics. Opportunity cost rests on the truism that using some resource, including one's time, in one way precludes using it in other ways. Purchasing an additional dialysis machine may require cutting back on maternity care, allowing fewer physical therapy sessions after knee surgery, or, if the health budget can be enlarged, postponing the purchase of new high school textbooks. Supplying an additional medical service that requires additional resources requires either enlarging the health care budget or cutting back on some other medical service. This is not to deny that it is sometimes possible to find ways to do more with fewer inputs. Reorganizing a hospital kitchen so that it provides the same mediocre food with fewer employees requires no sacrifice on the part of the hospital, but when the hospital administrators decide what to do with the increased resources, the necessity of trade-offs reasserts itself.

In considering any policy, one is comparing its benefits to the benefits of using the resources in some other way. Because the health budget is fixed, the

---

[5] "The focus of marginal CEA is on using a threshold for making discreet choices. This works as intended, however, *only if we are already at the optimal position*. It works, in other words, only when we do not need to confirm (or reverse) past decisions and can focus exclusively on the decision under consideration. . . . In other words, we have the 'correct' threshold only when we have already maximized health, either because the health system happens to have been optimized as it were 'by accident' or because we have gone through the exercise of performing a generalized CEA" (Lauer et al. 2020, p. 79).

comparison must lie between the mainly health benefits of the policy and those health benefits that could be obtained from an alternative use of the resources. My description of the bookshelf analogy was too simple. If one places additional books on the shelf to the left of the budget cutoff, one has to make room by moving other books to the portion of the shelf to the right of the threshold. The thicker (more costly) the books one places to the left, the greater width of the books that need to be moved to the right.

It is easy to overlook the opportunity costs of a decision to provide a new drug or surgical procedure because what will not be provided is often unspecified. A hospital may need to postpone upgrading its X-rays machines. A vacancy for a physical therapist may not be filled. The anonymous losers typically have no voice and little capacity to organize compared to the lobbying of manufacturers of new treatments and their prospective beneficiaries.[6]

2.4 Incremental Cost-Effectiveness and Opportunity Cost

When considering providing some new treatment or clinical strategy S, the choice is not between providing S or not providing S. It is instead providing S in place of X, where X consists of what will be defunded in order to pay for S. But what "X" should one decide to defund? One appealing option is to pick an existing treatment S^* for the very same condition that S treats. If S treats the same health condition that S^* treats, then the health care system is not leaving those who have been using S^* in the lurch. Although convenient, it is not necessary that a new treatment addresses a condition for which a treatment already exists.

The most sensible way to compare the new treatment S to the old treatment is to measure the incremental cost-effectiveness of S compared to S^*: $(C_S - C_{S^*})/(Q_S - Q_{S^*})$—the extra cost divided by the additional benefit. Q_S consists of the health benefits S provides in units such as QALYs. If $C_S = C_{S^*}$, then one should adopt S if and only if $Q_S > Q_{S^*}$. If $Q_S = Q_{S^*}$, then one should adopt S if and only if $C_S < C_{S^*}$.

Because new treatments or procedures typically promise greater benefits at a greater cost, merely recognizing that S will replace S^* as a treatment for the particular ailment fails to capture the opportunity cost of making S available. Defunding S^* might cover only a portion of the costs in terms of QALYs lost as a result of shifting resources from other treatments to pay for treatment S.

---

[6] According to Bryan et al. (2007, p. 191), members of NICE Appraisals Committees expressed concern that "no explicit consideration was therefore given to the sacrifice that would be required in order for the additional resources to be made available (assuming that the incremental cost is positive [of some new treatment with an incremental cost-effectiveness below the threshold])."

COST-EFFECTIVENESS, WELL-BEING, AND FREEDOM   31

Consider Figure 2.3. The top panel shows the status quo, with T the threshold treatment and S a new more expensive proposed treatment that might replace S^*. Because the budget does not grow, S needs to replace some other health care, labeled with an X, in addition to S^*. Replacing S^* and X with S will result in more QALYs if the area of S is larger than the area of S^* and X combined.

One can then derive the following criterion governing incremental cost-effectiveness—that is, $[C(S) - C(S^*)]/[Q(S) - Q(S^*)]$, where $C(S)$ and $C(S^*)$ are the costs in some monetary currency of some new treatment S and some existing

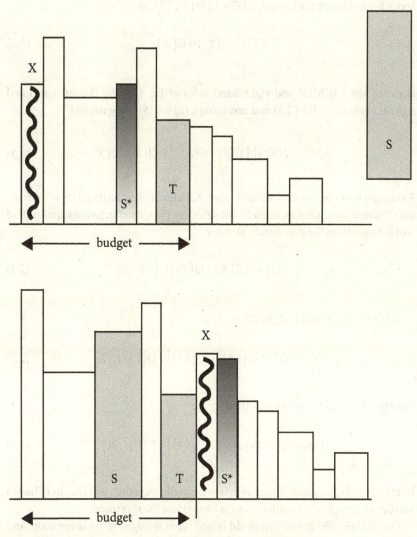

Figure 2.3 Opportunity costs and incremental cost-effectiveness.

treatment S^* of a health problem, and $Q(S)$ and $Q(S^*)$ are measures of the value of the health improvements S and S^* provide in some unit such as QALYs. If, as I am assuming, $C(S) > C(S^*)$, then the benefits of S should be no less than the sum of the benefits provided by S^* and X. So $Q(S) \geq Q(X) + Q(S^*)$, or in other words,

$$Q(S) - Q(S^*) \geq Q(X) \tag{2.1}$$

Because both the set of treatments including S and the previous set including S^* and X both exhaust the budget, $C(S) = C(S^*) + C(X)$, or

$$C(S) - C(S^*) = C(X) \tag{2.2}$$

Dividing the left-hand and right-hand sides of Eq. (2.1) by the left-hand and right-hand sides of Eq. (2.2) and assuming $C(S) > C(S^*)$, one derives

$$[Q(S) - Q(S^*)] / [C(S) - C(S^*)] \geq Q(X) / C(X) \tag{2.3}$$

Assuming that the unknown health care, X, that may be sacrificed to accommodate the new treatment, S, is itself cost-effective (that its effectiveness per unit of cost is larger than the threshold), we have

$$Q(X) / C(X) > Q(T) / C(T) \tag{2.4}$$

Equations (2.3) and (2.4) imply

$$[Q(S) - Q(S^*)] / [C(S) - C(S^*)] > Q(T) / C(T) \tag{2.5}$$

Equation (2.5) is of course equivalent to

$$[C(S) - C(S^*)] / [Q(S) - Q(S^*)] < C(T) / Q(T) \tag{2.6}$$

In other words, new health care provisions should be more cost-effective (have a smaller incremental cost-effectiveness ratio) than the threshold.

Determining what the threshold is and what it ought to be is not easy, and there are political forces pressing for a higher cost-effectiveness threshold to permit more treatments. To clarify the discussion, it helps to distinguish three notions of a cost-effectiveness threshold. First, there is the *announced threshold*, such as NICE's vague threshold of £20,000 to £30,000 per QALY. Second, there is a threshold that is implicit in the budget allotted to health care. If the announced threshold is higher than the threshold that is implicit in the budget, too many treatments will be authorized, and there will be a budget shortfall. Call the threshold that is implicit in the budget the *actual threshold*. Determining the actual threshold is a subtle technical task. Finally, there is what I call the *normative threshold*—the threshold that reflects the marginal value of health expenditures compared to the value of non-health expenditures. The determination of the normative threshold is a normative social choice, unlike the determination of the actual threshold. Ideally, the actual and announced thresholds should be close to the normative threshold. When the normative and actual threshold differ, too many or too few resources will be devoted to health care, and, as Lauer et al. (2020, pp. 79–80) note, when the actual and announced threshold differ, incremental cost-effectiveness will fail to maximize health.

One way to make c-e allocation practical is thus to determine the actual threshold and then to check whether the incremental cost-effectiveness of new treatments is within that threshold. Basing c-e allocation on comparisons of incremental cost-effectiveness to a threshold value also has political advantages because for the most part it only defunds existing treatments explicitly when more cost-effective treatments for the same ailments are available. In fact, as Figure 2.3 illustrates, other treatments (the "X" in the diagram) have to be cut to pay for the greater cost of new treatments, but these losses are more difficult to detect and give rise to less focused complaints.

2.5 Conclusion: The Attractions of Cost-Effectiveness

If the incremental cost-effectiveness of a more expensive replacement, S, for the existing treatment, S^*, is below the threshold, then S will provide greater benefits than S^*. Whether adopting S makes more efficient use of the budget is not certain, because if S is more expensive than S^*, something else besides S^* must be abandoned, whose identity and cost-effectiveness are typically not known. But there is a presumption that adopting new clinical strategies whose incremental cost-effectiveness is below the threshold makes a better use of the health care budget. Unless cost-effectiveness reflects background injustices, allocation guided by it (c-e allocation) assesses claims to health care on relevant criteria—cost and effectiveness—and it does not depend on other features of individuals that might compromise its impartiality.

C-E allocation is flexible. It is compatible with discounting future health care benefits or with not discounting them. It is compatible with weighting health benefits and problems at different ages differently or with rejecting age weighting. Effectiveness can be measured in terms of public rather than private value (of which more will be said in Chapter 3). If there are reasons for prioritizing the treatment of individuals on the basis of age, severity of health problems, or other special claims to consideration, different thresholds can be assigned to different groups. Furthermore, there is nothing stopping policymakers from taking into account other factors apart from the cost of treatments and magnitude of their health benefits. Cost-effectiveness appears to be a handy addition to the policy assessment toolbox.

However, in light of the many problems with the determination of quality weights by means of preference elicitation sketched in Chapter 1, one should question whether small differences in cost-effectiveness are meaningful. The three digits of quality weights that the EQ-5D preference surveys assign to health states give an illusion of greater precision than the data justify. Even if the surveys were better conceived and executed, it is doubtful whether even two digits of the quality weights are significant. Recognizing these problems, critics of cost-effectiveness might argue that the practice is a waste of resources. When cost-effectiveness differences are large enough to be meaningful, they will be obvious without need for calculating incremental cost-effectiveness ratios. And when the cost-effectiveness differences are not that large, they are unlikely to be meaningful.

A cynical response to this critique points to the advantages of an impartial mechanism for ranking health care policies, even if only very large differences in calculated cost-effectiveness tell us anything about which policies are better or worse. A choice among policies has to be made, and reliance on calculations of incremental cost-effectiveness has the appearance of rational assessment, however arbitrary it may actually be. If there is no other good reason to prefer policy P' to policy P, then the greater cost-effectiveness of P is a useful way to make the decision, even if one is cynical about whether there is good reason to believe that P' is the better policy. Even if cost-effectiveness information is often a poor basis for evaluating health care policies, it might be a useful procedure.

3
Conceptual, Technical, and Ethical Problems with Cost-Effectiveness

Although Chapter 1 did not dwell on the problems with the so-called "quality weights" used to calculate the effectiveness of health care, its brief presentation suggests that the numbers assigned to health states are not accurate measures of their values. These qualms about the measure of effectiveness raise doubts about whether cost-effectiveness is a good guide to the allocation of health-related resources.

This chapter explores further conceptual problems that need to be resolved before cost-effectiveness can be put into practice, and it introduces the ethical objections to which the rest of this book is devoted. Sections 3.1 and 3.2 return to the questions concerning what sort of generic health measure provides the information wanted for the purposes of allocating health care. Sections 3.3 and 3.4 discuss technical questions that must be settled before cost-effectiveness can be calculated. Section 3.3 discusses discounting: Should a health benefit that is not available until some point in the future be as valuable as the benefit would be if it were available now? Section 3.4 is concerned with age weighting: Should an additional quality-adjusted life year (QALY) be equally valuable regardless of the age of the recipient? Section 3.5 presents four "fairness" objections—*fair chances*, *severity*, *aggregation*, and *discrimination*—to which Chapters 6–9 are devoted. Section 3.6 concludes the chapter.

3.1 Personal and Public Values

As explained in Chapter 1, generic health measures assign quality weights to health states by eliciting preferences among health states. The numbers are supposed to indicate the health-related quality of life (HRQoL) associated with each health state in some health state classification system. The values of changes in the qualities of health states are found by subtraction. Health economists have had little to say about why they take HRQoL to be the measure of the value of health states or why they take preferences among health states to be the best indicator of HRQoL. Chapter 1 expressed serious qualms about whether preference elicitation is an appropriate or accurate way to measure HRQoL, and Section 1.6

touched briefly on the question of whether HRQoL is the right measure of the value of health states for the purposes of guiding the allocation of resources. In other words, is the relevant value of health state H (call it "$V(H)$"), the HRQoL, $Q(H)$, associated with health state H? Does $V(H) = Q(H)$? Chapter 1 also said little about the assumption that the value of a change that improves someone's health from its untreated level $V(H_U)$ to its treated level $V(H_T)$, is $Q(H_T) - Q(H_U)$. Is $V(\Delta H) = \Delta(V(H))$?

Answering these normative questions concerning how health states and their changes should be valued requires a decision concerning what health care should aim to accomplish. For example, suppose that policy were governed by a quasi-utilitarian aspiration to maximize the satisfaction of health state preferences. Then HRQoL, as a measure of the average preference satisfaction that accompanies health states, might provide exactly the measure of the value of health states that the health utilitarian wants. From this perspective, health care should aim to improve the total HRQoL as much as possible.[1]

This adaptation of utilitarianism is naive and is intended only to provide a simple baseline. It ignores the ways that distributions of health care affect individual behavior and social solidarity and, in these ways, indirectly enhance or diminish well-being. Unless policy is governed by a naive preference utilitarianism, it must also address the question of whether the state should promote whatever individuals prefer. Even if one maintains that what is relevant to the social evaluation of health care is its value to individual recipients—its personal value—it is questionable whether personal value should be measured by preference satisfaction. The Introduction argued that health care is valuable from a personal perspective mainly in its relief of pain and distress and in its restoration and enhancement of people's abilities to evaluate alternatives and to bring about the outcomes they favor. These two values are direct personal benefits. Benefits to individuals that come with a lessening of the limitations imposed by illness or injury are typically also improvements in well-being, but they need not be. The relief of pain and enhancement of abilities are tangible benefits to individuals, regardless of whether the health care is provided as part of a publicly affirmed health care system or whether the health care is provided by a stranger that a tourist encounters on a hike, who happens to have some bandages handy to treat a cut. In virtue of providing these direct benefits to individuals, health care is

---

[1] One problem with this conclusion, which James Hammitt pointed out to me, is that relieving short-lived pain, such as a severe migraine headache lasting 4 hours, will typically not be cost-effective. The quality weight of severe pain in the EQ-5D (without problems in the four other dimensions) is .345 so that complete relief of pain would be an increase of .655. Because this lasts only 4 hours (or 1/2190 of a year), the QALY increase is approximately 0.0003. If the pain medicine costs $30, the cost-effectiveness of providing it would be 30/0.0003 or $100,000 per QALY. The cost-effectiveness of administering Novocaine when extracting a tooth would be closer to $1,000,000 per QALY.

also instrumental toward many other social goods from economic growth to childrearing.

I have not said much to defend this account of the personal value of health care, apart from arguing near the end of the Introduction against lumping together enhancing well-being and enhancing freedom. I hope that there is little need to argue that health care is valuable in these ways, but one might wonder whether there are other independent values that health care addresses. The enhancement of human capabilities might be a third value, but I will not venture into these questions.

Exclusive attention to enhancing personal value, whether it is focused exclusively on welfare or also on choice and opportunity, allows for a very intrusive state. If the objective of the state is to maximize the total personal value of health, then the state could potentially become a partner in everyone's lives. A benevolent, competent, and powerful partner might be welcome, but we cannot be confident that the state is either competent to direct individuals to their benefit or motivated to do so. A utilitarian may wisely back away from a "nanny state" and, with John Stuart Mill (1859), argue that many things should be left to individuals to do for themselves, even if government might do them better.

Given a more cautious view of the appropriate role of the state in the lives of individuals, what should be the objectives of the health care system, and how should alternative health care policies be assessed? What are the *public values* of health states—that is, the values of health states that are relevant to allocating health care? What objectives should the state pursue in protecting and enhancing the health of the population (Scanlon 1975)? Even if there is a conceptual distinction between the public value of health and the average personal value, will their pursuit differ significantly?

In the midst of the COVID-19 pandemic, which is raging as I write, it might seem obvious that personal value and public value differ. Vaccination provides protection from serious illness to the vaccinated individual. That is the largest part of its private value, although individuals may also seek to be vaccinated in order to protect friends and family members. Because vaccination diminishes the probability that individuals will infect others and slows the rate at which the disease is transmitted, it might appear that its public value is much greater than its private value.

However, this is not the distinction between private and public value with which I am concerned. In this example, what is called "the public value" of vaccination is a sum of private values. Recognizing that the value of vaccination does not accrue exclusively to the individual who is vaccinated relies on the personal values attached to health states. Appreciating the externalities that come with treating individuals has nothing to do with the values assigned to health states.

A utilitarian who cares only about the consequences of policies for individual happiness can easily appreciate the importance of externalities.

I am concerned instead with the value of an individual's state of health *from a public perspective*, not with the causal consequences of an individual's state of health for others. Deciding what information about health ought to influence the allocation of health care requires some commitments concerning political philosophy, which I shall sketch without a discussion of the complexities of the issues. There is significant overlap between the personal and public value of health states because every decent state has an obligation to its residents to lessen their pain and distress.[2] There are constraints that limit how far the state can go in helping those who are suffering. Assistance requires resources that must come from others, and help may intrude on individual privacy. But it is difficult to think of any government that completely turns its back on the distress of residents. Defining precisely the obligation to alleviate suffering is difficult. Distress at failures and grieving at tragedies are healthy; the state should not be handing out opioids to disappointed suitors. Distress *about* some health problem, such as embarrassment about incontinence, has a different status than distress that is part of the problem, such as the terror provoked by hallucinations. Pain and suffering that are parts of illnesses are harms from both a personal and a public perspective.

Things are more complicated with respect to choice, the other direct personal value of health. An intrusive illiberal paternalist state might view itself as a senior partner in the activities of its residents, directing their actions and helping them achieve their state-approved goals. From such a perspective, the public value of the limitations poor health imposes on choice may overlap heavily with the personal value. But if one holds a liberal view of the state that discourages interference in individual choices beyond the protection of individual liberties, then personal and public value come apart. Apart from the alleviation of distress, the personal value of health care lies mainly in assisting individuals to bring their projects to fruition, whereas the public value of health care lies in providing individuals with a wide range of possible projects and the all-purpose means to pursue them. This distinction should not be exaggerated. The flexibility that comes with having many paths open matters to individuals, not just the ability to pursue fixed aims.

For example, consider someone who, due to a stroke, has difficulty following logical arguments. Some people would find this a devastating state of affairs, whereas others might not be so distressed. Regardless of what the average

---

[2] Callahan exaggerates when he writes (1994, p. 463), "The first goal of a health care system should be the relief of suffering, and the greater the suffering the greater the claim upon the rest of us to respond," but his willingness to overstate matters this way testifies to the importance of relieving suffering.

HRQoL loss might be, cognitive functioning has a very large public value because it is crucial for citizenship and instrumental to a huge variety of activities. As a second example, consider where to locate deafness among the health states defined in the EQ-5D. Recall that the EQ-5D has three levels (no problem, moderate problem, and severe problem) along five dimensions: mobility, self-care, usual activities, pain/distress, and anxiety/depression. Along most of these dimensions, deafness involves no problems at all.[3] The only way in which deafness could count as a disability would be if it limits "usual activities." From the perspective of someone who has adapted to deafness, the inability to hear does not limit usual activities. The personal value or quality weight for someone who has adapted to deafness and is otherwise healthy is 1.0. Deafness does not involve suffering, and it does not stand in the way of the goals to which individuals have confined their aspirations. From the personal perspective of those who have successfully adapted, deafness is no disability at all.

From the public perspective, in contrast, the value of health states does not depend on their contribution to the chosen goals and activities of individuals. From a public perspective (in a society in which most people can hear), "usual activities" include many that deafness impedes. What makes deafness a disability from a public perspective is not its effect on well-being or HRQoL (if indeed deafness has any effect on the quality of life). What makes deafness a disability from a public perspective are the limits it places on the range of activities individuals can engage in (where that range depends in part on shared views of the differing components of a good life).

In my view, although a liberal state has stringent duties to protect and expand opportunities and secure individual rights, it should not take responsibility for the success of individual projects or the happiness of those who undertake them. The state is a protector and a facilitator. Its role is to create an environment in which individuals can safely and successfully pursue different valued objectives. There should be a robust safety net so as to lessen the risks of experimenting and to ensure that everyone, apart from those who violate the rights of others, can respect themselves and be sure of respectful treatment. From a public perspective, what is important about health care, in addition to the alleviation of suffering, is its role in expanding opportunity, enabling self-determination, and securing individual dignity and self-respect. Expanding opportunity and enabling self-determination are public objectives of health care, whereas securing individual dignity and self-respect are either side effects of promoting opportunity and self-determination or constraints on their promotion.

---

[3] Someone might be distressed at being deaf (or, indeed, at not being deaf), but this distress is a reaction to the health condition, not a part of the condition.

From a personal perspective, health care is important because of its bearing on well-being and on the ability to pursue one's chosen aims. From a public perspective, health care is important in alleviating suffering, enhancing opportunities, facilitating choice, and demonstrating equal respect and concern. Whatever virtues HRQoL and its measurement by preference elicitation may have as indications of the personal values of health states, they are inappropriate ways to specify the public value of health—and it is the public value rather than the personal value of health that is relevant to the allocation of health care.

In speaking of the dependence of the public value of health states on the scope of alternatives available to individuals, it sounds as if the objective is to maximize the number of available opportunities, without respect to their value. But opportunities are not all equal. Some are important and extremely valuable to a large number of people. Others are less important but still widely valued or important only to a few. Still others are of little value to anyone in the given society. There is no way for a health care system to maintain complete neutrality concerning what kinds of activities are valuable and hence which opportunities are more important to protect. Although thus not neutral concerning the values of different ways of living, the health care system does not shape its treatments to further the efforts of computer programmers over athletes or musicians over automobile mechanics. The personal values of health states differ from person to person, and health care can only improve average values or standard values (see Section 1.5). Although the public value of a health state or a health change may also be sensitive to context, it does not depend on individual objectives and is thus uniform across individuals within a given community,[4] even if they have radically different interests.

As a first approximation, it is plausible that one should measure the improvements or failures of treatments by subtracting the value of the pretreatment health state from the value of the health state that results from the treatment. But the value of some health improvement, $V(\Delta H)$, need not equal the difference between the values of the untreated and treated health states ($\Delta(V(H))$) if the change has morally significant properties of its own. From a personal perspective, treatments that bring about the same improvements in health may be more or less painful, invasive, and humiliating. From a public perspective, *how* the health of individuals improves or declines takes on an even greater importance. Treatment may reaffirm the equality of respect and concern owed to each, or it may treat individuals like cattle. The public value of *health care policies* thus depends on more than the differences in the values of the pre- and

---

[4] Public values may exaggerate the significance of minor disabilities when they are the object of popular prejudices, such as dislike of crooked teeth. It may be better public policy to combat the prejudice than to assign a high public value to orthodonture.

post-treatment health states. The assessment of health care policies depends on considerations such as fairness, respect, solidarity, and sensitivity to the wishes and fears of patients as well as improvement in health. My claim is that public, rather than personal, values of the contribution to health are relevant to the assessment of health care policies, even when it is not curative. Having determined the public values of the improvements in health that various policies promise, one is not done. Other more procedural considerations must be addressed concerning whether the health care system treats individuals fairly and with respect, and whether it is sensitive to the concerns of those who need health care.

Although public values differ from private values, public and private values are not generally opposed to one another nor orthogonal; and one might wonder whether average private value might not be a close approximation to public value. Because no one has attempted to measure public values (with the exception of the highly speculative suggestion in Chapter 14 of my *Valuing Health* [Hausman, 2015]), it is difficult to say whether they are approximated by average personal values. What is needed is a measure that is sensitive to the bearing of health on the range of opportunities. When asked their preferences among health states, individuals are not making the relevant comparisons. How many people have thought through what matters about health or have considered how to trade off lessening distress against expanding opportunities. It would thus be surprising if the results of surveys of preferences among health states approximated public values. Even if people did aim to rank health states on the proper grounds, few people understand in any detail the impact of health states on the range of things people can do.

These comments about the public value of health are not specific enough to characterize exactly what facts about health states and health care are relevant to determining the effectiveness of health care. Nor do they provide guidance concerning how to assign a scalar measure to health improvements. It is possible to devise methods that will roughly measure public values, but no one has yet done so. Consequently, there is little alternative than to proceed with the health-state values we have. Rather than talking about cost per QALY, we ought to be talking about cost per "PVALY" (public value-adjusted life years). But because there are as yet no PVALYs, most of this book treats changes in QALYs as if they were the relevant measure of the effectiveness of treatments.

3.2 Social Values of Health Improvements

The same improvement from an untreated health state, H_U, to a treated health state, H_T, may be brought about through methods that differ in morally significant ways. In addition to its non-health consequences, such as its effect on financial security, health care has morally significant properties that are separate from its success in taking individuals from H_U to H_T. In particular, health care can be fair, respectful, personal, and sensitive to individual choice and values, or it can treat individuals as malfunctioning machines.[5] In focusing on health care rather than on public health measures in general, I am emphasizing the importance of care. Health care policies that diminish suffering and expand opportunity are morally objectionable if they are cold, unfeeling, or disrespectful.

One response to this conundrum, which has been defended by Erik Nord, is to adjust the values attached to health states so as to incorporate some of these concerns. Nord does not maintain that all of the relevant moral considerations can be satisfied in this way, but he argues that two important fairness issues can be addressed by shifting one's concerns from maximizing the total improvement in the individual values of health states (i.e., QALYs) to maximizing the total *social value* of the health improvements (Menzel 1999). In fact, he would place other constraints on maximizing social value, but my concern here is to distinguish Nord's notion of the social value of health states from what I have called their "public value" and to argue against attempts to incorporate concerns such as fairness or respect into measures of health or of the effectiveness of health care.

Nord begins by noting that there is extensive evidence showing that individuals think it is better, for example, to improve someone's health from 0.2 to 0.4 than it is to improve someone's health from 0.4 to 0.7.[6] These quality weights are on a scale like the EQ-5D's, with $Q(\text{death}) = 0$ and $Q(\text{full health}) = 1$. In Nord's view, the social value of an increase in HRQoL of 0.2 if someone starts at a low level of HRQoL is larger than the social value of the same or a somewhat larger increase in HRQoL if it comes to someone who starts at a higher level. In Nord's view, HRQoL is a measure of individual welfare, and by itself it says nothing about trade-offs between different individuals. Dan Brock puts the point this way,

> Do people who assign the utility level of 0.95 to requiring equipment to see or hear or speak mean by that assignment that saving one healthy person's life is of equal importance to keeping 20 persons from having to use eyeglasses or a hearing aid? It is highly doubtful that people are thinking of such trade-offs between or among different persons or groups when they assign utility levels to the different attribute levels. . . . They do not understand or intend their assignments to have those implications, and they reject in their explicit trade-offs these inferred trade-offs from their utility assignments.[7]

---

[5] I thought of writing "or it can treat individuals as if they were animals." But the veterinarians who have treated my dogs have been on the whole more engaged with them and more concerned to allay their fears than some of the doctors I have seen.

[6] See Chapter 8 for discussion of this concern to give great priority to treating those in worse health.

[7] 1998, p.75. The quality weight comes from the Quality of Well-Being Index, a competitor to the EQ-5D.

In Nord's and Brock's view, those who would maximize QALYs are, as it were, health utilitarians, who seek to maximize welfare linked to health. But people care about fairness, too, and they would not allow someone to die in order that 20 others can have eyeglasses.

Effective treatments may provide fewer benefits to some people, owing to their disabilities, age, or other reasons. For example, curing someone who would otherwise die of COVID-19 results in fewer additional QALYs when the person who is ill is a paraplegic or a septuagenarian than if the person is in their 40s and free of any disabilities. Deciding on this basis to prioritize treating individuals without other disabilities would be extremely unfair. The source of the unfairness, Nord maintains, is focusing merely on the QALY gain rather than taking into account the differing capacities to benefit. Saving either individual's life provides them with all the benefit of which they are capable and, other things being equal, generates an equal or nearly equal claim for treatment.[8]

One way to accommodate these data concerning the distributive preferences of the population is to assign distributive weights to QALYs that strengthen the claims of those whose conditions are severe or who cannot benefit to the same extent. By means of these distributive weights, Nord derives social values from the individual quality weights assigned to health states by generic health measures such as the EQ-5D. Alternatively, Nord suggests that social values can be measured directly by a technique known as a person trade-off. For example, in Brock's case, one can ask respondents to compare two health care interventions. One extends the life of 100 healthy people for 1 year. The second provides corrective glasses for a year to X individuals suffering from severe myopia. Respondents then need to state what value of X makes them indifferent between the two plans. Suppose they say that $X = 100,000$. Then if the social value of saving a life is 1, the social value of alleviating myopia will be 0.001. So the social value of a health state marred only by myopia will be 0.999, which is much higher than the quality of well-being's estimated HRQoL of 0.95.[9] Nord et al. (1999, p. 30) accordingly argue,

> If values with convexity and strong upper end compression are used to weight life years, there is no need to add separate equity weights to account for

---

[8] Nord does not consider whether there might be other reasons to favor directing life-saving treatment to some rather than others, such as those who have suffered from poor health or other deprivations. See John, Millum, and Wasserman (2017).

[9] This version of a person trade-off is known in the literature as PTO2. In earlier work by the World Health Organization, respondents were asked PTO1 questions. In terms of this example, they were asked to state a value for X that would make them indifferent between a policy that saves the lives of 1,000 healthy individuals and a policy that saves the lives of X myopic individuals. Nord (1999, pp. 122–123) and others (Anand and Hanson 1997) objected to these PTO1 questions on

concerns for severity and realization of potential. Instead, QALYs themselves become a comprehensive measure of societal value rather than a measure of the simple sum of individual health gains.[10]

Due to upper-end compression and the diminishing social value of health improvements, the social value of an improvement in individual health from 0.2 to 0.4 can be larger than the social value of an improvement of HRQoL from 0.4 to 0.7.

Like the public values discussed in the previous section, the social values of health states that Nord would use to guide the allocation of health care differ from their HRQoL. But the similarity stops there. The social values of health states derive from their HRQoL with an adjustment for fairness. The public value of a health state may have some correlation with its HRQoL because both are sensitive to pain and distress, but the public value of a health state is not derived from its HRQoL, and it does not incorporate a concern for fairness. The thought behind the notion of a public value is that the values needed to allocate health care in a liberal political order should measure pain and the curtailment of overall opportunity, whereas HRQoLs measure instead pain and the frustration of specific aims. In contrast, the thought behind social values is that the priorities calculated from HRQoLs are in need of correction to avoid unfairness.

Nord's social values are built on top of individual values (HRQoL), adjusting them in order to encompass aspects of fairness. Public values, in contrast, rest on the view that what is of concern about health from the perspective of public policy only partly overlaps with what is of concern about health from the perspective of an individual. To illustrate the difference between Nord's social values and the public values to which I allude, consider the following: [11]

---

the grounds that individuals might reasonably maintain that it is of equal value to save the life of a healthy individual as to save the life of a disabled person, even if the disability is much more serious than myopia.

[10] Nord should have written "social values" here instead of QALYs. The convexity Nord mentions is the diminishing marginal value of health improvements to progressively better untreated health states, and "upper-end compression" refers to the compression of social values near the top end of the 0–1 scale as compared to QALYs.

[11] These are two health states from the Global Burden of Disease Study 2016 (Global Burden of Disease Collaborative Network, 2016), respectively, "intellectual disability/mental retardation, mild" and "alcohol use disorder, very mild." I am assuming that, as "very mild," her alcohol use disorder allows Sarah to be sober most days at work. The disability adjustments, from which I inferred the quality adjustments, are 0.043 and 0.123. This example assumes of course that the disability values provided by the Global Burden of Disease studies are credible.

> **Isaac and Sarah**
>
> Isaac "has low intelligence and is slow in learning at school. As an adult, [he] can live independently, but often needs help to raise children and can only work at simple supervised jobs." Sarah "drinks alcohol daily and has difficulty controlling the urge to drink. When sober, [Sarah] functions normally." The quality adjustments for these health states are respectively 0.957 and 0.877.

It is not unreasonable that Isaac's HRQoL is high His limited cognitive ability need not cause him distress or limit his ability to carry out his (quite limited) objectives. Because the quality of both states is high, Nord's transformation from quality adjustments to social values will only slightly diminish the difference between them. The public values, on the other hand, would be very different. Isaac is far more limited in the range of activities available to him than is Sarah, who is also better able to contribute to democratic decision-making.

Social values are meant to capture aspects of fairness that constrain the maximization of health state value, whereas public values are meant to change the criteria with respect to which health is valued. Unlike public values, social values are not intended to provide an alternative standard of the efficacy of treatments. In Nord's view, if one sets aside questions of fairness, the value of a change in health state is the same from the perspective of the policymaker as it is from the perspective of individuals. My view, in contrast, calls for public values because they assess health from the proper perspective. In Nord's view, if one wants to know which health care policies are more efficient at enhancing health, one needs to look to QALYs rather than to social values.

Rather than attempting to build considerations of fairness into the values of health improvements, the public value of health is consistent with the view, which I defend in Chapters 9 and 10, that considerations of fairness and efficiency should be separated, and the trade-offs between them should be explicit. Public values reflect my view that health has a different value from the perspective of a liberal state than it has from the perspective of an individual. If the distribution of health care were entirely fair or if instead one did not care about fairness, then Nord would have no objection to relying on QALYs to allocate health-related resources, whereas from my perspective health care policy would be responding to the wrong values.

I think it is a mistake to incorporate concerns of fairness into the value of health states, although I think that a case can be made for incorporating fairness into the value of health *care* (Cookson et al. 2014). The transformation of HRQoL into social values that Nord espouses may guide policy, but does the fact (if it is a fact) that, due to considerations of fairness, an improvement of 0.2 units in the value of health in someone whose health is terrible is more important than an improvement of 0.3 in someone whose initial health state is not so awful tell us anything about the value of health *states*? Fairness is not something that makes health better. Nord doubts that the value of health improvements should equal the difference between the values of the treated and untreated health states.[12] Fairness influences what we should do, not how good or bad health states are.

3.3 Discounting

Some health care brings concrete benefits immediately. An antacid relieves heartburn this evening, but it has no further effects. Other treatments have lasting benefits. The successful surgical removal of a malignant tumor may change an individual's whole future. The benefits of other treatments are dispositional, like the resistance to disease that vaccinations confer. The values of treatments with different time patterns to their benefits must be assigned scalar values if their cost-effectiveness is to be measured. For example, an expensive one-time treatment may be more cost-effective than a cheap treatment that must be repeated often, and the quantitative value of treatments with lasting effects is typically uncertain. Computing incremental cost-effectiveness poses technical problems concerning how to compare the values of benefits and risks that are spread out over time.

Exactly how one's appraisal of treatments should depend on probabilistic and uncertain information about their efficacy and side effects is a complex matter that is relevant to this book only insofar as it raises ethical questions. The standard way economists appraise uncertain prospects relies on the calculation of expected values. If one knows all the possible outcomes and each outcome's probability and value, then one can take the value of the treatment to be the sum of the values of the outcomes weighted by their probabilities. These are big "ifs." It is not too unrealistic to suppose that one knows the probabilities and values of the outcomes of treatments that have been widely used and that are short-lived in their effects. The estimation of risks and benefits is then straightforward. T^*, the treatment with the largest expected value, is then often the best choice, but there may be other considerations that weigh against choosing it. For example, T^* might have a much larger variance than some alternative T' or it might, unlike T', cause occasional fatalities.

---

[12] "In the standard QALY procedure, there is no utility elicitation on gains in health resulting from interventions, even if such utility estimation is actually the aim of the procedure.... The 'subtraction procedure' is understandable on grounds of data collection feasibility.... It is nevertheless a proxy approach, which has not been discussed, let alone validated, in the health economics literature" (Nord, Daniels, and Kamlet 2009, p. S12).

When a health care intervention today has benefits tomorrow, next year, and even decades in the future, there is a further problem concerning how to determine the present value of future health states. Standard practice in economics is to assign a value today to future benefits and costs, such as returns to investment or repayments of loans that is "discounted." For example, suppose that I am purchasing a car for $20,000, and the rate of interest is 5%. Suppose also that there is no inflation. The price of the car and everything else is the same next year as this year. If I pay for the car now, it costs me $20,000. If, on the other hand, I plan to purchase it in a year, I need to deposit in my savings account only $19,047.62, which at 5% interest will yield $20,000 in a year. So the present value of the $20,000 cost of the car next year is $20,000/(1 + r)$, where r is the "discount rate," which in this case is the rate of interest. I am indifferent between paying $19,048 today and spending $20,000 next year. Similarly, the present value of a car that will cost $20,000 when I buy it 2 years from now is $18,140.59 ($20,000/(1 + r)^2$ and so forth). Notice that I am not at this point asking how much to pay now for a car delivered next year compared to how much to pay now for a car delivered this year. What is in question is instead the dependence of how much to pay for a dated benefit on *when* I pay.

Because the interest rate is 5%, I may not care whether I have to pay $19,048 now or $20,000 next year. And if I am indifferent, then I am discounting the cost by 5%. But the rate by which costs are discounted need not equal the rate of interest. It can be rational to pay less or more than $19,048 this year rather than paying $20,000 next year. If, for example, agents anticipate having a larger budget next year or strongly want other things that must be paid for this year, then they may prefer paying $20,000 next year to paying a good deal less this year. If, on the other hand, they anticipate being poorer next year, they may prefer to pay $19,048 this year rather than $20,000 next year.

What about benefits? Should they be discounted? Suppose that the cost of curing a child of leukemia is $50,000 and there is a choice between curing 20 children now and curing 21 children of leukemia next year. Assume that there will be no other funds for treating leukemia next year and no medical advances in treatment. For purposes of illustration, I am assuming, unrealistically, that there is no uncertainty. Note that what is at issue is whether it is better to treat Albert now or treat another child next year whose circumstances are just the same as Albert's circumstances today. The question is *not* whether it is better to treat Albert sooner rather than waiting a year, by which time Albert's prognosis may be worse. What is in question is whether the location in time of exactly the same benefit matters. In Erik Nord's terminology (2011, p. 18), the question is whether there is "a benefit time difference" in value and how large it may be. If one believes that the value of curing a child's leukemia does not depend on the date when it occurs, then one denies that there is any benefit time difference, and one will not discount future health benefits. That means that if one aims to maximize the benefits of treatment, then one should cure 21 cases next year rather than 20 cases this year. If, on the other hand, policymakers maintain that there is a benefit time difference and they discount benefits by 5% per year, then they should be indifferent between curing 20 this year or 21 next year.

There are several general reasons why individuals may want to discount future *consumption*. Economic growth means that people will be richer. Given diminishing marginal returns to consumption, the fact that one will be richer next year constitutes a reason why present consumption is likely to contribute more to well-being than future consumption. The risk that humans will blow themselves up provides an additional reason to prefer receiving benefits while the benefits are to be had. Moreover, although of questionable rationality, people prefer to consume things sooner rather than later.[13]

These general reasons to discount future consumption do not constitute a decisive argument for discounting the benefits of health care. In my view, policymakers should discount health care costs but not health care benefits. Greater future wealth does not mean that specific health care benefits—whether they be cesarean sections or treatments for back pain—will be any less valuable. In addition, unlike individuals, policymakers should not favor one moment in time over another, which rules out pure time preference and undermines the catastrophe rationale. Needs for health care do not diminish over time, and there seems to be no general reason from an impersonal policy perspective to value health care benefits more at one time than another.

On the other hand, the facts that we will be richer and that funds can be invested and earn interest provide reason to discount costs. I do not know how large the discount rate for health care costs should be, and fortunately I do not need to say, because the discounting of health care costs has limited relevance to the current allocation of a given health care budget. Investing some of it so as to have a larger budget in succeeding years is not on the table, and I am setting aside questions concerning how much should be invested in research. The commitments that

---

[13] Economists do not typically discount for uncertainty, which should usually be incorporated into the model. But Owen Cotton-Barratt has argued that the broad and shared uncertainties that are difficult to model justify discounting the benefits of health care (2020, pp. 247–248). Greaves (2020) argues for discounting on both this ground and on the basis of the instrumental value of earlier as opposed to later health improvements. She remarks, however, "Alternatively, one could (1) *explicitly* represent the various possible effects of one's intervention and their probabilities, and perform a corresponding explicit expected value calculation, eschewing the use of the 'naive calculation' as an estimate of affects and future health and (2) *explicitly* model the instrumental as well as intrinsic benefits of the health improvements. . . . If we did both of these things there would be no reason of the kind we have accepted for discounting future health" (2020, p. 231).

I am inclined to follow the more orthodox view of the grounds for discounting in the way Greaves here suggests and to deny that health benefits should be discounted. Fleurbaey and Zuber (2020) disagree and argue for discounting, albeit at a very low rate.

some policy choices imply concerning future expenditures will be affected by the rate at which future costs are discounted, but the discounting of future health care costs is mainly relevant to setting the budget for health care, rather than to the allocation of that budget (Claxton et al. 2007; Claxton et al. 2011).

Discounting the future costs of treatments but not future benefits leads to an apparent paradox (Keeler and Cretin 1983). Consider the following fable, which illustrates the paradox. Suppose I am in charge of a health care system and someone comes to me with an investment that is guaranteed to earn 100% interest. If I invest the health care budget rather than spending it on health care, then I will be able to afford to provide twice as much health care next year or 50% more health care during the 2-year period. If I have got the same investment opportunity next year, I can provide more than twice as much health care over the 3-year period[14] (although none of it will be accessible until the third period). If I want to maximize the value of the health care that is provided to the population and I do not discount the value of future health care benefits, then I should keep deferring actually providing any health care until the magical investment opportunity dries up.

This fable makes the deferral paradox vivid, and it also shows how to respond to it. Suppose in the real world, not the fable, that costs are discounted at some moderate and realistic rate, r, which is also the rate of interest. That means that the present value of a surgery that costs \$10,000 this year is of course \$10,000, while if the price is unchanged, the present value this year of the cost of the surgery next year is $\$10,000/(1 + r)$. If the benefits of treatments are not discounted, I can get the same benefit next year for a cost today of $\$10,000/(1 + r)$, which is less than I have to pay to have the surgery today. So one gets more value per dollar by deferring the treatment to next year. Next year, the same logic applies, and maximizing health benefit leads to deferring endlessly without actually providing any benefits! The conclusion Keeler and Cretin (1983) draw is that to avoid endless deferral of benefits, one needs to discount benefits at the same rate as costs.

In response to this argument, Nord points out that what is at issue in allocating the health care budget is a benefit time difference, whereas the Keeler–Cretin paradox involves what Nord calls a "start time difference." Those who are allocating the health care budget do not usually have the choice of deferring health care expenditures or of investing rather than spending the budget (and of course they do not have magical investment opportunities that double their money). A more important problem lies with the supposition (which Nord rejects) that

---

[14] Let \$X be the budget allotment for each year. The proceeds of the investment of the first year's budget is \$2X. Adding the second-year budget allotment (\$X) to the proceeds, a total of \$3X can be invested. So at the beginning of the third year, there will be \$7X available to spend on health care.

one should assess outcomes purely in terms of the total value of the health they provide from a fixed budget.

This problem is easy to see in the fable. Suppose we are at the beginning of period 3 with seven times the budget that would otherwise have been available and more than double the total health care budget, averaged over the 3 years. So now at the beginning of period 3, entrepreneurial health care administrators can do *far* more to improve the health of the population in period 3 than would have been possible if they had spent the allotted budgets in periods 1 and 2. If all that matters are total health benefits, the administrator's choices are a glorious success.

But there is an obvious fly in the ointment. What about all those who needed treatment in periods 1 and 2 and did not get it? The possibilities for increasing benefits in the investment story have a distributional dark side. If distribution does not matter, then this dark side is covered by the bright rays of greater future benefits. However, if one cares about both health benefits and their distribution, then the case for deferral collapses. Fairness rules out endless deferral.[15] The Keeler–Cretin paradox is not a good argument in favor of discounting health care benefits at the same rate as health care costs, and for the reasons already given, I think that health care benefits should not be discounted, unlike health care costs, which should be discounted.

3.4 Age Weighting

Suppose that an intervention brings about the same personal health improvement to individuals of different ages. If the health improvement is persistent, then its magnitude from both a public and a personal perspective depends on how long it lasts, which will generally be longer in those with longer life expectancies. Because those who are younger on average have longer remaining life expectancies than those who are older, the same lasting health improvement usually counts for more if it is given to younger individuals.

Setting aside for the moment whether this form of priority to the younger, which is built into the QALY, is justified, should age affect the value of health states in any other way? There is an intuitive case in favor of weighting health benefits differently in individuals of different ages, even if their life expectancies do not differ. Extending the life of a toddler or an octogenarian by a year seems on average to be less urgent than extending the life of someone in

---

[15] I am indebted to John Roemer for this response to Keeler and Cretin, although he is not responsible for the terminology or the fable. The same response can be given to the objection that most health care resources should be devoted to disease eradication because eradicating a disease brings benefits to all future generations (Murray and Schroeder 2020, pp. 39–40).

the prime of life. Otherwise, if in addition there is no discounting of health benefits, saving the life of a newborn would provide roughly twice the benefit as saving the life of its 42-year-old mother. From neither a personal nor a public perspective does this implication of rejecting age weighting and discounting seem plausible. At different ages, individuals and the society at large have invested different amounts in life projects, which are in turn subject to greater or lesser disruption by disease or death. Individuals are more productive at some ages than others, and the extent to which they contribute to the lives of others differs. Lives are finite, and it seems more important to add to the life spans of individuals who have not had their "fair innings"—that is, the life span required for a typical full human life—than to extend the lives of those who have already had their fair innings (Willliams 1997). Without age weighting and without discounting health benefits, treatments that save the lives of the very young become disproportionately important. Because age is itself one of the factors defining the reference classes with respect to which health is defined, there seems to be strong reason to weight the life years that health care contributes to those of working age more heavily than additional life years going to the very young and very old.

Although age weighting is plausible, it is problematic. The global burden of disease studies in the 1990s incorporated age weights and then abandoned them (Murray 1996). What makes age weighting problematic is that the reasons that make it seem plausible support different weights and call upon different values. I think it is better to regard the question of whether to assign different weights to the values of health improvements going to those of different ages as a question about how to treat the claims of those at different ages fairly, rather than a question concerning the dependence of well-being or opportunities on age. Both the personal and the public values of a health improvement depend in complicated ways on age, but instead of attempting to capture those relations with a set of weights, I think that it is more fruitful to ask more localized questions about whether it would be fair to refuse to do kidney transplants in individuals older than age 80 years or whether to invest in more beds in neonatal intensive care units. Clearly, these comments are not definitive. There is much more to be said about age weighting and the badness of both death and illness at different ages (Gamlund and Solberg 2019; Kamm 2020a, 2020b).

3.5 Is Allocation by Cost-Effectiveness Fair?

Few would deny that a health care system should be fair, but there is less consensus concerning what a fair allocation of health care might be, and there is little discussion of whether and how philosophical accounts of fairness justify criticisms of cost-effectiveness (c-e) allocation. When is it fair to withhold treatment from some people in order to treat others? A full answer requires a serious inquiry into the fairness of the whole health care system, not an individual allocation. Those who would have benefitted from a treatment for hearing loss, which the health authority refuses to pay for, may benefit from a treatment for ulcers or for something else that cost-effectiveness favors. Some of those whose hearing loss might have been ameliorated by the treatment that is not incrementally cost-effective may have the good luck never to need any other health care, but even they benefit from the security that the health care system provides, which may require drawing a line between those treatments that are paid for and those that are not. What appears to be an unfair provision of treatment of a particular claim may be part of a policy that treats sets of claims fairly.

In a classic essay (2003a), Dan Brock presents four regards in which using cost-effectiveness information to guide the allocation of health care appears to be *unfair*. These are criticisms of how cost-effectiveness works, rather than criticisms of the resulting allocations, which may be objectionable on many grounds, whether or not they result from cost-effective considerations. For example, from the perspective of cost-effectiveness, it does not matter whether a distribution of health care is unequal, and as a result a cost-effective allocation may be unfair, owing to its inequality (Voorhoeve 2020b). This is an objection to a particular outcome and a warning against relying on cost-effectiveness as the sole consideration guiding health care resource allocation, but it is not an objection to the use of cost-effectiveness information as one of the main determinants of health care policy.

Brock's objections are instead directed toward the workings of cost-effectiveness assessments themselves. In particular, he maintains that (1) c-e allocation is discriminatory, (2) c-e allocation fails to give a fair chance of being treated to those whose treatment is a little less cost-effective than those who are treated, (3) c-e allocation places insufficient weight on the claims of the more severely ill or otherwise badly off, and (4) allocating treatment by cost-effectiveness allows treating a large number of minor health problems unfairly to take priority over treating a small number of serious problems.

These criticisms of allocation by cost-effectiveness do not merely complain that a cost-effective allocation may be objectionably unequal or lead to worsening of the circumstances of those who are already badly off. I have no quarrel with the assertion that what is cost-effective may sometimes offend against other ethical norms. The four criticisms I address in contrast maintain that there is something ethically unsatisfactory built into the consideration of cost-effectiveness, whether or not cost-effectiveness allocations turn out to be otherwise ethically acceptable.

3.5.1 How Might C-E Allocation Be Unfair? Discrimination

As attractive as cost-effectiveness may be as a rubric for evaluating health policies, it appears to be intolerably discriminatory. Vaccinating someone suffering from post-traumatic stress disorder against COVID-19 is less cost-effective than vaccinating someone at the same age who is otherwise healthy, because it averts the loss of fewer QALYs. Saving the life of a non-disabled person results in a larger number of QALYs than saving a disabled person. Similarly, saving the life of a child who has a life expectancy of 40 years can be expected to result in fewer QALYs than saving the life of another child with a life expectancy of 60 years. The discrimination objection extends to those who suffer from non-health disadvantages, although this discrimination, unlike assigning a lesser value to saving the life of someone with disabilities, is an objection to possible outcomes of employing cost-effectiveness rather than a flaw built into cost-effectiveness itself. It may be more expensive to treat disadvantaged individuals because they live in difficult-to-reach places. Owing to poverty or the exigencies of taking care of others, disadvantaged individual may find it difficult to conform to treatment regimens. It appears that c-e allocation may unfairly pile deprivations on those who are already unfortunate.

3.5.2 How Might C-E Allocation Be Unfair? The "Fair Chances" Complaint

Brock calls this complaint "the conflict between fair chances and best outcomes" (2003a, p. 305). He presents it by means of the following example:

> **Brock's Case**
>
> "Suppose two patients are each in need of a heart transplant to prevent imminent death, but there is only one heart available for transplant. Patient A has a life expectancy with a transplant of ten years and patient B has a life expectancy with a transplant of nine years . . ., with no difference in their expected quality of life. Maximizing health benefits or QALYs, as a CEA standard requires, favors giving the organ to patient A, but patient B might argue that it is unfair to give her no chance to receive the scarce heart. (p. 305)

Norman Daniels presents a similar case: "Suppose that Alice and Betty are the same age, have waited on queue the same length of time, and will each live only one week without a transplant. With the transplant, however, Alice is expected to live two years and Betty twenty. Who should get the transplant?" (1994, p. 27). In Brock's view, a concern with fair chances demands in his case a lottery, possibly weighted toward A, whereas the best outcome in both cases demands that the heart be given to the individual who will live longer. The fair chances objection argues that the difference in cost-effectiveness should not eliminate B's and Alice's prospects of treatment.

These examples are imperfect, because (a) unlike typical health policy decisions, they involve a single indivisible good; (b) they are each a one-time decision, in which there is no way to provide any compensation to the individual whose treatment is less cost-effective; (c) in Brock's case, it is difficult to be confident that there would be a higher QALY total if A were treated: 9 and 10 years are on a par (Chang 2002); (d) there may be special obligations to individual patients; and (e) decisions in particular cases should be governed by general policies, whose adequacy rests on how well they deal with a range of cases, not just one.

It is not clear what the fair chances objection is. In Brock's case, the problem might be that one is depriving B of a chance at a life-saving surgery on the basis of an arbitrary difference: Who can tell whether A's 10 years will be better than B's 9 years? B's life or death should not depend on such a slender reed. Daniels' case avoids this problem: It is reasonable to suppose that 20 years is a greater health and well-being benefit than 2 years. What then is the objection to c-e allocation? Daniels puts it this way: "But Alice might complain, 'Why should I give up my only chance at survival—and two years of survival is not insignificant—just because Betty has a chance to live longer?'" (1994, p. 27). Is Alice's complaint against cost-effectiveness, or is she complaining specifically about how life-saving is valued? Her point seems to be directed to the measure of effectiveness. She appears to be arguing that saving a life should have the same value, provided that the additional period is substantial.

A third interpretation of the fair chances objection is as a complaint about c-e allocation's indifference to the distribution of goods or chances of goods. On that interpretation, the fair chances objection is related to a classic objection to utilitarianism presented by Peter Diamond (1967). He asks the reader to consider two allocations, A_1 and A_2, of a single good to two equally deserving individuals, I_1 and I_2, in two equally probable states of affairs, S_1 and S_2. In A_1 and A_2, a single good provides one unit of welfare to either individual, as shown in Table 3.1, which adds two options, A_3 and A_4, that Diamond does not discuss.

Diamond suggests that A_2 is morally preferable to A_1 because it gives both individuals equal expectations. It is apparently fairer. Diamond argues that fairness concerns expectations as well as outcomes. From a utilitarian perspective, in contrast, A_1, A_2, and A_3 are equally good, whereas for any epsilon (ε), no matter

Table 3.1 Diamond's Example Extended

	A_1		A_2		A_3		A_4	
	I_1	I_2	I_1	I_2	I_1	I_2	I_1	I_2
S_1 (Pr = 0.5)	1	0	1	0	0.5	0.5	$1+\varepsilon$	0
S_2 (Pr = 0.5)	1	0	0	1	0.5	0.5	$1+\varepsilon$	0

how small, A_4 is better. One way of understanding the fair chances objection maintains that A_2 is better than A_4, because A_2 provides a fair chance of benefitting to I_2. For small values of ε, many would maintain that A_3 is also better than A_4 because it provides I_2 with a fair share of the good. This criticism applies both to the inequality of the outcome and to the unfairness of the treatment of the claims of the two individuals.

Norman Daniels offers a second illustration of a fair chances objection, this time at a macro level. His case suggests that the fair-chances objection to cost-effectiveness concerns its indifference to the distribution of benefits or chances:[16]

Daniels's Case

To see the problem in its macroallocation version, suppose our health care budget allows us to introduce one of two treatments, T_1 and T_2, which can be given to comparable but different groups. Because T_1 restores patients to a higher level of functioning than T_2 [at the same cost], it has a higher net benefit. We could produce the best outcomes by putting all our resources into T_1; then patients treatable by T_2 might . . . complain that they are being asked to forgo any chance at a significant benefit.

Let us modify the example and suppose that it is possible to provide a mixture of both T_1 and T_2. The unfairness alleged in the fair chances objection lies in the "forgoing of any chance at [or portion of] a significant benefit" on the part of those whom it is less cost-effective to treat. As in the comparison of A_3 and A_4 in Table 3.1, the problem is not that no probabilistic device is used. What Daniels is objecting to is instead that benefits to those needing T_2 are ruled out. Providing

---

[16] (1994, pp. 27–28); see also Kamm (2002a). I have altered Daniels' example so that it is possible to divide the budget and provide a mixture of T_1 and T_2, but not in quantities sufficient to meet the needs for both.

those who need T_2 with "a chance of benefit" may require the provision of a mixture of T_1 and T_2 rather than any specifically probabilistic procedure to determine who gets what. The fundamental problem is that cost-effectiveness, like utilitarianism, is indifferent to distribution of health improvements or of chances of improvements.

On this interpretation, the fair chances objection constitutes a criticism of any distribution of health care that does not provide a chance or share of treatment to all ailments. The objection is most potent when addressed to cases in which the claims of those whose treatment is only slightly less cost-effective are drastically discounted because the purported unfairness brings only a small increment in better health. With reference to Alice and Betty, Daniels writes that "few would agree with Alice [who complains that she has no chance at having the transplant], for example, if she had very little chance at survival; more would agree if her outcomes were only somewhat worse that Betty's" (1994, p. 28).

3.5.3 How Might C-E Allocation Be Unfair? The Severity Complaint

If A and B are in need of treatment, and A is in greater need than B, then it seems that (other things being equal) treating A should take priority over treating B. Cost-effectiveness often yields this verdict. For example, if A, unlike B, is likely to die if not treated immediately, then by treating A first, a hospital can save two lives rather than one. Treating A is more cost-effective. Moreover, if both A and B can be restored to full health, and A is in worse health, then curing A rather than B brings about a greater health improvement. In these ways, c-e allocation prioritizes the treatment of the more severely ill.

However, suppose that A's and B's health can be improved by the same amount by some treatment T^*. Because both cost and effectiveness are the same, whether A or B is treated is from the perspective of cost-effectiveness morally indifferent. But if A is worse off than B, then it seems fair that treating A should take priority over treating B. Indeed, fairness allegedly demands even more. Critics of allocation by cost-effectiveness maintain that those who are more severely ill should have priority even if treating them provides a somewhat lesser benefit. For example, Callahan writes, "Our bias, I contend, should be to give priority to persons whose suffering and inability to function in ordinary life is most pronounced, even if the available treatment for them is comparatively less efficacious than for other conditions" (1994, p. 463). In thinking about giving priority to those who are worse off, what Callahan has in mind is prioritizing those whose health prospects are worse at the time when the allocation is to take place. Others have argued that priority should be given instead to those who have had harder lives, whether or not the source of their problems lies in their health. The latter invoke more consistently egalitarian or "prioritarian" intuitions that favor equalizing well-being or assigning a greater weight to benefitting those who are badly off (Parfit 1991). Although these concerns are very different, both object to the insensitivity of cost-effectiveness to the untreated health states of individuals rather than to the post-treatment distribution of health. Clearly, a great deal more needs to be said to disambiguate these claims about severity. But for now, let us settle for the following ambiguous statement of the criticism:

> *The severity criticism*: C-e allocation fails to place sufficient weight on how badly off individuals are and will be if untreated.

The various construals of the severity objection and their justifications hinted at above are different, and in Chapter 7, I consider whether any of them are sustainable.

3.5.4 How Might C-E Allocation Be Unfair? Against Additive Aggregation

Consider the following remarks of Frances Kamm concerning the question of whether to incur the additional deaths in order to lessen the economic impact of COVID-19:

> Bloom added up all the years of life that would be lost given 40 million jobs lost in the last three months of economic distress [owing to the response to COVID-19] and came up with 40 million life years lost. The aim was to translate economic losses into the language of life....
>
> But some might be tempted to go further and conclude that the large total of life years lost (40 million) outweighs the deaths of individual people. But in translating economic loss into life years lost, we must not lose sight of the fact that if 40 million people each lose one year of life no one of those people will suffer a loss as great as someone who, for example, dies at the age of forty, thereby losing thirty years of life. It is a mistake in what is called "moral mathematics" to aggregate in an additive fashion small losses to many people,... There is no one person who suffers the loss of 40 million years of life and there may be no one in the large group who dies at 40 rather than 70. This kind of "interpersonal aggregation" is morally misguided. (2020c, pp. 2–3)

Kamm's case, like most real cases, is complicated, because sheltering in place also causes deaths, owing to a variety of causes, such as failures to treat other dangerous health problems or violent domestic quarrels.

The central idea in this example should be clear: The sum of comparatively small benefits, no matter how numerous they may be, allegedly should never outweigh comparative large benefits such as saving a life. Here is a simpler hypothetical example to which I return in Chapter 8:

> **Aspirin* or Ambulance**
>
> Some money is left in a state's health budget. There are two ways to spend the money. Either (a) it can be spent on building a factory to produce millions of doses of aspirin*, a new more effective treatment for minor pains, or (b) the funds can be used to install new defibrillators in ambulances, which will save a few lives. Adding up all the small contributions that aspirin* makes to the HRQoL of many individuals, the health policymaker may conclude that it is more cost-effective to build the aspirin* factory. Critics of aggregation maintain that it is unfair to favor a large number of small benefits over a large benefit such as saving a life.

Clearly, saving someone's life, which upgrading ambulances makes possible, is immensely more valuable than curing a single headache, and saving lives is of greater concern to the health care system. Nevertheless, if one adds up all the benefit from each of the millions of minor pains relieved, building the aspirin* factory may be more cost-effective than upgrading the ambulances. C-e allocation presupposes that many small health improvements can constitute an aggregate health care contribution that can outweigh the benefit of a major improvement in someone's health or saving that person's life.

The aggregation critique denies that small benefits add up in this way. To the contrary, Kamm and others argue that comparatively small benefits, no matter how numerous, *never* justify failing to save a life or failing to avert a major loss of QALYs. As Kamm elsewhere states, "There is no number of headaches such that we should prevent them rather than certainly save a few lives (2002a, p. 691). On such a view, the incremental cost-effectiveness of aspirin* compared to defibrillators is either irrelevant, because there is never any occasion on which providing minor treatments is defensible, or it is relevant only in special circumstances when there are no opportunities for using health-related resources to treat major health problems.

The view that some benefits or burdens are relatively too small to count when major health losses are in question is problematic: Where is the boundary between harms that are relevant and those that are too small to be relevant (Voorhoeve 2014)? How should one deal with the intransitivities that arise when a small harm, H, is relevant to medium harm, H', which is relevant to extreme harm, H'', but H is not relevant to H'' (Kelleher 2014)? What should be done in cases in which there are many different complaints of differing degrees of severity (Tomlin 2017)? Is a small lessening of a *risk* of serious harm equivalent to the alleviation of a small harm and equally irrelevant to major harms (Voorhoeve 2017, Lazar 2018, Steuwer 2021a)?

3.5.5 Summary: The Fairness Challenges to C-E Allocation

Although not unrelated, none of the four complaints about the unfairness of c-e allocation entails any of the others, and it is consequently possible for applications of cost-effectiveness to run afoul of only any one of the four objections, even though many applications of cost-effectiveness are objectionable on multiple grounds. For example, in Daniels' case, it could be that those who need T_2, who are excluded from treatment, are victims of discrimination— that there is a failure to prioritize the greater severity of their health problems and that the greater cost-effectiveness of T_1 results from aggregating many small benefits. In that case, c-e allocation would be objectionable in all four ways. On the other hand, it could be that Daniels' case runs afoul only of the fair chances objection. One can make a similar argument for the distinctness of each of the other objections.[17]

Modifications of c-e allocation that address one of the fairness objections sometimes wind up responding to others at the same time. For example, Nord intends his proposal to assess policies by their social value to respond to the objection that c-e allocation fails to prioritize severity. But in compressing values near the top, it also diminishes the gap between the benefit of saving the life of the healthy and saving the life of the disabled; and it makes it less likely that small improvements in the health of those who are already quite healthy will add up to a larger total benefit than some major health benefit, such as saving a life. In that way, Nord's proposal makes it less likely that c-e allocations guided by social

---

[17] One might question whether an allocation can be objectionable on the grounds of aggregation without at the same time running afoul of the severity objection, because the small benefits that are aggregated will go to individuals whose health problems are not severe, whereas the major benefit that the small benefits are mistakenly allowed to outweigh must come to someone whose health state is severe. But the small benefits of some treatment could come to those whose health is worse than those whose health could be significantly improved. For example, it could be that only those who are suffering from severe emphysema get a specific annoying rash that is alleviated by an inexpensive cream, which does nothing to lessen the main symptoms of emphysema. If not spent on this cream, the resources could prevent a few cases of quadriplegia. I am indebted here to Frances Kamm.

values will run afoul of the aggregation objection, and it takes some of the sting out of the discrimination objection.

In thinking through the objections to the fairness of c-e allocation, we should be careful lest our reactions to stark hypothetical cases mislead us. We may judge that those excluded from benefits today did not have a fair chance, but it might be that they were favored by cost-effectiveness considerations yesterday. There may be no tenable objection to relying on c-e allocations, except where those excluded from benefits today are the same as those excluded yesterday and the day before. And in that case, what is objectionable may be discrimination rather than unfair chances. We should be suspicious of our intuitions in Daniels' example because needs for T_1 and T_2 do not exist in a vacuum. Where the deprivation suffered by those who need T_2 is not systematic, it may not be morally objectionable, and where it is systematic, it likely constitutes discrimination. The fair chances objection applies only when there is reason to believe that the losers from a particular application of cost-effectiveness analysis are not consistent losers and thereby victims of discrimination.

3.6 Conclusion and Additional Qualms About the Fairness of C-E Allocation

Determining what would be a cost-effective allocation of health care depends on nitty-gritty knowledge of the efficacy and side effects of alternative clinical strategies and a classification of health states to which values are assigned. Because health care is hugely expensive, it is important that it be efficient, whether it be funded via private insurance or through some form of state provision. Otherwise, the populace will suffer from inadequate health care or from wasting resources on health care that does little good.

Looking to cost-effectiveness to guide the allocation of health-related resources is accordingly tempting. But it is difficult. There are conceptual, technical, and ethical hurdles. One needs to define and measure "effectiveness." One needs to decide whether health benefits and costs should be discounted and, if so, at what rate. One needs to decide whether gains and losses should have different weights at different ages. Crucially, one also needs to allocate health care fairly and respectfully. There are questions to be asked concerning the fairness of age weights and discount rates. Questions about fairness also arise concerning the assignment of values to health states. Is it fair to treat health as a separate sphere—that is, to appraise health care narrowly by its consequences for health? Is it fair to focus exclusively on the direct benefits to the recipients of health care and to leave out of account the further indirect benefits that an improvement in A's health may provide for B or C (Brock 2003b)?

To understand whether c-e allocation is unfair, to characterize that unfairness, and to lay out a fair procedure for allocating health care resources require an understanding of fairness. To that philosophically demanding task, I turn in Chapter 4.

4
Theories of Fair Distribution

Despite a recent flurry of work on distributive fairness,[1] the philosophical literature is unsettled, and there is no consensus concerning what constitutes fair distribution of benefits and burdens. One minimal notion of fairness consists of following established rules and norms. This "formal fairness" is not sufficient: The impartial enforcement of the Fugitive Slave Act (requiring that runaway slaves be returned to their owners) did not make its enforcement fair.

The paradigm case in which questions of distributive fairness arise involves multiple agents who have "claims" to goods, which may be divisible or indivisible. One widely accepted general principle maintains that in the absence of reasons favoring some other distribution, an equal division is fair. Other things being equal, it is fair to distribute benefits and burdens equally. The other things that may not be equal include rights, responsibility, desert, entitlement, and needs. These often justify inequalities and sometimes make them fair. Fairness demands giving these factors an appropriate weight, which may differ from the weight to be placed on those factors when one takes into account the full range of ethical considerations. One can say truly, but unhelpfully, that a fair distribution is properly responsive to relevant properties of claimants and their circumstances, and it is not responsive to irrelevant properties. Although fairness concerns burdens and costs as well as benefits, I assume that what is said in this book about the fair distribution of benefits can be extended to cover burdens and costs.

Allocations of health care are typically unequal, and appropriately so, because health care should be responsive to people's needs, which are commonly unequal. Most of the population does not need gallbladder surgery. Although typically unequal, a cost-effective (c-e) allocation (an allocation guided by cost-effectiveness) is impartial, at least in intent. The properties of claimants it depends on are relevant: namely how much they can benefit from health care resources and the opportunity cost of those resources measured by their expense. By placing equal weights on benefits to different individuals whose health conditions are the same, c-e allocation avoids relying on many characteristics of

---

[1] See Broome (1990), Curtis (2014), Elster (1987), Heilmann and Wintein (2015), Henning (2015), Hooker (2005), Kirkpatrick and Eastwood (2015), Kornhauser and Sager (1988), Lazenby (2014), Paseau and Saunders (2015), Piller (2016), Reiff (2009), Sharadin (2016), Sher (1980), Stone (2007), Tomlin (2012), Vong (2015), Wasserman (1996), and Wintein and Heilmann (2018a, b).

claimants that, as a matter of fairness, ought to be irrelevant to the allocation of health care. Moreover, the inequalities of c-e allocations have a justification—they maximally enhance health.

In what regard, then, might a c-e allocation be unfair? By assumption, entitlement and desert are not usually relevant to the distribution of health care,[2] and the relevance of responsibility is a matter of debate. I also assume that no one has special rights over the health care resources to be distributed. In examples such as Daniels' case from Section 3.5.2, what is the basis for the accusation that c-e-allocation is unfair?

We have already seen a partial answer: The aggregation, discrimination, fair chances, and severity objections allege that despite its intent, cost-effectiveness turns out either to depend in part on irrelevant characteristics of claimants, such as independent disabilities, or fails to respond adequately to relevant characteristics of claimants, such as the severity of illness. In the case of indivisible benefits or burdens, such as Brock's heart-transplant example, the fair chances objection is directed to the distribution of expectations or chances, rather than to the distribution of hearts. Concerns about fairness appear to be directed to outcomes, expectations of outcomes, and procedures.

People use the adjective "fair," the adverb "fairly," the noun "fairness," and their negations in many ways. Sometimes "unfair" is used loosely to refer to any sort of wrong (Hooker 2005). Sometimes it is not directed toward any *wrong* at all, as when a short friend complains that it is unfair that he is so much shorter than others. I am concerned with fairness as a moral notion in terms of which to evaluate the distribution of benefits and burdens. This chapter develops the main contemporary theories concerned with the fair distribution of both divisible and indivisible goods. How these philosophical accounts bear on the allocation of health care will wait until the chapters that follow.

I begin in Section 4.1 with vague generalizations about fairness, which guide the formulation and assessment of more specific theories. Section 4.2 characterizes problems of fair division, a simple example of which is presented in Section 4.3. Section 4.4 presents John Broome's influential account of how to allocate divisible goods fairly among the claimants. Section 4.5 turns to Broome's view of the fair distribution of indivisible goods. Section 4.6 discusses problems for Broome's theory. Section 4.7 considers what fairness requires when claims to goods differ both quantitatively and in strength, and it defends a fragment of a theory of fairness. Section 4.8 sketches two other philosophical theories of fairness, and Section 4.9 concludes the chapter.

---

[2] This is not true of the conventional or legal entitlement or desert that is established by health insurance policies or by legislation specifying legal rights to health care. What should not bear on access to health care in my view is moral deservingness or social status. For a contrary view of the relevance of moral deservingness, see Larry Temkin's views, which are discussed in Section 4.8.

4.1 Suggestive Visions of Fairness

At the most general level, I suggest that fairness in the relations among individuals is a matter of mutual recognition as "rational" beings—that is, as beings who are able to monitor their actions and reactions to one another and to justify their actions to one another. One might say that fairness is a matter of equal "baseline" or "recognition" respect.[3] Showing equal baseline respect arguably encompasses more specific but still quite general claims about fairness, such as that fairness requires impartiality, that it places greater weight on the interests of those who are worse off, that it gives to individuals what they deserve, that it manifests reciprocity, and that it recognizes the separateness of persons and refuses to sacrifice the important interests of some for the mere benefit of others.

What I am calling "baseline respect"[4] is not the sort of respect or esteem we show toward brilliant athletes or musicians, skilled negotiators, gifted architects, brave firefighters, or the heroic nurses who are, as I write these words, putting in 12-hour shifts in intensive care units treating COVID-19 patients. The esteem we have for achievements, skills, courage, character, effort, uprightness, self-sacrifice, and so forth is won from us by what people do and are able to do. It can be lost when we learn other facts that diminish our esteem for individuals, such as the almost daily news reports about how badly formerly admired male figures in politics, sports, and the arts have behaved toward women in their private lives.

Baseline respect, in contrast, is not something that people earn, and it is very difficult to lose it. Criminality is not enough, for we show baseline respect to criminals when we regard them as persons liable to punishment rather than as merely threats to be neutralized, like the threats posed by wild animals.[5] Unlike "appraisal respect" (Darwall's term), which is responsive to excellence, baseline respect centers around acknowledging the authority of rational persons to make demands of one another. In Kant's view, beings who are capable of rational

---

[3] What then of young children and the cognitively disabled who are not in this sense rational beings? On this account, rational agents extend to infants and the comatose or extremely severely demented portions of the baseline respect due to rational agents. But for the existence of rational agents and their extension of something like that status to humans who are not rational agents, treatments of those humans would be neither fair nor unfair.

[4] "Baseline respect" is what Stephen Darwall (1977) calls "recognition respect for persons." "And recognition respect for that fact consists in giving it the proper weight in deliberation. Thus to have recognition respect for persons is to give proper weight to the fact that they are persons" (1977, p. 39). This discussion is, however, more heavily indebted to a later essay of Darwall's, "Respect and the Second-Person Standpoint" (2004). Darwall does not explore the connections between respect and fairness.

[5] "For centuries no jurisdiction has countenanced the execution of the insane, yet this Court has never decided whether the Constitution forbids the practice. Today we keep faith with our common-law heritage in holding that it does" (Justice Marshall writing in *Ford v. Wainwright*, 1986). The confinement of the criminally insane for the protection of others is not punishment, as one can see when one recognizes that it is not dependent on having committed a crime.

supervision of their own conduct are entitled to the baseline respect of other beings with similar capabilities. To be eligible for baseline respect is to be capable of rationally appraising one's own activities and thus capable of justifying one's actions with reasons that one judges that all rational beings can endorse. In making that judgment, one subjects one's actions and reasons to the scrutiny of other rational beings. The flip side of this subjection to rational scrutiny by others is the authority not just to express one's wants but also to make *demands* of others. "The dignity of persons consists, not just in requirements that are rooted in our common nature as free and rational, but also in our equal authority to require or demand of one another that we comply with these requirements" (Darwall 2004, p. 44).

Fairness as equal baseline respect is not necessarily comparative, because there are cases in which what is at issue is the treatment of just one single individual. But fairness and unfairness are typically comparative matters. It is unfair that African Americans are much more likely to die of COVID-19 than are Americans of European ancestry because the disparity reveals a failure to treat the most fundamental demands citizens make of one another as equally weighty.

What is at issue in this book is not the overall fairness of the relations among individuals but, instead, the narrower questions of whether health care institutions and policies and those who administer them treat individuals fairly. Whether policies themselves are fair depends on whether they are in accord with the equal authority of rational agents to make demands of one another. Whether the administration of policies is fair is a narrower question. The respect it shows to individuals turns in part on whether benefits and burdens are distributed as the policies require.

Although Rawls does not speak of baseline respect and in his later work adopted a much more political construal of his theory of justice, he called his account "justice as fairness," where fairness is implicitly defined by considering what would be chosen in the "original position" behind a hypothetical veil of ignorance, where it is impossible not to recognize the rational authority of others.[6] The veil of ignorance guarantees both impartiality and, less obviously, reciprocity.[7] Rawls describes reciprocity as follows:

> Fair terms of cooperation specify an idea of reciprocity: All who are engaged in cooperation and who do their part as the rules and procedures require, are to

---

[6] Rawls could complain that the discussion here abuses his framework, which is meant to apply only to the *basic structure* of society, and it is unclear from such a perspective whether one should take people's claims to health care as givens. I make no appeal to Rawls' authority.

[7] Rawls also defines what he calls "the principle of fairness," which requires that individuals do what just institutions require of them if they have accepted the benefits the institutions provide (1970, pp. 111–112). This principle is not germane to this book.

benefit in an appropriate way as assessed by a suitable benchmark of comparison....

The idea of reciprocity lies between the idea of impartiality, which is altruistic (being moved by the general good),[8] and the idea of mutual advantage understood as everyone's being advantaged with respect to each person's present or expected future situation as things are. (1993, pp. 16-17)

Although it is easy to see how a veil of ignorance guarantees impartiality, what is impartially beneficial to most of the population might demand indefensible sacrifice from those at the bottom. Reciprocity rules this out. It demands of a fair distribution that it be in accord with impartial principles that do not require such abusive sacrifice. According to fairness as reciprocity, if a principle is impartial among individuals and does not demand abusive sacrifice of any, then it is fair, and, other things being equal, it is morally permissible to rely on the principle to govern the distribution of benefits and burdens among those individuals. Note, however, that it might not be justifiable *tout court* because of other moral considerations, such as its implications for outsiders or nonhumans.

I think of reciprocity as an aspiration, rather than as a practical guide to the evaluation of institutions and policies. The general idea needs to be realized in much more specific conditions, such as Rawls' "difference principle," Broome's view (discussed later) that claims should be satisfied in proportion to their strength, or in an adaptation of Scanlon's contractualism.[9] Rawls' difference principle rules out sacrifice for the benefit of those who are better off by demanding of a just distribution D that there is no other distribution D' in which those who are worst off in D' receive a larger bundle of primary goods than those who are worst off in D.

What is at issue in evaluating whether principles are in accord with impartial reciprocity or baseline respect is whether institutions governed by those principles countenance an overall sacrifice of the fundamental interests of some members of society, not whether on one occasion or another, an allocation permitted by the principles sacrifices the interests of some while promoting the interests of others who are better off. In repeated interactions, there is give and take. Taking turns can be fair even though on any particular day the allocation is unequal.

Philosophers such as Aristotle and, more recently, Larry Temkin maintain that fairness consists in treating individuals as they deserve. Although ambiguous,

---

[8] Rawls has a more demanding notion of impartiality than merely the absence of bias, which is all that I mean.

[9] On Scanlon's view (1998, p. 153), a distribution is unfair if and only if it would be disallowed by principles governing the distribution of benefits and burdens that no one could reasonably rejected as a basis for "informed, unforced general agreement."

this view complements the vision of fairness in terms of baseline respect. Fairness on either view is not necessarily comparative. If I break my promise to everyone in some group, I have failed to treat them as they deserve, although I have shown no partiality toward anyone. Linking fairness to desert, one can say that I have also treated them unfairly, although in an absolute rather than a comparative sense of fairness. I am concerned with comparative fairness.

The notion of desert is ambiguous. Consider the following interpretations:

Rule-determined desert: Each of us deserve what the legitimate institutions and practices in society promise to us.

Duty-defined desert: We deserve what others are obligated to do for us (Hooker 2005; Vong 2020).

Intrinsic or rule-determining desert: This is a matter of moral merit or virtue (Temkin 2017). The distribution of ill fortune is in this sense fair if and only if an individual's moral failings are met with "equivalent" suffering. Retributive theories of punishment rely on this notion of desert.

Kantian desert: This is another way to describe the baseline respect that is due to rational agents in virtue of being self-assessing rational agents.

One helpful aspect of this discussion of different conceptions of desert is the distinction between judging whether distributions are fair—that is, whether they give people what they deserve (in a rule-dependent or duty-defined sense of desert)—and judging whether the principles governing distributions are fair—that is, whether they successfully define what people deserve (in a rule-determining or Kantian notion of desert).

Although vague, the conception of fairness as baseline respect explains why fairness requires reciprocity rather than merely impartiality, and it identifies the notions of desert that are relevant to comparative fairness. Let us then turn to well-defined problems of fair distributions and the solutions philosophers and economists have proposed.

4.2 Problems of Fair Distribution

Following John Broome, whose views are discussed at length in Sections 4.4 and 4.5, I focus on the question of how to satisfy *claims* fairly. The debts owed to creditors are examples of claims. An individual such as Barb has a claim to possess or receive x from Bob just in case Bob has a pro tanto duty *owed to Barb* that she possess or receive x. These duties are weaker than the virtually inviolable "side constraints" that are, according to some philosophers (Nozick 1974), the correlatives of rights. Claims carry normative force, and their satisfaction is often morally as well as conventionally or legally obligatory. Note that the "satisfaction" of Barb's claim has nothing to do with whether she *feels* satisfied or even knows whether her claim is satisfied. Charley's claim against a thief to return his wallet is satisfied if the thief returns his wallet—even if, owing to a stroke, Charlie never knows that the wallet has been returned.

Broome maintains that fairness is exclusively concerned with satisfying claims, but he says little about the sources of claims, the magnitude of claims, and what determines their strength. This is problematic because the assignment of claims may itself be fair or unfair. Which health care needs give rise to claims is a critical question.[10] Patrick Tomlin distinguishes what he calls voluntary and non-voluntary claims as follows: "Some claims just exist—other people don't need to do anything for us to get them. Other claims are distributed to us by other agents, through promises, contracts or other voluntary acts by others" (2012, p. 203). Claims based on need are examples of non-voluntary claims, whereas claims deriving from promises are instances of voluntary claims. I think that the distinction should be stated somewhat differently because needs often give rise to claims in a social context in which duties to attend to certain needs are specified. Although the distinction between voluntary and non-voluntary claims is helpful, the distinction does not explain how and when either need or promising gives rise to claims.

One can give both consequentialist and deontological accounts of what generates claims. Because keeping promises and some conventions concerning the duties of meeting needs have better consequences than alternatives, consequentialists can argue that needs, promises, and so forth should give rise to claims. Deontologists can maintain that in virtue of their capacities to make rational and unbiased appraisals of the actions and wants of both others and themselves, persons are entitled to make claims of one another. On either view, what allows facts such as needs and promises to give rise to socially recognized claims are the laws and conventions that govern social interactions, which are in turn justified by moral principles that in turn have some sort of consequentialist or deontological justification. The rules of the Supplemental Nutrition Assistance Program (food stamps) coupled with a family's size and income determine whether and how much food assistance the family can claim. On this view, fairness in distribution is closely related to the formal fairness of impartial administration of rules.

The rules themselves must also pass moral muster, and both consequentialist and deontological concerns govern which rules are acceptable. It is

---

[10] One may also question whether fairness is only concerned with the satisfaction of claims. Are there no questions of fairness concerning the treatment of interests? Because this book argues that health care needs give rise to claims, there is no need to explore questions about the fair treatment of mere interests.

perfectly reasonable to apply the terms "fair" and "unfair" to the rules that determine what claims individuals have as well as to the outcomes those rules lead to. Nevertheless, an ethical evaluation of the rules determining what claims people have is a different inquiry than the assessment of whether their claims have been fairly satisfied. Just as one can distinguish between a rule-dependent notion of desert (e.g., the value of food stamps a family deserves) from a rule-determining notion, like that invoked by those defending a retributive theory of punishment, so one can distinguish a rule-dependent notion of fairness, which is concerned with the satisfaction of already specified claims, from a rule-determining notion of fairness, which determines what people can claim and how strong their claims are. The former takes claims as given and asks whether their satisfaction has been in accordance with the principles specifying their strength and what is required to satisfy them. Tomlin's complaint, "fairness responds to claims and so claims do not respond to fairness" (2012, p. 212), is thus a request for an additional theory: In addition to an account of whether responses to claims are in accord with the principles governing fair distribution, a theory of fairness needs to evaluate those principles.

4.3 Assigning Distributive Shares

Before turning to more detailed philosophical accounts of fairness, let us consider a simple case that reveals some of the complexities in assigning distributive shares fairly:

> **Bankruptcy**
>
> A firm is unable to pay its creditors, Alan, Barb, and Chad, all that it owes to them ($9,000, $3,000, and $15,000, respectively). None of its creditors has a stronger reason to be compensated than others. The firm has $18,000 to pay off its creditors.

The fair thing to do looks as if it is simple: Because only $18,000 is available of the $27,000 the firm owes Alan, Barb, and Chad, each of the creditors should receive two-thirds of what they are owed, or $6,000, $2,000, and $10,000, respectively. Although the creditors all come up short, it is plausible that the distribution in proportion to what each is owed does not sacrifice anyone's interests in order to benefit others.

However, there are alternatives to proportional satisfaction of claims. It could be instead that what remained in bankruptcies is owed to the state, which in turn uses those funds to benefit customers, laid-off workers, communities, suppliers, and creditors, where the criteria for reimbursement is need. I am not proposing such a bankruptcy policy. The point is that what the creditor is owed—the size of the creditor's (normative) *claim*—depends on the rules governing bankruptcies, and there are alternative rules that also define desert in a way that is consistent with the fundamental demands of reciprocity. Which individuals are recognized as deserving depends both on the facts that the institutions count as relevant and on the rules of those institutions. Whether providing individuals with the payments the institutions take them to deserve is morally defensible depends on the justice of the institutions. It was not morally defensible to satisfy what the institutions in pre-Civil War recognized as the claims of slave owners to the return of their runaway slaves.

Given the actual rules determining the claims Alan, Barb, and Chad can make of bankrupt firms, which I assume are morally defensible, one can argue in favor of the proportional distribution on the grounds that each makes an equal proportional sacrifice and each receives the same proportion of what each is owed. Given our rules governing bankruptcies, the fact that Alan is a compulsive gambler, Barb is a volunteer at a homeless shelter, and Chad is a billionaire is irrelevant to what constitutes a fair distribution from the bankrupt firm. If all are paid two-thirds of what they are owed, the claims that the institutions define are treated with equal concern and respect. None is favored. Proportional satisfaction of debts, needs, promises, and so forth appears to conform to the basic intuition that, given the constraints and the relevant sense of desert, a fair distribution gives individuals an equal proportional satisfaction of their claims.

The Bankruptcy case is much simpler than distributional problems in health care. Each of the debts carries the same obligation for repayment. Moreover, $2,000, two-thirds of what Barb is owed, provides, intuitively, two-thirds of the benefits that $3,000 provides, whereas two-thirds of a surgery is likely to be of no value at all. Later in this chapter and in Chapter 5, we will tackle these difficulties, but for now there are advantages to focusing on a simple case.

4.3.1 Cooperative Game Theory and Fairness: The Nucleolus

It is not obvious that fairness requires proportional satisfaction, even in such a simple case. From the perspective of cooperative game theory, the repayment of debts or the division of the proceeds from a joint endeavor can look very different. In cooperative game theory, agents, who are pursuing their own interests, are able to make binding agreements. In thinking about distribution of the proceeds of any common endeavor, the game theorist needs to consider whether subsets of the group of agents might form groups—that is, "coalitions"—that will do better for their members than does the "grand coalition" consisting of all the individuals. Although many of the concerns of cooperative game theory are not relevant to the problem of how to allocate health care fairly, it is possible to view the division of health care resources as a cooperative game, and some of the concepts from cooperative game theory are valuable as alternative ways to think about fairness.[11] For example, "Yet it is by no means obvious that this [proportional division] is the only equitable or reasonable system. For example, if the estate [the quantity to be distributed] does not exceed the smallest debt, equal division among the creditors makes good sense" (Aumann and Maschler 1985, p. 1950). If the firm in the Bankruptcy case had only $1,800 instead of $18,000 with which to pay its debts, would payments of $600 to each of the three creditors be fairer or less fair than paying Alan $600, Barb $200, and Chad $1,000? An equal division seems consistent with the notion of reciprocity, which I have argued is fundamental to fairness.

There are other ways to distribute repayments among creditors that appear to be fair. One of these alternative conceptions of fairness, which is implicit in an ancient text in the Talmud (Aumann and Maschler 1985), is called the "nucleolus." Begin by considering how much money the three creditors, singly or in pairs, can demand of the bankrupt firm, if it reserves sufficient assets to repay the other creditors. When, for example, Barb asks the firm for the $3,000 it owes her, the firm refuses to pay her anything because even if it gives Barb nothing, it does not have enough to pay Alan and Chad what it owes them. On the other hand, when Chad asks for what he is owed, the firm can release a partial repayment of $6,000 without compromising its ability to repay Alan and Barb. If Alan and Chad approach the firm together, the firm can release $15,000 and still retain enough to repay Barb fully. One can thus specify a set of what I call "guaranteed entitlements" of the "coalitions"—that is, the individuals, the pairs of individuals, and the grand coalition consisting of all three. For any arbitrary allocation of $18,000, one can examine how much more (or less) it provides to each coalition than the guaranteed entitlement. The nucleolus is the allocation that maximizes the minimum surplus over the guaranteed minimum an allocation provides to any individual or coalition and then maximizes the minimum second smallest

---

[11] For this thought, I am indebted to Heilmann and Wintein (2017) and Wintein and Heilmann (2018a, b).

surplus and so forth. In the Bankruptcy case, the nucleolus allocates $6,000 to Alan, $1,500 to Barb, and $10,500 to Chad.[12]

4.3.2 Fairness and Cooperative Game Theory: The Shapley Value

Let us consider one other view of fair allocation—the Shapley value. We can think of the creditors arriving individually at the bankrupt firm, asking for their money back. As each arrives, the firm pays the individual as much as it can, subject to the constraint that it retains enough to repay all the other creditors (as shown in the second row of Table 4.1). One can then examine what difference a creditor makes to the repayment to a group or coalition, depending on the order in which the creditors arrive. The average of the differences creditors make to the amount to be repaid to the coalitions they join is the Shapley value.

---

[12] Consider Table 4.1:

Table 4.1 The Nucleolus

Coalition	A	B	C	AB	AC	BC	All Three
Minimum	$0	$0	$6K	$3K	$15K	$9K	$18K
$V(S) - (6, 2, 10)$	–$6K	–$2K	–$4K	–$5K	–$1K	–$3K	$0
$V(S) - (6.5, 1.5, 10)$	–$6.5K	–$1.5K	–$4K	–$5K	–$1.5K	–$2.5K	$0
$V(S) - (6, 1.5, 10.5)$	–$6K	–$1.5K	–$4.5K	–$5K	–$1.5K	–$3K	$0

The second row shows the guaranteed minimums. The remaining three rows in Table 4.1 illustrate the thinking behind the nucleolus. Start with any proposed allocation to Alan, Barb, and Chad of the $18,000 available to repay the creditors. I've chosen to start with the proportional allocation ($6K, $2K, $10K), but one could begin with any allocation. This allocation gives every individual and pair more than what they can guarantee to themselves. But it benefits some more than others, and the inequality in surplus is arguably unfair, unless it is unavoidable. In the third row, the pair consisting of Alan and Chad receive a smaller amount of the surplus than does any other individual or pair. Even though Alan and Chad are both as individuals getting a larger surplus over their minimums than is Barb, the Alan-Chad pair is doing worse. To increase the surplus going to this pair, one must decrease Barb's surplus. However, one cannot lower Barb's surplus by more than $500, or else she will wind up with the smallest surplus. By adding $500 to the surplus going to the pair consisting of Alan and Chad, one maximizes the minimum surplus going to any individual or pair.

But we're not done. It is not a matter of indifference whether one adds the $500 taken from Barb's repayment to Alan's allocation or to Chad's allocation. The fourth row in Table 4.1 shows the repayment if the $500 goes to Alan, and the fifth row shows the allocations if Chad gets the extra $500. The latter maximizes the second lowest surplus in a repayment and is thus arguably fairer than the former. The nucleolus is that allocation that lexicographically maximizes the minimum surplus over the guaranteed minimums. In this case, the nucleolus would distribute $6,000 to Alan, $1,500 to Barb, and $10,500 to Chad.

In this particular example, the Shapley values are $5,000 for Alan, $2,000 for Barb, and $11,000 for Chad.[13] The Shapley values differ from both the proportional shares ($6,000, $2,000, and $10,000) and the nucleolus distribution ($6,000, $1,500, and $10,500). Which of these three allocations is fair (or fairest)?

The answer depends, I maintain, on the details of the problem, and it depends more on the case for the different distributive principles than on uncertain intuitions about which distribution is best. In this case of bankruptcy, coalitions are of no importance, and the fact that the nucleolus is sensitive to the differences in surpluses going to coalitions as well as to individuals is a vice, not a virtue.[14]

Consider, in contrast, the following variation on the Bankruptcy problem:

Investor's Loss

Alan and Chad invest respectively $9,000 and $15,000 in a company. It does badly and is on the verge of a complete collapse, with no value left. Barb is an optimistic investor who thinks that with her $3,000 investment, she can turn the company around. The firm winds up failing despite Barb's investment, but it now has $18,000 in assets to be divided among its three creditors, which it would not have had without Barb's investment. How should the $18,000 be divided among the three creditors?

---

[13] Consider Table 4.2:

Table 4.2 Shapley Values

Order of Arrival				Alan	Barb	Chad
ABC	A	AB	ABC	$V(A) = \$0$	$[V(AB) - V(A)] = \$3K$	$[V(ABC) - V(AB)] = \$15K$
ACB	A	AC	ABC	$V(A) = \$0$	$[V(ABC) - V(AC)] = \$3K$	$[V(AC) - V(A)] = \$15K$
BAC	B	AB	ABC	$[V(AB) - V(B)] = \$3K$	$V(B) = \$0$	$[V(ABC) - V(AB)] = \$15K$
BCA	B	BC	ABC	$[V(ABC) - V(BC)] = \$9K$	$V(B) = \$0$	$[V(BC) - V(B)] = \$9K$
CAB	C	AC	ABC	$[V(AC) - V(C)] = \$9K$	$[V(ABC) - V(AC)] = \$3K$	$V(C) = \$6K$
CBA	C	BC	ABC	$[V(ABC) - V(BC)] = \$9K$	$[V(BC) - V(C)] = \$3K$	$V(C) = \$6K$
Shapley value				$5K	$2K	$11K

[14] Starting with the proportional allocation, a concern with maximizing the minimum surplus *to individuals* would transfer $1,000 from Chad's proportionate share to Barb, rather than, as shown in Table 4.1 in footnote 12, transferring $500 from Barb to Chad. Similarly, in this case, marginal contributions are not important, and allowing them to determine the allocation seems to be arbitrary.

Now it seems that Barb should get more than $2,000—that is, two-thirds of what she invested—because it was only due to her timely investment that there are assets worth $18,000 to be divided among the three creditors. Defenders of proportional repayment might attempt to accommodate the intuition that Barb should get more by arguing that Alan and Chad have a debt to Barb. But what is owed to her, and how is that amount to be determined? In a case such as this one, the sensitivity of the Shapley value to marginal contributions makes a case for the fairness of the Shapley values (which give $3,500 to Alan, $8,000 to Barb, and $6,500 to Chad).[15]

The nucleolus for the Investor's Loss problem differs from the Shapley value, allocating $4,500 to Alan, $6,500 to Barb, and $7,000 to Chad.[16] Apart from believing that in the Investor's Loss problem, Barb should get more of the

---

[15] Since the value of any coalition that does not contain Barb is zero, one gets the Shapley values shown in Table 4.3:

Table 4.3 Shapley Values for the Investor's Loss Problem

Order of Arrival	Alan	Barb	Chad
ABC A AB ABC	$V(A) = \$0$	$[V(AB) - V(A)] = \$3K$	$[V(ABC) - V(AB)] = \$15K$
ACB A AC ABC	$V(A) = \$0$	$[V(ABC) - V(AC)] = \$18K$	$[V(AC) - V(A)] = \$0$
BAC B AB ABC	$[V(AB) - V(B)] = \$3K$	$V(B) = \$0$	$[V(ABC) - V(AB)] = \$15K$
BCA B BC ABC	$[V(ABC) - V(BC)] = \$9K$	$V(B) = \$0$	$[V(BC) - V(B)] = \$9K$
CAB C AC ABC	$[V(AC) - V(C)] = 0$	$[V(ABC) - V(AC)] = \$18K$	$V(C) = 0$
CBA C BC ABC	$[V(ABC) - V(BC)] = \$9K$	$[V(BC) - V(C)] = \$9K$	$V(C) = 0$
Shapley value	$3.5K	$8K	$6.5

[16] The second row in Table 4.4 gives the values of the coalitions in light of the fact that B's investment is essential. The third row then looks at the differences between the guaranteed values and an arbitrary allocation—in this case an allocation that gives everyone the same amount. That distribution awards too little to the pair Barb and Chad, which can be repaired only by decreasing the allocation to A, as in the fourth row. This goes too far, making Alan worst off. Shifting the distribution so that Alan gets $4,500 and Barb gets $6,500 maximizes the minimum benefit among the whole set of coalitions and also the second highest minimum surplus.

Table 4.4 The Nucleolus of the Investor's Loss Problem

Coalition	A	B	C	AB	AC	BC	ABV
Value	0	0	$0	$3K	0	$9K	$18K
$V(S) - (6, 6, 6)$	−$6K	−$6K	−$6K	−$9K	−$12K	−$3K	0
$V(S) - (4, 7, 7)$	−$4K	−$6K	−$8K	−$8K	−$11K	−$5K	0
$V(S) - (4.5, 6.5, 7)$	−$4.5K	−$6.5K	−$7K	−$8K	−$11.5K	−$4.5K	0

bankrupt firm's assets than in Bankruptcy, I have little intuitive sense of how much Barb should get. Should she profit, where Alan and Chad lose? The best one can do, I think, is to consider whether the considerations driving the Shapley value and the nucleolus are relevant and how plausible they are as principles of fairness. On that basis, I would be inclined to favor the Shapley values in the Investor's Loss problem, and proportional repayment in the Bankruptcy case.

It would be great to have a general theory of fairness that favors proportional distribution, the Shapley value, the nucleolus, or some other criterion, depending on the context. But it seems to me that there are several different ways to specify what constitutes an impartial distribution that does not sacrifice anyone's interests in order to benefit better-off others. Moreover, it seems to me that which of these ways is most satisfactory depends on the context. Because this is a book concerned with the principles governing the distribution of health care, not a treatise on fairness, it will suffice if I can clarify what constitutes fairness with respect to health care. From that limited perspective, I am initially inclined to identify (comparative) fairness with the proportional satisfaction or proportional chances of satisfaction of health care claims. The nucleolus and Shapley value capture concerns about fairness in contexts in which payoffs to groups, as well as payoffs to individuals, matter. But questions about how fairly health care is distributed are typically questions about the fairness of the distribution of health care among individuals, and concerns about increasing the marginal contribution individuals make to coalitions or the minimum surplus of an allocation seem to be of lesser relevance than proportional satisfaction.

The discussion of the nucleolus and the Shapley value is not, however, a digression because it makes clear the conceptual difficulties in defining a fair distribution and helps overcome the temptation to regard a proportional distribution as automatically a fair distribution. This has considerable importance because, as discussed later, a proportional distribution in the case of health care is often unavailable and even undefined.

4.4 Broome's Theory: Divisible Goods

John Broome (1990) maintains that distributive fairness requires that "claims" be satisfied in proportion to their strength. The debts owed to Alan, Barb, and Chad in the Bankruptcy case are examples of claims. In Broome's view, merely assigning *weights* to claims in proportion to their strength fails to treat them fairly. In taking some interest to have the moral force of a claim, the agent upon whom the claim is made has a duty to the claimant to satisfy the claim. If a claim is outweighed, then it is not satisfied, even in part. Claims that are outweighed receive no further consideration. Broome maintains that when goods are divisible, all claims, weak or strong, should be satisfied in proportion to their "strength." Broome's view is plausible and attractive, but it is not supported by much argument or beyond questioning. Why shouldn't the rules that specify what claims individuals have and how strong those claims are also dictate other ways in which those claims should properly be satisfied? For example, rather than requiring proportional satisfaction of weaker claims, fairness might instead be manifested in rules governing compensation to those whose claims are not satisfied. If claims are fungible in the currency in which compensation is provided, then compensation can be regarded as a partial satisfaction of a claim that should be proportional to the strength of a claim. But claims to health care are often not compensable, and when they are, it is questionable whether compensation can be regarded as a way of satisfying them.

The following case illustrates the contrast Broome draws between weighing claims and satisfying them proportionately:

> **Hips and Ankles**
>
> Suppose that funds become available to pay for additional physical therapy. Those with hip problems and those with ankle problems have unmet claims to physical therapy. The claims to hip therapy are twice as strong as the claims to ankle therapy. The additional physical therapy is not sufficient to satisfy all the claims.

Following Broome, I am assuming that there is some individual or institution that distributes a divisible good among a predetermined set of claimants, whose claims and their strength are predetermined and fixed. *Weighing* the claims implies satisfying claims to hip therapy first and then satisfying claims to ankle therapy if and only if there are resources left over. In contrast, *satisfying the claims proportionately* implies providing two-thirds of the additional physical therapy as hip therapy and one-third as ankle therapy.[17]

This contrast between weighing claims and satisfying them proportionately is central to Broome's account. Allocating nothing to any of the claimants provides each with the same proportional satisfaction, and hence it is comparatively fair, even though it is rarely the right thing to do, all things considered. In Broome's

---

[17] On the assumption that two-thirds of the therapy provides two-thirds of the benefit. It is unclear what it means to provide twice the hip therapy as ankle therapy. What if the hip therapy is much more expensive than the ankle therapy? I address these puzzles in Chapter 5.

view, fairness is entirely comparative, but it generates only pro tanto reasons that compete with and may be defeated by other moral considerations. It could be better, all things considered, to put all the additional resources in the Hips and Ankles case into hip therapy, even if it is unfair.[18]

Broome's view of fairness in distribution as entirely comparative has been challenged by Vong (2020), who cites Feinberg (1974), Hooker (2005), and Temkin (2011) (see also Curtis 2014). In their view, intentionally failing to satisfy an individual's claim is (non-comparatively) unfair, regardless of how the claims of others are treated. I am inclined to think that whether they are right is more a question of terminology than of substance.

Whether or not the (non-comparative) extent to which a claim is satisfied counts as a question about fairness, it is clearly morally relevant, and it may be more in accord with ordinary usage to call both comparative and non-comparative injustices unfair. No sensible health care system can be unconcerned about how well health care meets (non-comparatively) people's needs. It is morally obligatory that allocations go as far as they can toward satisfying claims. However, this book is mainly concerned with the comparative fairness of different allocations of health care, although unlike Broome, it inquires into the fairness of the assignment of claims as well as the fairness of their satisfaction. I postpone until Chapter 5 an examination of what claims individuals have to health care. For now, I am identifying health care needs with claims.

There are a few things that one can say very generally about what determines how strong claims to health care are. If treatment can significantly improve people's health, then their claims will be stronger than the claims of those whose health cannot be greatly improved. One might propose that fairness in health care requires that the same health needs for divisible health care benefits should be satisfied in the same proportion. But demanding equal proportional satisfaction of claims does not explain how to compare how well a partial dose of analgesics satisfies claims to pain relief to how well a partial dose of antibiotics satisfies claims for protection from infection. The demand for proportional satisfaction also says nothing about costs, and it does not say how to distribute health care when it is indivisible, as much of it is. Clearly, more needs to be said before one can apply Broome's theory to evaluate the fairness of health care allocation.

---

[18] Vong argues that it is not a terminological matter (2020, p. 327). He presents a case in which I have promised to give Laura lunch. If I give her $10 instead, she is equally well off, but failing to do as I promised is still a distinct wrong. This example supports the view that the objection to the partial repayment cannot be explained entirely in terms of the harm it may do. Even if I have not made her worse off, I have been unjust to her. But the example does not show that I have been *unfair* to her.

4.5 Broome's Theory: Indivisible Goods

What is to be distributed is not always divisible without loss of value. Half an apple is roughly half as good as a whole apple, whereas half a baseball is no good at all. When two individuals are in need of a transplant, they cannot each be given half a heart. What constitutes fair treatment of competing claims to indivisible goods?

When claims to an indivisible good are equal in strength, and there are no issues of overlapping groups (about which more is said below), then it seems pretheoretically to be (comparatively) fair to give each claimant an equal chance. Whether it is comparatively unfair simply to pick who wins and who loses is more controversial, with Henning (2015) and Eyal (n.d.) arguing that there is nothing wrong with simply picking, as long as the picking is not guided by properties of claimants or desires of allocators that should not be relevant.

Even if not required, random devices such as lotteries are attractive ways of distributing indivisible goods. A lottery is an easy way of getting a definite answer that is impartial and reasonably safe from tampering. Lotteries are transparent, inexpensive, and decisive. However, in c-e allocation, policymakers already possess a definite, clear-cut, and arguably impartial way to determine what mix of treatments to provide—namely by considering cost-effectiveness. Because costs and capacity to benefit are relevant properties to rely on in an impartial determination of who is to benefit, those who question the fairness of c-e allocation apparently deny that an impartial determination guarantees fairness.

Broome (1990) makes a different case in favor of employing a chance mechanism when claims to goods cannot be satisfied in proportion to their strength:

> In that case, the candidates' claims cannot all be equally satisfied, because some candidates will get the good and others will not. So some unfairness is inevitable. But a sort of partial equality in satisfaction can be achieved. Each person can be given a sort of surrogate satisfaction. By holding a lottery, each can be given an equal *chance* of getting the good. This is not perfect fairness, but it meets the requirement of fairness to some extent.
>
> It does so, of course, only if giving a person a chance of getting the good counts as a surrogate satisfaction of her claim. This seems plausible to me. After all, if you have a chance of getting the good you may actually get it. It is quite different from merely giving the claim its proper weight against other reasons; that does not satisfy it in any way. Suppose, in the example of the dangerous mission, that the talented candidate was sent because of her talents. She could make the following complaint. She has as strong a claim to staying

behind as anybody else.[19] Her claim was weighed against other reasons. But this [weighing] overrode her claim rather than satisfied it. It was never on the cards that she might actually get the good she has a claim to. But if she was sent because a lottery was held and she lost, she could make no such complaint. (pp. 97–98)

Broome maintains that the distribution of chances to receive an indivisible good in proportion to the strength of the claims of individuals provides a proxy, stand-in, or surrogate satisfaction of a claim. What is that? It is not simply a chance of getting the good that is proportional to the strength of the claim, which would make it a definitional truth that receiving such a good provides a surrogate satisfaction of a claim, which thus cannot explain or justify distributing chances one way or another.

Broome intends instead to make a substantive normative assertion about how chances should correspond to claims. Let us examine the passage carefully. First, Broome apparently thinks of the fair apportionment of chances as echoing the fair division of the good itself, were that good divisible. Second, Broome intends his account to apply to cases of both equally and unequally strong claims to indivisible goods. He does not discuss claims of different sizes like those in the Bankruptcy case. If chances are surrogate satisfactions of claims, then to provide a surrogate satisfaction, lotteries should give weaker claims a lesser but non-zero chance of getting the good.[20] The case for weighted lotteries is problematic because their outcomes may be unsatisfactory, at least with regard to efficiency (1990, p. 99) and non-comparative fairness. If the winner of a weighted lottery has an appreciably weaker claim to the good, then the outcome seems clearly worse than jettisoning the lottery and giving the good to the individual with the stronger claim to it (Hooker 2005, p. 349). But does the unsatisfactory outcome impugn the comparative *fairness* of the procedure that got us there?

Stone (2007) argues that a weighted lottery

does violence to the whole idea of impartially considering the strength of claims. Any grounds that an agent could have for assigning a higher weight to the chance that x will get the good than the chance y will get the good should count as grounds for simply giving x, and not y, the good outright. (p. 285)

---

[19] Although plausible, in Section 5.4 I challenge Broome's assertion that the talented candidate's claim is equally strong, when I argue that the cost of satisfying claims weakens them.

[20] Broome is hesitant to defend weighted lotteries and may only intend to defend lotteries among equal or almost equal claimants, because he is concerned that the good may go to lesser claimants (1990, pp. 98–99). But are his qualms about proportional lotteries qualms about their *fairness*?

However, Broome distinguishes the assessment of the distribution of chances from the assessment of the resultant distribution of the indivisible good. He regards the distribution of the good as unfair because only the lottery winner gets the indivisible good to which all the parties have a claim.[21] If one adds to Broome's theory the view that it is *more* unfair for those who have a weaker claim to be awarded an indivisible good than for those with a stronger claim to get the good, then a weighted lottery risks an *outcome* that is less fair than simply awarding the good to the individual with the stronger claim. But Broome says little about how to rank the fairness of unfair outcomes. Moreover, even if the outcome in which the claimant with the weaker claim is awarded the good is less fair, the chance procedure that resulted in that outcome may still be fair.

One might think that because the lotteries are weighted, unfortunate outcomes would be rare. But in circumstances in which there are many claimants, the fact that it is more likely that a strong claimant gets the good than any individual weak claimant does not imply that it is likely that a strong claimant gets the good. For example, if Elena has a claim that is four times as strong as each of eight other claimants, her probability of getting the good will still be only one in three. Simply giving the good to the strongest claimant may seem to be the fairer option. However, the intuitive attraction of giving the good to the strongest claimant might reflect a concern about efficiency or non-comparative fairness, rather than (comparative) fairness.

We have not yet figured out what is the surrogate satisfaction of a claim. Commentators have disagreed. Hugh Lazenby suggests that a surrogate satisfaction of a claim is either a partial satisfaction or it is an "improvement in fairness without satisfaction" (2014, p. 337). Neither interpretation is satisfactory. The second interpretation does not tell us *how* chances contribute to fairness if they do not contribute to satisfying claims. On the first interpretation, receiving a lottery ticket with a chance c^* of getting some good G provides an agent with a partial satisfaction of his claim and hence something with some positive value, $V(c^*)$. When the winning ticket is drawn and one has lost, then $V(c^*)$ and the chance c^* are both zero. (If not, one would have to explain how lottery winners manage to gain more than they would have if they had simply been awarded the good.) The chance each lottery ticket provides does not seem as if it goes any way toward satisfying the claim to the good, as it would have to if it were a partial satisfaction.

Gerard Vong (17) reads Broome as maintaining that the surrogate satisfaction of a claim *voids* the claim without satisfying it. On this interpretation, Broome's account is untenable. This might be a reasonable view of so-called consensual

---

[21] I am indebted to John Broome's objections to a previous formulation of the argument in this paragraph. I do not know what Broome would think of this version.

gambles (Henning 2015, p. 195), where individuals who have lost a lottery have agreed to surrender any further claim to the good. However, if there is no such agreement, as in a case in which an allocator employs a random device without consulting the claimants, it is implausible to maintain that losers no longer have any claim to the good. Suppose that Jack and Jill have equal claims to some good, whether it be a soccer ball or a heart transplant. I flip a fair coin with their names on the two sides. Jill's name shows, and I am committed to give the good to Jill. On Vong's interpretation, after I have flipped the coin, even if the good has not yet been distributed, Jack no longer has a claim to the good. However, suppose that after the flip an additional unit of the good becomes available. It is implausible to maintain that Jack has no claim on it, which is what, on Vong's interpretation, Broome's view of surrogate satisfaction implies.[22] Moreover, if outcomes satisfy all non-voided claims, then the outcomes would be fair, which Broome denies.

Vong offers his own view of the value of chances, which I find persuasive both as an account of the value of chances and as an interpretation of "surrogate satisfaction" (even though Vong does not intend it that way). On this view, individuals have two kinds of claims: benefit claims to the good to be distributed and procedural claims to have their benefit claims treated fairly and with respect. Although procedural claims are parasitic on benefit claims, it is possible for either to be satisfied without the other. Procedural claims to indivisible goods are satisfied in proportion to their strength only in the case of goods that are distributed by lotteries. A fair lottery satisfies procedural claims, but it does not satisfy the benefit claims of losers, which are unsatisfied and undiminished. Conversely, if a transplant surgeon has a heart for you, the only person who can use it, and instead of giving you the heart straight off, she flips a coin with the intention of giving you the heart if and only if the coin lands heads, then, even if you are lucky and she gives you the heart, she has not satisfied your procedural claims. Although interpreting lotteries as satisfying procedural claims revises Broome's theory, it seems to me to capture what Broome intends by "surrogate satisfaction".

Speaking of chances as in some way satisfying claims suggests that chances are themselves goods, whose fair distribution ameliorates the unfair distribution of tangible goods, without, however, making the distribution of tangible goods fair, or voiding anyone's (benefit) claims. Unable to distribute G fairly among those with claims to G, the allocator distributes $ch(G)$, a surrogate for G, in proportion to the strength of claims and thereby satisfies procedural claims fairly. On this interpretation, it seems that what matters is the distribution of objective chances, not evidential or subjective probabilities.

[22] Cf. Vong's "Extra Buoy" case (2015, p. 474). One might attempt to defend the view that lotteries void the claims of losers by arguing that the lottery does void Jack's claim to that particular token good. But if Jill dies before the good is distributed to her, Jack still has a claim to it.

It might appear that few (or perhaps none, as Michael Otsuka [n.d.] suggests) of the chance mechanisms that we possess confer objective chances on their outcomes. Moreover, it has been questioned whether fair division needs objective chances: Some have argued that epistemic probabilities provide all that fairness requires. If the satisfaction of a procedural claim is a matter of showing proper baseline respect, then perhaps epistemic probability is all that is needed.[23] On such a view, it makes no difference whether the lottery that determines who gets the good has already been carried out, provided that its results are not yet known. After all, gamblers seem to draw no distinction between tickets for a future drawing and "scratch cards,"[24] whose payoffs are already printed on the card but concealed. If unexposed scratch cards have no less value than do tickets to a lottery with the same prize that has not yet been drawn, then it would appear that a fair lottery requires only equal (or perhaps merely unknown) epistemic probabilities.

One might argue that satisfying procedural claims requires only providing assurance that no one's claim has a greater chance of being satisfied than is proportional to the strength of their claim. In that way, equal respect is shown to all claimants. On this view, only beliefs concerning the chances of getting the benefit are being distributed, and proponents can argue that respect and impartiality require nothing more than shared beliefs about the chances of winning. However, consider the following case:

> **Brian and Betty's Coin Flip**
>
> Whether Brian or Betty gets a good is to be determined by flipping a coin that is believed to have "Brian" printed on one side and "Betty" printed on the other. However, due to a manufacturing malfunction of which no one is aware, both sides have Brian's name on them.

No one has any better reason to believe that Brian will win than that Betty will win. But even if no one ever finds out that Brian's name is on both sides of the

---

[23] Wasserman (1996), Stone (2007), and Sher (1980). With respect to cases involving equal claims, Stone maintains that "if the warrant for predicting that one outcome will occur is exactly the same as the warrant for believing that any other outcome will occur, then the lottery is a fair lottery" (2007, p. 280). Wasserman grounds this view as follows: "Lotteries are fair if they respect the claimants' equal entitlements to the scarce good; they do so simply by distributing the scarce good in a way that cannot reasonably be seen by the allocator or the claimants as favoring any claimant" (1996, p. 48).

[24] I borrow this example from Otsuka (n.d.).

coin, and everyone believes the procedure to be fair, it isn't. [25] To the extent of their abilities, everyone expressed equal concern for each claimant. But fairness demands more.[26] The claimant's procedural claim demands a genuine—that is, objective—chance proportional to the claim's strength. What justifies the use of a lottery does not lie entirely in the attitudes that a lottery expresses toward the claimants or in the beliefs of those in possession of lottery tickets or in charge of the lottery. Lotteries are an especially good way of showing that no claimant is favored. But the proper epistemic probabilities are not sufficient for the fairness of the procedure that distributes indivisible goods. In Brian and Betty's Coin Flip, "It was never on the cards that she might actually get the good she has a claim to" (Broome 1990, p. 98). The procedural claims of the claimants are not satisfied by merely epistemic probabilities of getting the good.

This case for the conclusion that fairness demands objective chances proportional to the strength of claims faces serious challenges. Consider scratch cards. The objective chance of their winning a prize is exactly 1 or 0. Yet individuals apparently treat them no differently than a lottery ticket that has a small objective probability of winning. Are people just confused? Not necessarily. Although the card gamblers hold in their hand have a probability of winning of 1 or 0, that is not the probability of buying a winning scratch card.

One might also object to the conclusion that fair lotteries must assign the proper objective probabilities on the ground that in a deterministic world, the only objective probabilities are 1 or 0. Suppose one flips a coin to decide which of two people with equal claims receives an indivisible good. Conditional on a perfectly precise characterization of how the coin is held, flipped, and allowed to fall, the turbulence in the air, the dirt and scratches on the coin, and indeed of everything that could influence whether the coin lands heads or tails, the probability that it will land heads is, let us suppose, either 1 or 0. But there is still a difference between flipping an ordinary coin, which lands heads, and flipping a two-headed coin.

The difference lies in the distribution of heads in those (many) states of affairs that are consistent with the (token) action of the person or device that flips the coin.[27] The specific individual state of affairs is consistent with intervals of the

---

[25] If the example involved instead a two-headed coin, objective chances might creep back in via the link between the individuals and the faces of the coin. Kornhauser and Sager defend a plausible thesis, which they call "convolution" (1988, p. 486), that says that if any essential step in a multistep procedure is random, then, other things being equal, so is the output of the procedure as a whole. *Brian and Betty's Coin Flip* is not subject to the complications of convolution.

[26] "Lotteries give good reasons to the losers for why they should accept being on the losing side. Namely, that a non-arbitrary procedure was used *that easily could have made them win*" (Spiekermann 2021, p. 1).

[27] To use some useful jargon, the distinction is between the probability of heads associated with a point in phase space and the distribution of the probability of heads associated with a region of phase space. With deterministic laws, the first will be 0 or 1, whereas the distribution of zeros and ones for the points in the region will be roughly equal. See Ismael (2009).

values of relevant factors. Conditional on the specific individual flip—that is, on the many values of the fundamental variables lying within these intervals—there is an *objective* probability distribution of heads and tails (Ismael 2009; Sober 1980). Such a conditional probability distribution for ordinary one-headed coins will have a peak close to 0.5. Given the range of values of variables consistent with coin flips, coin flips provide an objective chance that is close to 0.5.

I conclude that Broome is right to maintain that the fairness of lotteries depends on whether they distribute the appropriate shares of a surrogate or proxy for shares of the indivisible good, but I construe "surrogate satisfaction" as the satisfaction of procedural claims. The chances that constitute these surrogates are evanescent: All except the winning lottery tickets become valueless, except as souvenirs, once it is known who has won. Moreover, in identifying the surrogate satisfaction that lotteries provide with a distribution of objective chances, one need not deny that lotteries also have benefits that require only epistemic probabilities, such as impartiality, expressing equal respect, and the subjective value of believing (and possessing evidence) that one has a chance to win.

Consider again Brian and Betty's Coin Flip. Using the coin that, unknown to all, has Brian's name on both sides shows no partiality on the part of the allocator, and (at least if the misprinting is never discovered) it expresses equal respect toward Brian and Betty. Moreover, there is value in the belief in the equal objective chance of Brian and Betty winning. But this spoiled lottery gives Betty only the false belief that her procedural claim has been satisfied.

4.6 Challenges to Broome's Theory

Gerard Vong (2020) has noted that it is not always possible to comply with the demand that equal claimants should have equal chances. Sometimes it is not possible to benefit one person without benefitting others in a group. If individuals belong to more than one group (if groups "overlap"), then it may not be possible to give equal claimants equal chances. For example, suppose one has a good that can be shared by one of four couples: A & B, A & C, D & E, and D & F (Vong 2020, p. 324). There is no way to distribute chances among the couples so as to give each of the six individuals an equal non-zero chance of getting the good.

One might conclude that all Vong shows is that it is sometimes impossible to satisfy claims in proportion to their strength, but Broome already concedes this in the case of indivisible goods. But in that case, unlike Vong's, there is the backup provided by surrogate satisfaction. In Vong's cases, Broome's theory provides no guidance. Presumably there are fairer and less fair ways to assign probabilities to groups, even when it is impossible to give equal chances to those with equally strong claims. Vong argues that what is fair in this example is to give each couple an equal (25%) chance of getting the good, which is impartial and maximizes the minimum chance each individual possesses, even though it gives A and D a 50% chance of getting a share of the good, whereas B, C, E, and F each have a 25% chance.

A theory of fairness should encompass goods that must be shared and that can only be enjoyed by some individuals if they are enjoyed by others. In the philosophical literature, cases involving a choice between helping different groups with exclusive memberships of different sizes have been discussed (e.g., in Kamm 1993 Chaps. 5–7), but prior to Vong's recent article, cases in which groups overlap have not been considered. In Vong's cases, each individual receives the full benefit of the good if awarded to any group to which the individual belongs, regardless of how large the group may be. So a choice among groups raises issues concerning the magnitude of benefit as well as how it is distributed. Vong (2020) defends a complicated view of how to assign chances of receiving the benefit to groups so as to treat their members in the fairest way, where fairness, in his view, is both comparative and non-comparative. For criticism of his proposal, see Hausman (2022).

As we have seen, Broome maintains that it is fair to give equal claimants for an indivisible good an equal chance of getting the good. However, this view, and Broome's theory, runs into problems not only when there are overlapping groups and equal distribution is impossible but also in cases such as the following:

> **Volcanic Rescue**
>
> Volcanic eruptions have placed the lives of many inhabitants in immediate jeopardy. A large number are gathered at the north end of the island, awaiting evacuation. A handful find themselves on the southern tip. Imagine the captain of the only Coast Guard evacuation ship in the area finding himself midway between. Where shall he head first? (Taurek 1977, p. 310)

Suppose there are 100 people at the north end and 5 at the south end, and those on either end will die if the ship goes to the other end first. If all the people on the island have, as I shall suppose, an equal claim to be rescued, then in Broome's view, the fairest thing to do is to refuse to save anyone. (Of course, this action is ruled out on the grounds of justice and benevolence.) Second fairest in Broome's view is to give equal claimants equal chances of rescue by, for example, flipping an unbiased coin. Because most people find this implication of Broome's view implausible, cases such as Volcanic Rescue challenge the view that fairness requires that equal claimants for some indivisible good should have equal chances of getting it.

If the captain has an obligation to save as many of the individuals on the island as possible, then allowing the deaths of 100 if the coin lands tails, when the captain could have guaranteed that only 5 individuals would perish, is unjust (or non-comparatively unfair) to scores of people the captain had an obligation to save. But the question is what is the (comparatively) fair thing to do, not what is just or optimal. Should one agree with Broome, or is there some alternative view whereby it is fair to give the 100 a greater chance or perhaps a certainty of being saved.

Although not specifically focused on fairness, Frances Kamm discusses a few alternatives (1993, Vol. 1, pp. 116–117), and defends one, which Scanlon also defends (1998, pp. 232–233):

> Consider a pair of such opposing individuals [such as those at different locations on the island]. Since their interests are opposed and of equal weight, it might be suggested *that they cancel each other out.* If we cancel them out, we will have counted each of these interests and given it all the weight it should be given consistent with equal treatment. . . . All the remaining interests (if any) will be for the same alternative. . . . The weight of these interests will decide the matter in favor of that outcome. (Kamm 1993, p. 116)

Kamm speaks of interests rather than claims, but I assume that she would say the same about the balancing of opposing claims. After the claims of 5 of the 100 on the north end have "balanced" the claims of the 5 on the south end, the claims of the others on the north end are (in Kamm's and Scanlon's view) impermissibly ignored by flipping a coin. Claims are like forces that, when oppositely directed, can balance one another and, when unopposed, determine motion. Call this policy (following Kamm) "majority rule." Showing equal baseline respect demands some responsiveness to the claims to be saved of the 95 on the north end whose interests or claims are not balanced by any conflicting interests or claims. In Kamm's view, to treat people (fairly) as equals requires focusing on their interests rather than the impersonal value of the objects of their interests. That means that when there are conflicting interests of the same magnitude, we treat people as equals by treating their interests equally. To treat their interests or claims equally is to weigh their conflicting interests against one another—which is precisely what Broome condemns.[28]

---

[28] Kamm denies that the opposing interests are literally canceled. "But, as noted above, the balancing of equal and opposites need not be understood as cancelation. . . . It can be understood, rather, as the recognition that neither of two equal and opposing claims can finally decide an outcome (the 'unbalanced' members of one side must do that), and, whichever side we help, we will satisfy an interest—it does not disappear as canceled out—that counts as much as any interest equal

A third alternative, "proportional chances," assigns chances to groups of equal claimants that match their proportion of the population. However, this alternative is difficult to motivate or defend. On the assumption that saving more people is better than fewer (which, as discussed in Chapter 8, Taurek denies), proportional chances has a much higher expected value than equal probabilities. But it is in this regard inferior to majority rule, and, in any case, why think that it is fairer than either equal chances or majority rule? Unlike majority rule, it gives a chance to those who are in the smaller group, but that chance is determined by the number of individuals in the respective groups, which appears to be irrelevant from the perspective of fairness. Moreover, proportional chances apparently implies that the greater number in a group strengthens the claims of the members of the group. If the unlikely outcome occurs and the good goes to the smaller number, then the defender of proportional chances must accept an outcome that they regard as less fair. As Kamm notes, it is possible to argue for proportional chances as the outcome of a series of equal-chance encounters. Moreover, if initially everyone has a chance of $1/n$ of being saved (where n is the total number of individuals involved) and individuals are able to pool their chances, then proportional chances follows. But the premises in these arguments are rarely true, and the expected outcomes appear less fair than those implied by majority rules.[29]

How can we determine whether Broome is right that fairness demands that the satisfaction of claims or the chance of satisfying claims be proportional to their strength or Kamm is right that fairness demands the balancing of strength-weighted claims? One possibility is to examine our intuitions concerning further cases. For example, what if instead of 5 people at the south end, there were 97 (with 100 still at the north end)? On Kamm's view, all that matters is whether the number of those at the south is fewer than those at the north. But is it fair to give the 97 at the south no chance of survival? Kamm argues for majority rule on the grounds that it is equally sensitive to everyone's interests—or (extrapolating) claims—whereas Broome's account insists on giving each person an equal chance.

Insisting, as Broome's theory implies, that it is fair for everyone in Volcanic Rescue to have the same chance of survival might appear to be a cavalier denial of strong intuitions. What is the point of asserting that fair division requires that equal claimants have equal chances, when equal chances is so

and opposite to it with which it is balanced" (1993, p. 117). Although this argues against regarding the interests or claims as canceling one another, it does not show that balancing is not a form of the weighing that Broome criticizes.

[29] Kamm also discusses another way of adjudicating between partially conflicting claims, which she calls "the ideal procedure" (1993, Vol. 1, Chapter 6), but it is not applicable to this case.

completely at variance with the policy virtually everyone would regard as fair, or at least not unfair? The best response to this objection lies in the moral bookkeeping that Broome's view permits. It is important both to treat people fairly and to save lives. It is important ("non-comparatively fair") to satisfy people's claims, regardless of comparisons to how others are treated. It is also important to treat claims of equal strength equally. It may be helpful for practical purposes in particular contexts to formulate criteria that are responsive to more than one of these considerations. But to address criticisms of the criteria and to extend one's moral theorizing from one context to another, one should recognize that these considerations of well-being, non-comparative fairness, and comparative fairness are separate. What is wrong with giving 100 people, who could have been saved for sure, only a one-half chance of living in order that 5 other people also have that chance is the expected harm and the non-comparative unfairness of exposing so many people to such a large risk. Because Broome's proportional-satisfaction or proportional-chances-of-satisfaction views fit our intuitions elsewhere, and its uncomfortable implications in cases such as Volcanic Rescue can be explained away, it seems to me at this point that Volcanic Rescue poses no serious objection to Broome's theory.

4.7 Fairness When Claims Differ Both in Size and in Strength

The view that shares in divisible goods as well as chances of obtaining indivisible goods should be proportional to the strength of claims fails to address questions concerning fair division when claims differ with respect to their size or quantity, as in the Bankruptcy example. Benjamin Curtis (2014) offers a reformulation of Broome's view that aims to cope with this complication. However, his reformulation ignores differing claim strength.

Following Wintein and Heilmann's presentation and adopting much of their notation, one can formalize the problems posed by claims to different quantities of a good as "claims problems" (2018a, p. 56):

> Definition 1 (Claims problems) A *claims problem* $C := (E, N, c)$ consists of a (divisible or indivisible) amount of good $E > 0$, also called the *estate*, a set of agents N, and a claims vector c specifying the amount $c_i > 0$ of the estate that agent i has a claim to and which is such that $\Sigma_{i \in N} c_i \geq E$.

In the case of fully divisible goods, Curtis defends the proportional view—that each individual i should receive $\alpha.c_i$, where $\alpha = (E/\Sigma_{i \in N} c_i)$. Each individual's claim must be satisfied in the same proportion (α) as the estate satisfies the total claims. In the case of goods that are not entirely divisible, each individual should receive the integer part of their proportional share, with any remaining units distributed via a weighted lottery in which the probability that an agent gets a further unit of the good is equal to the fractional part of the agent's proportional share.

If, like Hooker and Lazenby, one rejects the use of weighted lotteries, then one must propose instead some rule determining who gets the units of indivisible goods remaining after providing the claimants with the integer part of their shares. The natural thought is to give them to those whose fractional remainder is largest. This largest remainder proposal runs into paradoxes, as Wintein and Heilmann (2018a) explain. What they propose instead is "Webster's method," which calculates $\alpha.c_i$ for all i, and then rounds the allocations going to individuals up or down to whole numbers depending on whether the fractional remainder is more or less than 0.5. If the resulting allocations do not exhaust the estate or sum to more than the estate, the method adjusts α up or down until the allocations going to individuals add up to the estate.[30]

As already mentioned, Curtis' extension of Broome's theory has nothing to say about circumstances in which some claims are stronger than others. Consider the following case:

Acne and Paralysis Pills

Albert has a claims to 10, 11, or 12 pills to alleviate his acne. A larger number of pills works better. Fewer than 10 pills does him no good, and more than 12 pills brings no more relief than 12 pills. Bonnie has a strong claim to 2 of the same pills to avoid her left foot becoming paralyzed. A single pill has only a small probability of working, and her claim to it is weak. She has no claim to more than 2 pills.

Bonnie's claim is *stronger* ($s_B > s_A$), whereas Albert's claim is *larger* ($c_A > c_B$). Wintein and Heilmann propose a way to attend to both the strength and the quantity of claims by reinterpreting the task as aiming at fairly satisfying "corrected claims" rather than claims simpliciter. A corrected claim, r_i, consists of the quantity claimed weighted by the strength of the claim ($r_A = c_A.s_A$; $r_B = c_B.s_B$).

---

[30] Webster's method is a method of apportionment (e.g., of seats in the U.S. House of Representatives), but the method can be reinterpreted to govern allocation. Rather than working with α, that is, $E/\Sigma_{i \in N} c_i$, it is cast in terms of "divisors," where the standard divisor is $\Sigma_{i \in N} c_i/E$ or $1/\alpha$.

Corrected claims problems reduce to plain claims problems when there are no differences in the strength of claims. Here is Wintein and Heilmann's definition:

> (*Corrected claims problems*) A corrected claims problem $C := (E; N; r)$ consists of a (divisible or indivisible) estate $E > 0$, a set of agents N, and a vector r specifying the strength-corrected claim $r_i > 0$ of agent i.

However, one loses crucial information in replacing the two variables, c_i and s_i, capturing respectively the size and strength of individual i's claim, with the single variable r_i, indicating i's "strength-weighted" claim.[31] Among other problems, corrected claims do not distinguish those circumstances in which claims problems are trivial, because there is more than enough to go around, and those in which $\Sigma_{i \in N} c_i \geq E$. Suppose that one has a full specification of a corrected claims problem: There are two agents; their corrected claims are each for 12 units of the good, and the estate consists of 14 units of the good. Lest one think that fairness requires that they each receive 7 units of the good, note that this corrected claims problem describes Acne and Paralysis Pills, with $c_A = 12$ and $s_A = 1$, whereas $c_B = 2$ and $s_B = 6$. In that case, of course, if 14 pills are available, Albert should get 12 and Bonnie should get 2. The values of E, N, and r are not sufficient to define a claims problem.

The complications of combining quantities and strengths or of dealing fairly with claims to different quantities of different strengths go deeper than the difficulties with determining whether all claims can be satisfied. To combine size and strength of claims supposes that quantity and strength are commensurable—that an increase in quantity somehow balances a decrease in strength. But if (in Acne and Paralysis Pills) Bonnie needs 2 pills to avoid paralysis, then it does not matter whether Albert needs 1,000 pills for his acne. The size of a claim is irrelevant to its strength, and the strength of a claim is irrelevant to its size.

Suppose that in Acne and Paralysis Pills, there are only 10 pills available. Bonnie has a very weak claim to 1 pill and a strong claim to 2 pills, and Albert has weaker claims to 10, 11, or 12 pills. If one were to ignore strength of claims and what the pills actually accomplish and look merely to their size, the extent to which their quantitative claims are met would be equal if Bonnie received 1.67 pills and Albert got 8.33. Because the pills are not divisible, Bonnie should get 1 pill with a two-thirds chance of getting a second, whereas Albert gets 8 pills with

---

[31] I am indebted to Emma Prendergast, who pointed out the problem to me. In correspondence, Heilmann and Wintein suggested (but only as a useful heuristic) that one think of strength-weighted claims as analogous to expected values that amalgamate the values of outcomes and the probabilities that outcomes will occur. Just as expected values suppress information that may be valuable, so do strength-weighted claims. The analogy is helpful, even though, unlike expected values, which often provide guidance, thinking about the satisfaction of strength-weighted claims is, as I argue in the text, often uninformative.

a one-third chance of receiving a ninth pill. But such a division would be senseless because a ninth pill does nothing for Albert. A fair allocation depends on the consequences of giving the 1 pill in question to Albert or Bonnie. Rather than proportioning pills to the size of the claims or to the strength of the claims, one needs to look at the extent to which a proportion of what is claimed translates to a proportion of the benefit that full satisfaction of the claim would provide. It is only in circumstances such as those in Bankruptcy, in which claims are of equal strength and the benefit of some good is proportional to the amount of it one has, that fairness demands distribution proportional to the size of claims. In Acne and Paralysis Pills, if there are 10 pills to be distributed, it does not matter whether Albert has a claim to 9, 12, or 500 pills. The fair allocation gives Bonnie an extremely large chance of getting 2 pills.

The relevance of size and strength to fairness appears to depend on the context. In Bankruptcy, providing the claimants with a portion of the money to which they have a claim constitutes a partial satisfaction of their claims. It might be the case in Bankruptcy that failing to repay fully one of the creditors is devastating to that individual, whereas the other creditors can easily absorb the loss. However, differences in need have little salience in commercial claims, unlike in claims to health care. These differences in the significance of partial fulfillment of quantitative claims cannot be captured by some single algorithm combining the differing roles of the size and strength of claims in fair distribution. But that is not necessary in order to apply a broadly Broomean account of fairness to the allocation of health care.

4.8 Other Theories of Fair Distribution

Often invoked, fairness is seldom analyzed. Unlike equality, which is the subject of hundreds of philosophical essays during the past four decades, there has been relatively little philosophical theorizing concerning fairness. As a sample of this small literature, I comment here on two other accounts of fair distribution that depend on different interpretations of desert and reciprocity. These views of fairness emphasize aspects that have not been prominent in previous sections, and, as shown later, these accounts lead to different conclusions concerning the fairness of specific allocations.

4.8.1 Larry Temkin: Fairness, Desert, and Equality

Larry Temkin links fairness to desert and equality. He writes, "*Undeserved* inequality is unfair, but deserved inequality is not" (2003, p. 767). A distribution is fair if and only if the distributive shares individuals possess (which Temkin takes to be levels of well-being) are in the same ratio as their desert. Desert here is something like "intrinsic moral excellence" rather than some status defined by social norms. If there is no free will and hence (in Temkin's view of desert) no desert, then fairness, one form of what Temkin calls "proportional justice," requires equality (2011, p. 56). Temkin writes,

> There are two main versions of proportional justice. The first corresponds to a conception of *absolute* justice or desert. . . . On this view, it is unjust when one fares either better or worse than one morally deserves to, where this is understood in *absolute* terms. (2011, p. 54)
>
> According to comparative justice, if two people are responsible for the extent to which they are virtuous, then one person should fare better than another in proportion to the extent to which she is more virtuous. (2011, p. 56)

More recently, Temkin has argued that fairness depends on responsibility in addition to desert. He maintains that it can be fair for two equally deserving individuals, Brett and Amy, to be unequally well-off, if the inequality results from their free choices. For example, it is fair for Brett to be worse off than Amy as a result of his choosing to make sacrifices to benefit others (2017, p. 58). Although Temkin now makes room for fair inequality among equally deserving individuals, he still links fairness closely to equality and desert.

Like Vong (who draws from Temkin), Temkin is concerned with both "absolute" and comparative justice. Although Broome, in contrast, does not regard absolute justice as a kind of fairness, he does not maintain that only (comparative) fairness matters morally. One might then attempt to reconcile Temkin's view of "comparative justice" to Broome's view of fairness by interpreting them as addressing different questions. One can interpret Temkin as addressing mainly questions concerning who has claims and how strong they are, which Broome sets aside, to focus on how claims should be satisfied. One might see a remaining disagreement about whether inequalities resulting from voluntary sacrifices are unfair, but one can reconcile Broome and Temkin here if one takes voluntary sacrifices as waiving one's claims.

Much of Temkin's argument addresses the question: What claims do people have? (albeit not in these terms). His answer is that individuals have claims to well-being proportional to their moral desert. This answer seems to me implausible. Against whom can these claims be pressed? They would appear to be directed toward God, who, despite an apparently spotty track record at apportioning well-being in proportion to desert, is purportedly the only agent able to look into people's hearts and judge what they morally deserve.

In earlier work, Temkin depicts individuals as making "complaints" against those who are better off than they are, rather than against the universe or God.

In Temkin's view, if the rainfall on one side of the hill is better than on the other, the greater prosperity of the lucky farmers on the better side of the hill justifies a complaint on the part of the less lucky farmers. These complaints do not reflect a prior normative principle embodied in their institutions; they are in force morally even if not embodied in law or convention, and they place pro tanto constraints on the institutions. However, this construction does nothing to explain what justifies any *complaint* about an inequality, unlike the view that well-being should be proportioned to desert.

Whatever merits Temkin's egalitarianism may have,[32] it is of little use in appraising the fairness of health care allocations. It is usually infeasible, unreasonably intrusive, morally questionable, and wildly presumptuous to condition health care treatment on what one can judge of the moral character of those seeking health care. The most notable attempt to take character into account that I know of occurred in Seattle, Washington, in a committee charged with deciding who would have access to dialysis (Alexander 1962). The committee was playing God—without the information, wisdom, and purpose that deities are supposed to have. As far as I know, the attempt to bring moral desert explicitly into the determination of who should be treated has not been repeated.

4.8.2 Matthew Adler: Fairness and Social Welfare Functions

Although Matthew Adler uses the language of claims, his notion of a claim has little to do with Broome's, and his view of fairness has nothing to do with proportional satisfaction. In Adler's view, developments in political philosophy during the past half century, especially with respect to the notion of a social welfare function, have gradually filled out the concept of fairness. (A social welfare function takes the appraisal of a society, or perhaps only of an aspect of a society, to depend exclusively on the well-being of its members.) If one takes fairness to be simply impartiality, then there is a famous argument due to John Harsanyi (1955) in defense of the fairness of a utilitarian social welfare function. From behind a veil of ignorance, where rational agents who are mutually disinterested suppose that with equal probability they might be anyone, a society governed by average utilitarianism maximizes expected well-being.[33] At the same time, the veil of ignorance guarantees impartiality and hence in this view fairness.

---

[32] Matt Waldren and I criticize Temkin's theory in Hausman and Waldren (2011). Although I have objections to other formulations of distributional egalitarianism, the argument here is directed solely toward Temkin's formulation.

[33] With a $1/n$ probability of being any of the n individuals in a society, my expected well-being is $(1/n)w_1 + (1/n)w_2 + \ldots + (1/n)w_n$, where w_i is the well-being of individual i. This quantity is average well-being. So average utilitarianism maximizes my expected well-being.

However, as Rawls pointed out in distinguishing his view from that of Harsanyi, this is a questionable interpretation of fairness. Policies that maximize average well-being are not ipso facto fair, regardless of how they distribute their benefits and burdens. What has gone wrong, in Rawls' famous terminology, is that utilitarianism fails to respect "the separateness of persons." Within a single life, one can prudently trade off a pain here for a pleasure there. But the enjoyment of slaveholders does not cancel out the suffering of slaves. Fairness requires reciprocity as well as impartiality. Utilitarianism can call for the sacrifice of some members of society purely for the advantage of others, and for that reason, maximizing expected benefits from behind a veil of ignorance does not imply fairness.

Taking his cue from arguments of Thomas Nagel (1991), Adler takes a different tack. He proposes that policies should be compared by the (welfare) claims of each individual. What Adler (2012) calls "claims" are welfare comparisons of states of affairs. Individual i has a "claim" for a state of affairs x over y if and only if i would be better off if state of affairs x rather than y were to obtain. Redescribing this interest i has in x obtaining rather than y as i's *claim* in favor of x permits Adler to assert that his framework takes the separateness of persons seriously, because its evaluation of outcomes is guided by the claims of each individual. However, there is nothing here that reflects any reason, other than the general grounds of benevolence, why individual i should get x. All that Adler's "claims across outcomes" framework implies is that policies should be compared by their welfare consequences.

Adler does not defend a utilitarian social welfare function. What keeps the framework from reiterating in different terminology a standard argument for utilitarianism is an additional moral premise: that the claims of those who are worse off are stronger than claims of the same magnitude of those who are better off. In other words, more weight should be attached to the welfare gains and losses of those who are badly off than is placed on the gains and losses of those who are better off. In this way, Adler concludes that a form of prioritarianism, or weighted utilitarianism, measures the fairness of institutions, policies, states of affairs, and outcomes. If one interprets the imperative to respect the separateness of persons as ruling out social arrangements that sacrifice the interests of the less well-off in order to benefit the better off, then one can provide some defense for Adler's claim that his prioritarian social welfare function respects the separateness of persons.

Indeed, Adler suggests that for welfarists—that is, those who would assess social policies exclusively in terms of their results for individual welfare—there are no trade-offs between fairness and efficiency: Fairness encompasses the whole of normative political philosophy (2012, pp. 338–339):

> But within the context of welfarism, it is hard to see—at least at the onset—why we should feel pressure to be pluralists. "Fairness," on the view tendered here,

provides an overriding structure for determining the normative significance of facts about human well-being. All of the various aspects of an individual's welfare determine the valence of her claim between a given pair of outcomes. (2012, p. 338)

For now, I assume that if x is at least as fair as y, in light of the claim-across-outcome understanding of fairness, then x is all-things-considered morally at least as good as y. (2012, p. 339)

Adler has more general aims than did Rawls, who sought principles of justice to govern only what he called "the basic structure" of society—that is, the pervasive institutions that determine the overall life prospects of members of the society. Rawls denied that one should assume that these principles are appropriate to problems of "local" justice, such as whether the national health system should provide dialysis to those who need it or whether there should be a legal market in kidneys for transplantation. Adler, in contrast, seeks a criterion with which to appraise both the basic structure and specific policies. The subtitle of his 2012 book, *Beyond Cost–Benefit Analysis*, announces his ambition to offer an alternative way to appraise policies.

Whatever the virtues of prioritarianism as a standard for evaluation of the basic structure of society, its claim to exhaust our concerns with fairness is untenable. Nothing in prioritarianism helps determine what is the fair division of the assets of the bankrupt firm or whether it is fair for a middle-income country to refuse to provide dialysis. Adler's prioritarianism is more promising as the underlying moral principle with respect to which alternative institutions can be evaluated—in other words, as a principle for determining what claims people have rather than how their claims should be satisfied.

Although Adler has a powerful argument for his version of prioritarianism, one of the premises it rests on asserts without much argument that the interests of those who are worse off should carry more weight. Adler's only defense of this crucial premise consists of the rhetorical question, "Shouldn't this further fact about well-being levels 'tip the balance' in favor of i [the worse off individual] having the stronger claim?" (2012, p. 340). How solid is this intuition? Is one inclined to favor the worse off because (as Adler maintains) the "claims" of those who are worse off are stronger, or does one favor the worse off because one is an egalitarian, or is it because one mistakenly imagines that there will be a greater benefit if the good is given to the worse off, or does one favor the worse off individuals because one assumes that they are suffering and one seeks to eliminate suffering? Adler's intuition is a slender reed upon which to build a theory of fairness, when there are competing plausible explanations for why we might favor those who are worse off in one circumstance or another.

A more serious problem for Adler's theory than its shaky foundation is the criticisms it faces. First, like utilitarianism, it says that the misery of some can be canceled out by the flourishing of others. Placing greater weight on the interests of the worst off does not rule out a society in which the well-being of many is obtained through the misery and degradation of a few. It will take more benefits for the lucky ones to outweigh the losses for the unlucky ones, but placing additional weight on the benefits and burdens to the worse off still allows for their interests to be sacrificed in order to benefit others.

Adler calls these interests "claims," but they are interests nevertheless: The strengths of these so-called claims in Adler's prioritarianism rest only on comparing levels and differences in well-being. His account has nothing to say about those interests that have a special normative significance because they are grounded in factors such as needs, promises, and past injuries—that is, Adler has nothing to say about what Broome calls "claims." In Adler's construction, it does not matter whether states of affairs fulfill the duties that Broomean claims impose. Without recognizing the existence of such claims, which, if Broome is to be believed, do not cease to call for satisfaction even when weaker than other claims, Adler does not consider that there are objections to weighing moral considerations against one another and setting aside those that are outweighed. Whether or not fairness requires placing greater weight on the well-being of those who are worse off, Broome argues that it requires more than weighing interests against one another.

I shall have more to say about prioritarianism in Chapter 7 when I discuss the allegation that c-e allocation unfairly fails to assign a sufficient priority to treating those who are more severely ill. Although I have pointed to problems in Adler's prioritarianism, it may be possible to salvage some of the theoretical structure he has assembled and to wed it to an account of rule-dependent fairness such as Broome's.

4.9 Conclusion

The philosophical and economic treatments of fairness canvassed in this chapter suggest that there is more than one kind of wrong, which philosophers and the public at large call "unfair," and that there may not be any single criterion determining what is fair or unfair, apart from the underlying concern that institutions should show respect for persons and their legitimate expectations by requiring impartiality and ruling out some sacrifices of individuals for the benefit of others. Cooperative game theory links fairness to the contributions individuals make to coalitions. Broome ties fairness to the proportional satisfaction of claims. Temkin links fairness to desert and equality. Adler maintains that fairness requires prioritizing the interests of those who are badly off. I suggested that one think of Temkin's and Adler's views as problematic accounts of what fairness demands concerning the assignment of claims and the determination of their strength. Rules or institutions that come up to snuff are "fair" in a rule-determining sense. The treatment of individuals and groups is then fair if it is in accord with fair principles specifying claims, their strengths, and what is required to satisfy claims. Given the norms specified by some set of institutions or conventions, the treatment of individuals or groups is fair only if it satisfies the claims that the norms assign to individuals in the way that the norms require.

Both the size and the strength of claims are relevant to whether they have been satisfied fairly. Wintein and Heilmann's attempt to bring magnitude and strength together into a single theory is unsuccessful, and I am skeptical about whether the theories that specify what is a fair response to claims of different sizes can be combined with theories that specify a fair response to claims of different strengths. At least with respect to a good such as health care, information concerning how *much* health care is needed bears on the specification of what is claimed rather than on how the claim is to be satisfied.

The application of philosophical accounts of fairness to the appraisal of c-e allocation is far from simple. Critics of c-e allocation have many different philosophical locations from which to begin their criticisms, and defenders have many philosophical redoubts from which to fight back. Chapter 5 explores some problems that arise when one attempts to determine what would constitute a fair allocation of health care, and it provides a first sketch of a theory of fair health care allocation. The four succeeding chapters examine specific complaints about the unfairness of c-e allocation in the light of that theory, with Chapter 10 concluding.

5
What Is a Fair Allocation of Health Care?

Chapter 4 examined theories of fairness with special attention to Broome's view that fairness requires satisfying claims in proportion to their strength or distributing chances of getting indivisible goods that are proportional to the strength of claims. I raised questions about the fairness of claims themselves, and I argued that there are other construals of fairness that, like Broome's theory, fill out and make specific the underlying view that fairness is a matter of treating persons with equal baseline respect. But Chapter 4 said little about how to allocate health care fairly.

Health care is a special good, whose distribution raises special puzzles about fairness. The goal of this chapter is to consider how to apply general accounts of fair distribution to the specific task of assessing the distribution of health care. The objective is to formulate a theory of fair health care allocation that can be used in later chapters to evaluate the criticisms of cost-effective (c-e) allocation presented in Chapter 3. Section 5.1 examines whether individuals have claims to health care and what determines the strength of their claims. Section 5.2 develops criticisms of the view that the fair distribution of health care involves proportional satisfaction of claims to health care. Section 5.3 shifts the problem from which distributions of health care are fair to the conditions in which *access* to health care is fair. Section 5.4 addresses the question of how the costs of treatments bear on the fairness of the combinations of health care to which individuals have access. Section 5.5 returns to the question of how to specify a fair distribution of health care in the light of the heterogeneity of health problems and treatments. Section 5.6 concludes the chapter.

5.1 Claims to Health Care

To simplify applying theories of fairness in the specific context of health care, I suppose that the allocation takes place within the centrally administered universal health care system of a reasonably affluent nation, which has an obligation to address the population's medical needs as fully and fairly as the resources devoted to health care permit. These assumptions imply that claims to health care are claims against the state agency administering the health care system. I shall simplify and assume that each individual's claims to health care and the strength of those claims depend exclusively on the (a) properties and consequences of their health deficiencies (the public value of their medical needs), (b) the availability and efficacy of treatments, (c) the principles governing the health care system, and (d) costs. I postpone the discussion of how costs bear on health care claims until Section 5.4. To assume that there is a centrally administered universal health care system simplifies the discussion but is not essential to its conclusions. I return in Chapter 10 to complications that arise when there are competing private insurers.

Let us call the assumption that individuals have claims to health care that depend exclusively on a public evaluation of medical needs, on which treatments exist, on the principles governing the health system, and on costs the "health claims assumption." As I argued in the Introduction, the crucial features of health deficiencies from both a personal and a public perspective are suffering and limitations on what one can do, and the crucial moral principles that give rise to claims to health care are benevolence (and compassion), fairness, freedom, and, as emphasized by Daniels (1985, 2007), a commitment to equal opportunity. These are not the only moral principles that can give rise to claims to health care, and indeed the health claims assumption is false. For example, providers may make promises to patients, which give rise to claims that are additional to claims based on needs. Patients may be injured by providers, and in that way, they may acquire additional or more stringent claims. Insurance policies specify entitlements to reimbursement, which may in turn determine what health care individuals have claims to. Individuals may perhaps forfeit some of their claims by careless behavior. It is debatable whether all these factors should affect the strength of claims, and I shall not examine their role. Instead, I rely on the health claims assumption as a reasonable first approximation. It is plausible that the main sources of claims to health care are needs, the possibilities of meeting them, costs, and the general principles of benevolence and justice that ground a pro tanto obligation to assist those who are suffering or whose choices are severely constrained.

In making the health claims assumption, I am offering a partial answer to the well-taken questions that Tomlin (2012) asks about what generates claims and whether there are fairness questions concerning the distribution of claims as well as their satisfaction.[1] One might question whether one makes any progress in substituting the problem of specifying what health care needs individuals have for the problem of specifying what claims individuals have to health care. Indeed, one might plausibly maintain that what distinguishes needs from wants is that needs justify claims on others to satisfy them, whereas mere desires do

---

[1] Broome recognizes this lacuna, "Consequently, I cannot pretend to have defined claims independently of the notion of fairness, and then shown how fairness applies to them" (1990, p. 96).

not. In that case, we would need to know what claims to medical treatment individuals have in order to determine what medical needs they have.

I think that one can nevertheless explain how medical needs give rise to claims to health care in the following way. The first crucial moral premise asserts that individuals have imperfect duties to assist those who have unsatisfied needs. By an imperfect duty to address someone's needs, I mean (as is standard in the literature) a duty that does not derive from or entail a corresponding right in the person whose needs are unmet. The duty to help those whose needs are unmet requires only that I help sometimes and that I not ignore every need, but it does not demand that I address any particular need. The second premise maintains that to satisfy their imperfect duty to help others who have medical needs, individuals employ the state (or some other encompassing institution) to act as their agent. Whereas individuals can only address a tiny portion of the needs for health care—and then only sporadically and unsystematically—the state or charitable organizations, as agents for individuals, can offer consistent and systematic help. To fulfill its role as the principal agent responsible for making good the imperfect duties of the members of the population and also to abide by requirements of impartiality and neutrality, the state should address as many of the health care needs that medical knowledge and the budget assigned to health care allow. Government should protect individuals from disease and disability, improve their health where possible, and provide comfort and care to those who cannot be restored to good health. These duties of government are controversial, and some libertarians deny that they exist. This sketchy argument shows how needs for health care give rise to claims on the state to provide health care.

If this argument is sound, it shows that the state has a heavy responsibility to protect and enhance the health of its population. This argument does not draw any precise line between those problems that are best left to individuals and those that demand a response from health care institutions. Moreover, this assumption concerning the obligations of the state leaves unanswered questions about which institutions best enable the state to make good on its obligations of care.

Determining what claims to treatments individuals have is a normative task that also requires knowledge of people's health and of what medical interventions are possible. Do individuals have claims to or needs for specific treatments, or are their claims instead for the outcomes that treatments may provide, and are those outcomes objective states of affairs or are they subjective reactions to states of affairs? Can one cure the *handicap* (not the impairment)[2] of a limp with a drug

---

[2] According to the *International Classification of Impairments, Disabilities, and Handicaps* (World Health Organization, 1980), handicaps, unlike impairments, reflect not only bodily conditions but also their psychosocial negative consequences.

that eliminates the emotional toll the impairment may have? How do mental and bodily complaints translate into needs?

These are difficult questions whose answers require specifying the moral principles that justify imposing obligations on public bodies to address shortfalls of health. The relevant moral considerations comprise at least compassion, solidarity, benevolence, justice, freedom, and opportunity. A mere desire, even if it is as strong as my father's desire for a cigar after a meal, which he conquered after decades of temporary defeats, gives rise to no claim because a frustrated desire does not appreciably limit one's activities and warrants only a slight benevolent concern. Other needs, such as for repair of a hernia, in contrast, bear heavily on opportunity, and for that reason give rise to a claim on the health care system (Daniels 1985, 2007). It is plausible that significant health deficiencies that are inexpensively treatable[3] give rise to claims due to their impact on opportunity or the suffering they involve. I will for the most part settle for a conventional (and hence vague) characterization of a medical need, returning to these questions only in Chapter 10 when I come back to the issues raised in Chapter 2 concerning the application of cost-effectiveness. Note that identifying health care claims leaves us with the further problem of estimating their strength, which Broome's account of fairness requires us to know. I assume that the strength of claims depends on how much individuals can benefit from treatment and, as I argue later, on the costs of treatment.

5.2 Satisfying Health Care Claims Proportionately

As discussed in Chapter 4, there are alternative conceptions of fair division. One plausible view defended by Broome holds that a distribution is fair if and only if the claimant's shares of divisible goods or chances of obtaining indivisible goods are proportional to the strength of their claims. In the case of health care, the size of a claim defines what is claimed, whereas strength determines the importance of satisfying the claim. Applied to health care, Broome's view of fairness requires that the satisfaction of claims to health care or the probability that claims be satisfied should be proportional to the strength of the claims.

Short of fully satisfying claims, it is difficult to say when a distribution of health care is proportional to the strength of claims, when, unlike cases such as Brock's and Daniels', there are myriad claims of different strengths to different quantities of different goods. It is difficult to specify how to make the satisfaction of different claims whose partial satisfaction has varying significance proportional to their strength. It is unclear how to compare how well the distribution of

---

[3] But not so inexpensive that individuals can easily provide for themselves.

health care satisfies different claims to different treatments. For example, when would the treatments of an infection and of a broken bone stand in the same proportion as the strength of claims to those treatments? How can one render commensurable the very different kinds of health care that satisfy diverse health care claims? Call this "the heterogeneity problem."

One should not think of the problem of allocating health care fairly as analogous to determining how many apples from a basket should go to individuals who have claims of different strengths to different numbers of apples. Maria may need surgery for her shoulder pain. Martha needs penicillin for pneumonia. Martin needs some combination of muscle relaxants and physical therapy to be able to walk. Marvin needs either penicillin or amoxicillin to protect his hearing. How does one allocate the surgery, physical therapy, penicillin, amoxicillin, and muscle relaxants fairly among Maria, Martha, Martin, and Marvin? How does one compare the strength of these claims and determine their proportional satisfaction?

The problem of fairly allocating health care is more like fairly distributing to individuals with differing tastes different quantities of commodities and services, some of which are substitutes or complements to one another. John hates peas, enjoys broccoli, and absolutely loves pedicures, whereas Joanna has no particular feelings about broccoli, peas, and pedicures but is instead passionate about sports cars and jazz. Just as consumers desire different commodity bundles, those sitting in the clinic waiting room need different treatments.

How should one allocate a heterogeneous collection of goods, where there are claims to different goods in the collection, of differing quantities and importance, with different costs, that may be substitutes or complements for one another? One possibility might be to focus on very specific claims. Some people have claims to pain relievers. Others have claims to blood pressure drugs. Others need insulin. One might propose to treat these claims as posing separate problems of fair distribution. Unfortunately, such a disaggregated approach is untenable because which resources are available to cope with Robert's cancer or Rhonda's hip depends on decisions about what other health care to provide. Costs tie together the specific distributional problems. Deciding to give an expensive treatment to Zach might make it impossible to treat some completely unrelated medical problem of Zelda's.

A different but equally unsuccessful way to respond to the heterogeneity of health care would be to proportion the cost of health care to which Robert is entitled to the strength of his claim. But the ratio between the expense of the health care one receives and the strength of one's claim to that health care bears no relationship to the extent to which one's health care claims have been satisfied. The cost of health care is not a measure of the strength of the claim to it or of the extent to which the claim is satisfied. Life-saving treatments may be cheap.

Possessing only half the cost of the suggested chemotherapy, Robert may be forced to use a less expensive chemotherapy that satisfies his claim almost as well, whereas possessing half the cost of a hip replacement is of no use to Rhonda.

One way in which economists have dealt with the problems of comparing the value or importance to individuals of bundles of differing commodities and services is by treating a distribution of commodities as fair if individuals do not prefer any of the commodity bundles others possess to their own. Such a distribution is described as "envy-free" in virtue of individuals not preferring the bundles of others, although the emotion of envy has nothing to do with it. When one moves from the simple context of consumption goods or resources to contexts in which there are more of the features of an actual economy, such as production, labor, and differences in talents, matters become more complicated and controversial, and envy-free distributions do not always exist (Varian 1974, 1975; Olson 2020).

One might suggest that a distribution of health care is fair whenever no one prefers the health care (or perhaps the health outcomes) that others receive to their own health care (or health outcome). But it is difficult to see how the notion of an envy-free allocation can be helpful in this context. The fact that Isaac, who is dying of an incurable cancer, prefers Isabel's health state tells us nothing about whether health care has been distributed fairly. Whether or not health care has been fairly distributed, Nathan will not prefer Natalie's health care to his own, regardless of its efficacy, if they do not have the same health problems. Whether or not Rhonda has received the hip replacement she has a claim to, she does not prefer the chemotherapy Robert is getting to whatever treatment she is receiving. Whether individuals envy the *improvements* in the health of others provided by a health care allocation to their own improvements is similarly irrelevant. Those whose health has not appreciably improved will prefer the substantial improvements others have experienced, regardless of whether the allocation has been fair.

To adapt Broome's theory to the question of how to allocate health-related resources fairly, one might suggest that it is a mistake to conceptualize the problem as involving claims to treatments such as antibiotics or physical therapy. Instead, one can attribute to those who are ill or at risk of illness claims to a single good—*better health*, whether secured by treatment or prevention. For practical purposes, this good might be identified with an improvement in quality-adjusted life years (QALYs), which have a scalar measure, and the strength of claims to better health could be measured by the improvements in health-related quality of life (HRQoL) that treatments can be expected to bring. Despite the problems with the concept and measurement of HRQoL discussed in Chapter 1, thinking about distributing improvements in QALYs might be a place to start.[4]

---

[4] However, not all of health care is curative.

As is implicit in Chapter 1, it is questionable whether the available measures of improvements in HRQoL are a reliable basis for measuring the strength of claims. HRQoL is measured (very imperfectly) by preferences, which vary across individuals, depending on culture, technology, geography, climate, and personal goals. Some of these factors are relevant to health care claims, whereas others are not. Moreover, grounding claims on the *average* strength or extent of medical needs of particular health conditions may attribute claims of mistaken extent and strength to everyone in a population. To suppose that one can represent the strength of health care claims by any scalar measure of claims to health care is a dubious simplification.

One might nevertheless forge ahead. In the absence of a well-supported set of public values for health states, we are stuck (or so Chapter 3 argued) with QALYs, which depend on both the severity of health deficiencies and their duration. Other things being equal, at least as a first approximation, the larger the increase in QALYs provided by some health care treatment T, the stronger the claim to that treatment.

However, although it is feasible to measure the strength of claims to health care by how much treatment can improve one's health, a little reflection reveals that the distribution of increases in QALYs tells one nothing about whether health care has fairly satisfied those claims. Because of the not-so-tender mercies of nature, the level and distribution of health outcomes may improve despite a worsening of the level or distribution of health care. Similarly, outcomes may worsen (as is the case in the current pandemic) regardless of any changes in health care. If some countries fail to reduce hospitalizations, due to unreasonable reluctance to be vaccinated on the part of a large minority, the resulting inequalities in health will not point to any unfairness in the allocation of health care.[5]

How can we judge whether the benefits provided by a health care system as measured in QALYs are fairly distributed? Ronald Dworkin (1994) proposes that one assess health care coverage by means of what he calls "the prudent insurance test":

> We should allocate resources between health and other social needs, and between different patients who each need treatment, by trying to imagine what health care would be like if it were left to a free and unsubsidized market, and ... [1] the distribution of wealth and income [were] as fair as it possibly can

---

[5] As Anders Herlitz pointed out to me, assessing the fairness of the allocation of health care by the fairness of the health outcomes is not as obviously hopeless when one is concerned with the performance of a health care system in a single country, rather than when one is attempting to make cross-country comparisons. But such an assessment will still face the problems of disentangling those aspects of the outcomes that are due to health care, as opposed to other causes, and of factoring in costs.

be,...[2] all the information... about the value and cost and side effects of particular medical procedures... is generally known by the public at large as well, [and 3] no one... has any information available about how likely any particular person is to contract any particular disease or to suffer any particular kind of accident....

Now suppose that health care decisions in this transformed community are left simply to individual market decisions in as free a market as we can imagine.... [H]owever health care is distributed in that society is just for that society.... We can speculate about what kind of medical care and insurance it would be prudent for most Americans to buy, for themselves, if the changes I imagined had really taken place; and we can use those speculations as guidelines in deciding what justice requires now....

[On] the prudent insurance approach... we would therefore accept certain limits on universal coverage, and we would accept these not as compromises with justice but as required by it. (pp. 7–11)

Whatever one's view of the plausibility of Dworkin's proposal,[6] it is far too vague to implement without specifying what determines whether an insurance purchase would be prudent under Dworkin's hypothetical conditions. Presumably, the seriousness and probabilities of ailments, coupled with the availability and cost-effectiveness or "net benefit" of treating them, would be the principal factors influencing prudent insurance purchases. Indeed, there may be an argument here that the most cost-effective set of treatments within the budget constitutes the fair set of treatments to which everyone should have equal access. Because costs and health improvements are major determinants of the strength of claims, criticisms of c-e allocation inevitably rely on much of the intellectual structure whose distributional implications they condemn.

Our central question remains unanswered: What is a fair allocation of health care?

5.3 Fairness and Equal Access

The main conclusion I draw from the previous section is that this chapter has thus far been barking up the wrong tree. What one wants of a fair health care

---

[6] In Dworkin's view, a fair distribution of income and wealth will not be an equal distribution. That means the choices concerning health care of those who are richer have greater influence than the choices of those who are poorer. Why should character traits that make one wealthier, such as greater industriousness or a greater interest in consumption rather than leisure, add weight to one's health insurance preferences? Moreover, as Debra Satz mentioned to me, why should one suppose that the outcomes of idealized market interactions should be fair to those who are not themselves participants but instead, like children and the cognitively impaired, depend on others?

system is fair *access* to health care. The distribution of health outcomes, however equal it may be, need not derive from fair health care. One cannot appraise the fairness of the allocation of health care by its distribution or by the distribution of outcomes. The focus must instead be on *access* to health care. What I mean by access to a treatment is that one can have the treatment without great sacrifice, provided that one has a medical need for it.

What is a fair allocation of access to health care? One answer is equal access. Equal access is apparently impartial. It seems to show equal respect. It is envy free. If individuals have equally strong claims to any specific treatment whenever their need is the same, then one might argue that equal access to health care satisfies claims equally. One might precipitously suggest that the distribution of health care is fair if and only if everyone has the same access to the same health care.

This criterion is inconsistent with Broome's view of fairness. Because the budget cannot cover all treatments that can be expected to be beneficial, equal access to some affordable subset of those treatments results in satisfying some claims and failing to satisfy others. Moreover, the proposal is insensitive to the strength of claims to health care. Those who are in agony will be no more or less likely to receive a painkiller than those who are merely uncomfortable. Equal access is in other ways obviously not sufficient for fairness. For example, suppose that a health care system provides equal access to a set of treatments that excludes treatments of health problems experienced only by women. Equal access to such a set would not be fair.

The only feasible way to make access to health care properly sensitive to the strength of claims is to allow the strength of claims to treatment to influence the set of treatments to which individuals have access. One might then suggest that access to health care is fair if everyone has access to the same "fair set of treatments," where, by a "fair set of treatments," I mean a set of treatments that is properly responsive to health care needs and costs. Such a system might very roughly operationalize Broome's view of fair distribution, but among the claims to treatments in the fair set of treatments, stronger claims are not prioritized, and claims to treatments that are not included in the fair set, because they are weak, are not satisfied at all, rather than satisfied in proportion to their strength.

5.4 Fairness and Costs

Costs obviously have a significant and unavoidable influence on the allocation of health care. Moreover, costs are crucial determinants of c-e allocation. I maintain that it is fair to allow costs to play a large role in the allocation of health care. Consider the following case:

> **George and Georgina**
>
> George and Georgina both need an antibiotic to avoid losing a leg. George needs a course of an inexpensive antibiotic. Georgina needs an expensive antibiotic, which she cannot afford, because she has an infection that is resistant to the inexpensive antibiotic. The health system refuses to pay for the expensive antibiotic, and she loses a leg.

George is treated and Georgina is not. Is that fair? If resources are limited, it seems that it could easily be morally permissible, all things considered, but is it fair? If the cost of Georgina's treatment weakens her claim to the antibiotic, then treating George but not Georgina might be fair. But can costs weaken claims? George and Georgina have the same need for treatment. The specific treatments they need are different, but they are of the same kind, similarly efficacious, operating by similar mechanisms. Although the exact treatments to which they have claims differ, because they are claims for different antibiotics, they seem to be equally strong and demand to be satisfied to the same extent.

It is untenable to maintain that because their needs are the same, fairness demands that either both or neither is treated, despite the intuition that fairness precludes any role for costs in the allocation of health care. Consider the following elaboration of the circumstances in which George and Georgina find themselves. Suppose that in order to make the expensive antibiotic generally available to those who badly need it, the health care system would have to refuse to provide an effective pain pill to a large number of individuals.[7] This is unrealistic. In practice, the opportunity costs of providing access to treatments are difficult to pin down. However, even if difficult to locate, opportunity costs are real. The choice of whether to provide the expensive antibiotic to Georgina (and to everyone else with the same needs) is at the same time a choice to refuse to provide effective pain relief to those in need of this pill. Refusing to take costs into account amounts to unfairly ignoring the interests of those who need the pain pill. Unless resources are unlimited, there is no way to respond fairly to claims to health care without taking costs into account. The fact that treating Georgina requires withholding a large benefit from others means either that she has a weaker claim to treatment than does George or that the claims of those in need of pain relief are given priority.

When we turn our attention from the distribution of health care to access to health care, we also need to know whether the difference in provision reflects a

---

[7] To simplify the example, I am assuming that it is not possible to provide a partial satisfaction of both claims to the pain pill and to the antibiotic or to make use of a lottery to determine which claims are satisfied.

difference in access. If the health system would have provided the expensive antibiotic to George (perhaps because of his gender or his influential friends), then not treating Georgina is unfair. If, on the other hand, Georgina would have received the inexpensive antibiotic, if her infection were not resistant to it, and George would not have received the expensive antibiotic, even if, like Georgina, he had needed it, then they both have access to the same treatments. If the restrictions on that basket of treatments is fair, then even though Georgina receives no treatment, one satisfies the equal access to a fair set of treatments condition, but not Broome's requirement that claims be satisfied in proportion to their strength. Even so, it seems that George and Georgina are treated fairly if they have equal access to a fair set of treatments. Neither's claims are treated as of lesser importance, and Georgina has no complaint that she is treated with less respect.

Without knowing costs, questions about limiting fairly which treatments individuals have access to cannot even be posed. Health systems must take costs into account both for the sake of efficiency and for the sake of fairness toward those who will not be treated because the resources have been used elsewhere. A complaint that it is unfair to allow cost to influence access to treatment is both mistaken and futile. Cost is relevant to fair distribution.

5.5 Access and Heterogeneity

At the end of the discussion of heterogeneity in Section 5.2, I proposed as a solution to the problem of heterogeneity that the strength of claims be determined by the expected QALYs individuals would have if untreated and by the improvement in QALYs that treatment brings. That proposal ran into trouble because outcomes and improvements depend on personal choices and the vicissitudes of nature as well as on the distribution of health care. The utilization of health care and health outcomes do not tell us how well claims are satisfied. Shifting the problem to specifying the set of treatments to which individuals should have access does not eliminate the problem of heterogeneity. Determining to which treatments fairness demands access is much the same problem as determining when an allocation of health care is fair. In both cases, health needs, improvement, and costs are relevant factors, and the heterogeneity of needs is just as problematic. However, shifting the focus from how things change or turn out in terms of QALYs to what health care is accessible mitigates the objections to the rough solution to the problem of heterogeneity sketched at the end of Section 5.2. One can measure the strength of claims as suggested there: by the improvement in QALYs that treatment can be expected to provide.[8] Then one can measure

---

[8] Ideally, the relevant information would concern public values rather than HRQoL and QALYs.

the extent to which the set of treatments to which individuals have access satisfy claims by the expected health improvement that access to that set provides.

Would it be fair to assess different ranges of access to health care by their cost-effectiveness—that is, to favor a set of treatments access to which maximizes health improvements? If sacrifices of those who are worse off in order to benefit the better off are ruled out as unfair, then the answer is surely "No." Just as utilitarianism may favor sacrificing some individual's life prospects so that others can thrive, so the most cost-effective distribution of health care—the distribution that maximizes health or well-being—might abandon some to serious illness in order to address the minor health problems of others.

However, there are reasons to doubt that a c-e allocation would often be in this way unfair. Ignoring the ill in order to benefit the relatively healthy does not in practice usually improve population health. Unlike well-being, whose upper bounds (if it has any) are seldom reached, a great many count as fully healthy without claim to further health care resources. Treatments of minor ailments are often cheap enough to be left to individuals to supply for themselves. Moreover, the security provided by universal health care is itself such an important benefit that it will be difficult to make good the complaint that some people's interests are being sacrificed without recompense in order to benefit others.

Once one recognizes the problems of heterogeneity and the relevance of costs to allocation, one sees that policymakers need to rely on something such as cost-effectiveness, cost–value, or cost–benefit analysis as a starting point for both the efficient and the fair allocation of health-related resources. In pursuit of fairness, one can modify how cost and effectiveness information is used, but without information about both costs and effectiveness, how could one determine the strength of claims to health care and the feasibility of satisfying them? Alternative ways of allocating health care, such as first-come, first-serve, which do not make use of anything like cost-effectiveness information, are both inefficient and difficult to defend on grounds of fairness. Policymakers can invoke concerns about fairness to constrain the reach of cost-effectiveness considerations and adjust the c-e allocation, but without the foundation that something like cost-effectiveness analysis provides, how could they sensibly determine which treatments individuals should have access to?

5.6 Conclusion

On the basis of the discussion of fairness in this chapter and Chapter 4, one might offer a preliminary sketch of a partial philosophical criterion for assessing the array of health care to which everyone should have access:

> **Abstract Principles of Fairness for the Distribution of Health Care**
>
> The satisfaction of claims to health care is fair, other things being equal, if and only if access to a set of basic treatments is fair.
>
> Access to a set of basic treatments is fair, other things being equal, if and only if
>
> - it is equal;
> - the set of basic treatments to which individuals have access depends exclusively on
>   - facts about health deficiencies and their consequences,
>   - what treatments can accomplish at what costs; and
> - the dependence is governed by moral principles that are impartial and that do not demand large sacrifices from the badly off for the benefit of the better off.

In addition, justice, but not (in my usage) fairness, requires that, other things being equal, claims to health care be as fully satisfied as the budget allows. Notice that unlike Broome's theory, this account does not require that claims be satisfied in proportion to their strength. We have already discussed some reasons to question Broome's account, especially its incompatibility with fairness as equal access to a fair set of treatments, and Chapter 6 provides others.

The next four chapters examine whether the complaint that c-e allocation is unfair can be supported by this account of fairness and whether in the light of the criticisms of c-e allocation this account of fairness requires modification. I begin in Chapter 6 with the "fair chances" objection.

6
Fair Chances

As discussed in Chapter 3, critics have alleged that (c-e) allocation is unfair in several regards. This chapter examines one of these. Section 6.1 defines more precisely what I have called the "fair chances" objection to c-e allocation, and it provides this criticism with a philosophical foundation in Broome's theory of fairness. Section 6.2 raises questions about whether the fair chances objection has much force, and it challenges Broome's theory. Sections 6.3–6.6 develop a hypothetical case that brings out some implications of the fair chances objection. Section 6.7 considers how moral concerns that are separate from fairness and enhancing health bear on the assessment of cost-effectiveness. Section 6.8 concludes the chapter.

6.1 Formulating the Fair Chances Objection

Consider Brock's case and Daniels's second case from Chapter 3, which are meant to illustrate the fair chances objection:

Brock's case: Because one transplant candidate is likely to benefit somewhat less than another, that candidate is given no chance of receiving the transplant.

Daniels case: Treatment T_2 is not provided to one group of people because the benefit it would provide to them is less than the benefit that another treatment, T_1, provides to another group of people, at the same cost.

Both Brock and Daniels think that those whose treatments are somewhat less cost-effective should receive some treatment or some probability of treatment. In Chapter 3, I suggested three interpretations of the objection: that it is a mistake to distinguish among alternatives whose cost-effectiveness is very similar; that life-saving for any significant period should be regarded as equally beneficial, regardless of how long the period is; and that c-e allocation is insensitive to the fairness of the distribution of benefits or chances of benefitting. Broome's view of fairness provides one way of specifying what is a fair distribution of benefits or chances of benefit. One can formulate the fair chances objection as follows:

> *The fair chances criticism*: C-e allocation is unfair because it allows stronger claims to *outweigh* weaker claims rather than satisfying claims in proportion to their strength or providing chances that claims will be satisfied in proportion to their strength.

When there is a large difference in cost-effectiveness between, on the one hand, devoting all the resources to the more cost-effective alternative (e.g., T_1 in Daniels's example) and, on the other hand, distributing the resources so that some portion of less cost-effective treatments are also funded, then there is a good case for accepting the unfairness. But when the more cost-effective treatment is only "somewhat more cost-effective," then the unfairness is egregious because no large benefit in overall welfare compensates for it.

If one regards the fair chances objection as coming from a pluralist view like the one sketched above, then, when there is a major difference in health and well-being, concerns about fairness should give way, whereas when one policy is only somewhat more cost-effective than another, then fairness should rule. In speaking of "the fair chances/best outcomes problem" (Daniels 1993, p. 225; 1994, p. 27) or "the conflict between fair chances and best outcomes" (Brock 2003a, p. 305), Brock and Daniels invite this interpretation. On this interpretation, *c-e allocation is almost always unfair*, even though it may often be morally permissible. Can that be right?

6.2 Another View of Fairness

An alternative way of specifying principles showing equal respect for persons is suggested by some of Daniels remarks on the fair chances objection to c-e allocation (1993). Consider again Daniels' case.[1] Those who need T_2 receive no treatment because T_2, although effective, is not as cost-effective as T_1, and the provision of T_1 exhausts the budget. Is this allocation truly unfair? On the assumption that those who need T_2 have claims to T_2, Broome's theory implies that it is unfair that they receive no treatment. But what if tomorrow it will be cost-effective to address some other need of those deprived today of T_2, whereas those receiving T_1 may have received the short end of the stick yesterday. Unless those who do not get T_2 are constantly getting the short end of the stick, what is unfair

---

[1] For the reasons I gave when introducing Brock's case, I shall say little about it here.

about their losing out today? General allocational principles are at least as relevant to the fairness of health care policies as are judgments about the fairness of particular allocations.

Broome would surely not condemn turn-taking as unfair even though every other week one-half of the population receives little or nothing while the other half receives a substantial allocation.[2] Taking the average across pairs of weeks as the allocation, everyone's claims are equally satisfied. Explicit turn-taking is exceptional, but considerable health care resources are typically devoted to treatments of some ailing individuals at the expense of taxpayers or those who pay insurance premiums, even if those who are paying are not at the moment in need of treatment. Of course, in compensation for their support of the health care system, the healthy receive the benefit of being insured. It is difficult to judge whether the extent to which their claims to risk reduction are satisfied is equal to the extent to which treatments satisfy claims to health care on the part of those who are ill. Broome's theory of fairness is difficult to apply to the assessment of health insurance.

A universal health care system establishes a prioritization of claims to treatment or, in other words, a list of treatments it will pay for, given various diagnoses. That list raises moral questions, including questions of fairness. Critics might, for example, maintain that some treatments are on the list because they provide greater benefits to the relatively advantaged or because of the political influence of a particular pharmaceutical company.

Is a health care system unfair if it refuses to provide treatments to weaker claims that are in proportion to their strength? As I noted in the discussion of desert, one can distinguish the fairness with which a judge is concerned from the fairness of concern to legislators in a constitutional convention. The allocator of some good, qua judge, knows what claims people have and the rules for satisfying them and faces mainly problems of applying those rules. The legislator, on the other hand, faces the question of determining what claims, if any, people have and what rules should determine how they are satisfied. This determination is of course constrained by all relevant moral principles (e.g., the requirements of baseline respect), but the principles will typically leave open many details that policymakers will need to fill in. Broome takes the moral questions concerning what claims individuals have as already settled and addresses only the question of how claims ought to be satisfied when they cannot be satisfied fully.[3] I maintain that in ongoing organized relationships, such as a health care system,

---

[2] I am here indebted to Nir Eyal.
[3] Broome's argument in defense of his proportional satisfaction account is that it provides the best explanation of the fairness of lotteries. That is one consideration in favor, but we have seen that there are other considerations that point elsewhere, and in any case, Broome leaves open the questions of which claims individuals have and how strong those claims are.

in which benefits and burdens for individuals shift over time, fairness does not demand that the allocation of particular benefits and burdens or their chances during limited time periods be in proportion to the strength of claims.

If the question is not how to apply to the case of T_1 and T_2 the already determined rules for distributing health care but, instead, to write those rules, one must decide which health conditions give rise to which claims of which strength and how claims are to be satisfied if they cannot be satisfied fully. If, under conditions of scarcity, every policy is going to deprive some individuals of treatment, the question is, Which policy is fairest? In answering this question, one cannot take for granted any specification of which claims individuals possess or how strong they are. Sometimes one person will benefit while another does not. Discounting treatments of claims whose cost-effectiveness ratio is not below the threshold is one way of prioritizing the treatment of claims, which is impartial and requires little sacrifice for the benefit of those who are better off. Looking at particular allocations, critics of c-e allocation may be appalled—and rightly so, if what were at issue were just that allocation—but they may be appalled because they do not see the larger picture.

To help determine how significant the fair chances critique is, let's explore a simplified (but far from simple) example of a difficult choice of how to allocate a medicine. It is atypical in many ways, not least because it involves exclusively risks of death, in which case later compensation for current deprivation is ruled out.

6.3 Epidemic

Consider the following problem, which is meant to illustrate the motivation and implications of the fair chances objection:[4]

Epidemic

You are responsible for health policy in a country with a population of 36,000,000. A terrible epidemic is coming that will kill 1 out of 10 members of the population—that is, 3,600,000 people (!)—if no action is taken. You have, at the current time, t_0, 18,000,000 doses of M, a medicine that reduces the odds of contracting the disease and dying from 1 in 10 to 1 in 10,000. In half

---

[4] This example is not intended to model the COVID-19 pandemic. It derives from Dan Wikler's "50 pills" case (2013). An animated version (with a Mahler sound track) can be found at https://vimeo.com/85057796.

> the population, a single dose of M is effective; the other half of the population needs two doses. One dose does them no good. There is no other difference between those members of the population who need one dose for protection and those who need two doses. Those who need only one dose of M are in no other way better off, healthier, or of higher status than those who need two doses of M. You cannot get more of M, and nothing else appreciably helps people survive the epidemic. How should you distribute the doses of M?

Receiving the doses of M does not guarantee survival; nor does not receiving the doses entail death, although it is certainly very bad news. The distribution of the doses of M is in effect a distribution of lottery tickets, some of which make survival extremely probable, whereas the others make death much more likely. Although stylized, this feature of the example reflects the fact that treatments rarely guarantee cures, and untreated people may recover.

It is cost-effective to give all the doses of M to those who need one dose. Yet, at least at first glance, it seems unfair not to give everyone in the society a chance of receiving the doses of M they need in proportion to the strength of their claims. How strong are these claims? The discussion in Chapter 5 suggests that claims to two pills are weaker than claims to one because providing two pills is more costly (in the additional deaths of others). However, to keep the focus on other aspects of the example and to avoid addressing the question of how much weaker claims to two pills might be, I shall suppose that the claims of those who need two doses of M to two doses of M are just as strong as the claims of those who need one dose of M to one dose of M. If the claims of those who need two doses are weaker, but not zero, it would still be unfair from Broome's perspective to do nothing toward satisfying them.

If the claims of those who need two doses are equally strong as the claims of those who need one dose, then Broome's view of fairness requires that those who need two doses of M should have the same chance to be protected from the epidemic as those who need only one dose of M. The fair policy would accordingly medicate one-third of those who need one dose and one-third of those who need two doses, and roughly 2,400,000 people will die. Fairness in this case is very expensive—an extra 600,000 lives compared to what would be the case with the cost-effective distribution of all of M to those who need only one dose.

The issue of fairness arises here with respect to the claims of *individuals*, not with how *groups* fare. This is not to deny that groups may have interests and even claims, but in this case the groups of those who need different doses have no structure or interests apart from the interests of their members. Prior to the anticipation of the epidemic, there were (by assumption) no known differences between those who need one dose of M and those who need two doses. Members of the two as-yet unknown groups did not and could not identify with the group. Giving each individual a one-third chance of being protected means that approximately one-third of the doses of M go to those who need one dose, and two-thirds of the doses go to those who need two doses. Those who collectively receive one-third or two-thirds of the doses constitute groups with no structure, interests, or importance, unless policies somehow make them salient.

Giving all of M to those who need only one dose allows the greater cost-effectiveness of treating them to *outweigh* the claims of those who need two doses, and the fair chances objection, like Broome's theory, would judge the cost-effective allocation to be unfair. Of course, Broome and other commentators on fairness recognize that there are other values that should govern social policy in addition to fairness. All I am attributing to the critic of c-e allocation is the judgment that giving M only to those who need only one dose is unfair. That unfairness constitutes a strong but not decisive reason to object to that allocation.

On the assumption that those who need a double dose have a claim to that double dose, Broome's theory implies that the only completely fair way to deal with the epidemic problem is not to treat anyone or to give everyone a useless half dose. Not to treat anyone is obviously unacceptable, due to how many deaths there would be. All the distributional policies result in outcomes that are arguably unfair, whether or not the doses are allocated as cost-effectiveness suggests. What is objectionable about giving all the doses of M only to those who need a single dose is not the distribution of life and death in the outcome. The unfairness of the outcome is unavoidable. The unfairness of any policy for distributing M, if there is any, resides in the distribution of chances.

6.4 The Lottery Backstory

Why does half the population need two doses and the other half only one? I consider two possibilities: an explicit prior lottery and, in Section 6.5, haphazard contingencies, which one might call a "natural lottery." Suppose first that the differences derive from a lottery held earlier:

The Lottery Explanation

The epidemic was anticipated at t_{-6} (6 months earlier). At that time, everyone needed two doses of M to reduce the risk of dying from 1 in 10 to 1 in 10,000. A total of 18,000,000 perishable doses of M were available at that time, and the pharmaceutical industry promised an additional 18,000,000 doses at t_0 (6 months after t_{-6}, shortly before the epidemic is due). The democratically elected legislature voted to hold a lottery at t_{-6} that gave everyone an equal chance of being treated—that is, of ultimately receiving two doses. Each of the winners was given the perishable first dose of the two-dose treatment. It is now t_0, and the epidemic is about to strike. The winners of the earlier lottery need their second dose, whereas the losers still need two doses.

Allowing the plan adopted 6 months ago to govern policy implies that at t_0 those who received one dose of M at t_{-6} get the second dose, and the other half of the population gets nothing. That is what the lottery 6 months before (in which everyone had an equal chance) decided, and it is the procedurally fair thing to do. The plan 6 months ago grounds the claims of those who now need just one dose, and it undermines the claims of those who now need two doses. Although the lottery 6 months ago fails to satisfy the interests of half the population to the benefit that M provides, it provides an equal satisfaction of all procedural claims. Those who need two doses now (at t_0) because they lost the lottery have no further procedural claim to M. The lottery 6 months ago has determined how M is to be distributed. If one were to insist on holding a new lottery at t_0 in which everyone has the same chance of getting the doses of M that they need, one would be rescinding the previous lottery, even though there are no new claimants and nothing in the situation that was not previously anticipated. The earlier lottery settled fairly the question of how to allocate the doses of M that are becoming available at t_0.[5] As argued previously, one cannot judge the fairness of an allocation in isolation.

Some may have doubts about the fairness of carrying out the policy determined by the lottery at t_{-6}. To determine whether there is anything to these doubts, consider two alternatives. First, suppose that the 18,000,000 doses available at t_{-6} had not been perishable and could have been stored. The lottery could then have been postponed until t_0, when all 36,000,000 doses were available. Would there have been anything fairer or otherwise morally better in waiting to hold the lottery (for two doses of M) until enough of M was available to give two doses to half the population? If such a lottery at t_0 is fair, as it appears to be, can it be unfair to have held basically the same lottery at t_{-6} and then carry out its result by distributing one dose of M immediately to half the population, and then 6 months later distributing the additional doses of M as envisioned?

---

[5] As Henning (2015, p. 195) notes, a lottery voluntarily entered into—"a consensual gamble"—can alter one's claims. If at the close of lunch together, Harriet and Barbara agree that the winner of a coin flip gets the restaurant's one remaining piece of pie, then the loser has no longer any claim to the pie. The coin flip at t_{-6} is a bit different because people were entered by their representatives into the lottery whether they chose to be or not.

Consider a second possibility: As in the original case, M cannot be stored, but instead of giving one dose to half the population, at t_{-6}, two doses are given to one-fourth of the population chosen by lottery. Now at t_0 a second lottery offers everyone who has not yet received any of M a one-third chance of getting two doses. Would that have been better or worse than giving a single dose of M to half the population 6 months before?

These are not rhetorical questions. Although the three lotteries offer equal chances of survival and have the same ultimate result, the procedures and interim outcomes are not morally on a par. Unlike a single lottery at t_0 in which everyone has an equal one-half chance of getting two doses of M, during the 6 months between t_{-6} and t_0, the other two procedures give members of the population a longer period with unequal prospects of surviving the epidemic. Distributions of subjective probabilities can themselves be interim outcomes, which have further consequences that may be unfair even if they result from fair procedures. If half the population knows at t_{-6} that they have a 10% chance of dying in the epidemic, whereas the other half knows they will almost certainly survive, the result will be, for 6 months, a strikingly unequal society. Such an inequality, even though it results from a fair lottery, could be a reason to have scheduled a second lottery, which would result ultimately in far more deaths and no greater equality of outcome. Although the point of the lottery is to determine the ultimate outcome, the lottery also affects what people believe—and their expectations have consequences for their social relations.

Chances in a lottery are preconditions to get the indivisible good or goods to be distributed, like can openers delivered to a set of people, only some of whom then receive a can of soup (Henning 2015, p. 173).[6] Just as the can openers are useless without a can to open, so it seems that chances or lottery tickets are of no value unless they win. Hugh Lazenby maintains plausibly (2014, p. 341) that losing lottery tickets that individuals never knew they had are of no value after the winning ticket is drawn. Yet without a can opener, there is no way to win: The can is worthless. Whether known or unknown, chances are valuable because they are necessary for winning, and knowing what chance one has of winning can be of great importance. As Michael Otsuka argues (n.d.), *beliefs* about chances have value. Knowing that one possesses a lottery ticket that may win has social and psychological consequences. Lottery tickets can be sold, and people take care to keep them safe and to prevent them from being stolen.

---

[6] As explained in Chapter 4, it is possible for chances to be unfairly distributed even when outcomes are fair. Suppose there are two kidneys and two claimants to them, Harriet and Barbara. A doctor who enjoys gambles decides to give them both a kidney if a coin lands heads but to treat only Harriet if the coin lands tails. That is unfair, even if the coin lands heads and both receive a transplant (Vong 2015, p. 471). Knowing the doctor's plans before the coin is flipped harms Harriet by making her fate so uncertain.

Differences in people's known allotment of lottery tickets may have significant consequences, especially if there is a substantial time interval between when the lottery tickets are distributed and when the lottery is held. It makes no difference to the satisfaction of claims to protection from the epidemic whether the 18,000,000 doses available 6 months ago could instead have been stored and the lottery determining who would be treated were postponed until all 36,000,000 doses were available. But deciding 6 months earlier who will be treated introduces deep inequalities in social relations by making the inequalities in the anticipated satisfaction of benefit claims known. There is thus a case to be made on grounds of fairness and an egalitarian concern with the character of social relations for postponing the first lottery until just before the epidemic, for keeping the results of the first lottery secret (perhaps by administering undetectable fake doses of M to those who lose the earlier lottery), or for holding a second lottery at t_0 that gives everyone a one-third chance of receiving the doses they need.

6.5 Satisfying Procedural Claims

Striking experimental results reported in Ubel et al. (1996) suggest that many people, including experts in bioethics, object to inequalities in people's chances even when the inequalities enhance everyone's expected benefit. Prospective jurors in Philadelphia, members of the American Association of Bioethics, and members of the Society for Medical Decision Making were presented with the following case:

> A group of doctors was formed to help the government decide which of two tests [to detect colon cancer] to offer the low-risk people.... The budget is just large enough to offer test 1 to all the low-risk people. With this approach, everyone can receive the test, and 1,000 deaths from colon cancer will be prevented. The budget is just large enough to offer [instead] test 2 to half the low-risk people. With this approach, half the people can receive the test and half cannot, and 1,100 deaths from colon cancer will be prevented. (1996, p. 1175)

If test 2 is adopted, a lottery gives everyone an equal chance of receiving the test.

Those surveyed were asked whether they favored test 1 or test 2: 56% of the jurors, 53% of the medical ethicists, and 41% of the experts in medical decision-making favored test 1. When those who favored test 1 were asked why, the overwhelming majority cited fairness as their reason. Their choices and their justification for their choices are puzzling. Although test 2 is given to only half the population, test 2, like test 1, gives everyone an equal chance of detecting colon cancer. The only other apparent difference is that test 1 gives the members of the population a smaller chance of finding a cancer.

If we set aside possible mistaken test results, individuals are saved from death by test 1 with probability $1{,}000/N$, where N is the size of the population. Test 2 is a compound lottery consisting of two stages: first something like a coin flip and second a $1{,}100/(N/2)$ chance of saving the life of those who win the coin flip. Before the first stage in test 2 is completed, administering test 2 gives everyone a greater equal expectation of avoiding a fatal case of colon cancer ($1{,}100/N$) than does test 1. Yet test 1 seems fairer to the survey respondents.[7] Why?

To believe that test 1 is fairer than test 2, survey respondents must believe that there is some difference between them other than the fact that test 2 saves more lives. Suppose that both tests consist of a single-use dropper containing a chemical that changes color (with some high probability less than 1) when applied to a feces sample from someone with colon cancer. Unbeknownst to both policymakers and the population at large, 5/11th of the droppers used in test 1 consisted of repackaged test 2 test droppers, whereas the remainder of the test 1 droppers contain inert chemicals. Although everyone will carry out the test procedures, only 5/11th of the population is actually tested. Because this fact is unrecognized, this difference among recipients of test 1 does not create any inequality in beliefs among individuals concerning whether they have been tested.

Initially, the adoption of test 2, like test 1, gives everyone an equal probability of being tested, but after the determination (via some random device) of who is assessed by test 2, the population bifurcates into two groups with unequal chances of being tested. If this difference explains why survey respondents judge test 2 to be less equitable than test 1, then it must be the case that the distribution of beliefs about whether one is tested is worth sacrificing 100 lives.

Although another experiment carried out by Ubel and co-authors provides some indirect evidence for my interpretation, there have been no tests of whether survey respondents would, as I predict, continue to assert that test 1 is fairer than test 2, even if the survey respondents were informed concerning the composition of test 1 (without knowing the composition of the specific test each has received). Experiments whose results confirmed these predictions would show how important equality in social relations, which depends on people's subjective probabilities, is to appraisals of the fairness of inequalities. I suggest that survey

---

[7] In a later study published in 2017, Li et al. asked the same questions of medical students, residents, and attending physicians at academic medical centers in Boston. Li et al. found that the percentage of those favoring test were 36%, 44%, and 53%, respectively, among medical students, residents, and attending physicians. They also found that women were more likely to favor test 1, and they noted that in Ubel et al.'s study, 64% of jurors and 22% of decision-making experts were women.

Table 6.1 Ubel et al.'s (2000) Results

Survey	Test 1 (1,000 Saved) % Receiving Test 1	Test 2 (1,100 Saved) % Receiving Test 2	Favoring Test 1 (%) Jurors	Physicians
1	100	50	56	59
2	50	25	27	26
3	90	40	28	38

respondents appear to be concerned about equalizing what people believe about their treatment as well as whether they have in fact been tested. A society in which half of the population has been tested and those tested are consequently better informed than the other half is an unequal society; and survey respondents appear to be willing to sacrifice lives to avoid this inequality in expectations and its consequences for social relations.[8]

A follow-up study carried out by Ubel et al. (2000a) on three samples consisting of jurors and members of "Physicians' Online" provides some evidence for this interpretation. In the first of three surveys, Ubel et al. replicated the results of the earlier study. In a second survey, Ubel et al. asked respondents whether they preferred giving test 1 to 50% of the low-risk population or giving test 2 to 25%, with test 2 once again detecting 1,100 cancers and test 1 detecting only 1,000. In a third survey, Ubel et al. elicited opinions concerning whether to give test 1 to 90% of the population or test 2 to 40%, with test 2 again detecting 1,100 rather than 1,000 cancers. The relevant results are shown in Table 6.1) (2000a, p. 369).

The percentage of the respondents favoring test 1 decreases in both experiments 2 and 3, and precipitously in experiment 2, where only a randomly selected half of the population receives test 1. Ubel et al. (2000a) explain these data with the hypothesis that "when neither test can be offered to everyone, both tests are seen as inequitable" (p. 370). "The central finding of our study is that preferences for equity are much stronger when 1 of 2 tests can be offered to an entire population" (p. 371). The account I have offered is consistent with that of Ubel et al., but it attempts to explain how sensible people can find test 1 to be more equitable than test 2: Equality in the distribution of subjective probability of survival in test 1 leads individuals to judge it to be fairer than test 2. But in

---

[8] Broome would regard the second step in the compound lottery constituted by test 2 as unfair whether or not individuals know whether they receive a real test or a fake one, because fair treatment requires equal objective probabilities. The consequences for social relations depend on people's expectations and hence their subjective probabilities.

experiment 2, both test 1 and test 2 impose inequalities in subjective probabilities of being tested. Concerns about avoiding inequalities in expectations are accordingly unimportant in experiment 2. There is no equity argument in favor of test 1, and thus individuals favor test 2 with its larger number of lives saved. The fact that approximately one-fourth of the population still prefers test 1 to test 2 in survey 2 is puzzling. Perhaps the respondents believe that testing a larger percentage of the population is fairer than testing a smaller percentage. Although this would explain their choice, normally providing a benefit to a larger percentage of a population does not diminish the total benefit, and in this case the greater benefit lies with test 2.[9]

6.6 "Natural Lotteries" and Fair Chances

The inequalities in subjective probabilities in Ubel et al.'s experiments or in the Epidemic case with the lottery explanation are due to the operation of known chance mechanisms. What happens in a case such as Epidemic if uncontrolled stochastic processes are the source of the differences in medical needs or claims? Those who need only one dose might be the lucky winners of a previous "natural lottery" (Daniels 1994, p. 28). This suggestion is reminiscent of Harsanyi's (1977) response to Diamond (1967). But, unlike Harsanyi's "great lottery of life," there is no invocation here of the chance of being one person or another—which raises vexing questions concerning *who* has this chance. This section is concerned with whether it is fair to treat the results of implicit unknown chance mechanisms, which are not explicit lotteries, in the same way that we treat the outcomes of explicit lotteries.[10]

Suppose that at some time t^* in the past, unknown natural processes that do not affect individual identities, such as dietary preferences and toxins in foods, gave everyone a one-in-two chance of needing only one dose of M to have effective protection against the epidemic striking now at t_0. The losers in this natural lottery need two doses of M. Even if this natural lottery is not biased in favor of any identified groups in the society, its outcome, like the outcome in the story of the explicit lottery at t_{-6} discussed above, is unequal and, on a view like Broome's, its outcome is ethically unsatisfactory and should be remedied if it is possible to do so.

---

[9] One might try to explain the shift by pointing to the preference for certainty that appears in responses in other contexts, such as the Allais paradox (Allais 1953), but it is difficult to see how a preference for *certainty* should influence judgments of fairness in this case.

[10] I employ this awkward expression because it seems to me that it is best to reserve "fair" and "unfair" and moral approbation or disapprobation in general to the actions and institutions of human beings and their consequences. Rather than pronouncing moral judgments on acts of nature such as lightning strikes or blizzards, I would reserve moral judgment to the responses to acts of nature.

There might appear to be a paradox here. On the one hand, many egalitarians maintain that what makes inequalities non-instrumentally bad is that they result from "luck"—that is, arbitrary factors, rather than their own choices, cause some people to get the short end of the stick. For example, Segall claims that "some inequalities, namely *arbitrary* ones, are bad in themselves, wherever and whenever we might find them" (2016, p. 2[italics in the original]). Segall continues, "Inequality is bad when and because it leaves some people worse off than others through no fault or choice of their own. The badness of inequality is thus anchored in *being arbitrarily disadvantaged relative to others*" (2016, p. 7 [italics added]). What could be more arbitrary than the results of an ideal lottery? Those concerned with the use of lotteries in fair distribution (e.g., Stone 2007; Kornhauser and Sager 1988; Sher 1980; Wasserman 1996; Henning 2015) have insisted that what makes lotteries fair is precisely the arbitrariness of the basis for the allocation—its insensitivity to any relevant differences apart from the claims themselves. In an ideal lottery, the allocator creates or selects some state or property with respect to which the claimants differ that is known to be irrelevant to their claims or to how those claims should be satisfied and makes the chance of winning depend on that state or property. Whether individuals are dealt a heart or a diamond from a well-shuffled deck does not reflect their needs, their desert, or the obligations others owe them. If before declaring that hearts are winners, the allocator checks who has them and decides whether hearts are winners on the basis of a correlation between hearts and previously identified properties whose distribution among the claimants is known, then the lottery is tainted and no longer succeeds in specifying winners and losers in an impartial way. The impartiality of lotteries depends on their arbitrariness.

In the case of so-called natural lotteries, nature rather than the allocator selects the winners. Apparent arbitrariness is no longer proof of impartiality, and one doubts whether nature is entirely arbitrary. The processes may have favored members of some salient social groups over others. In a natural lottery, there is no reason to believe that people have had equal objective chances of needing one or two doses of *M*. Unlike a constructed lottery, there is also no assurance in natural lotteries that the unknown processes that favor some group of individuals today will not do so tomorrow and the day after. There is no assurance "*that the losers could easily have been the winners* (Spiekermann 2021, p. 2 [italics in the original]). What makes some individuals into winners could be some property that is linked to oppression and stigma.

One might wonder how arbitrariness can contribute to fairness while aggravating the injustice of inequality, especially given the common view that unfairness explains what is wrong with inequality. There is no real paradox because the egalitarian who regards arbitrariness as bad and the theorist of fairness who regards arbitrariness as good are answering different questions. The egalitarian is concerned with how good or bad, just or unjust, are the results of lotteries, whereas the fairness theorist is focusing on the evaluation of lotteries themselves. An ideal lottery that gives everyone the same one-half chance of surviving the epidemic results in an extremely unequal state of affairs.[11]

Although the difference in the questions resolves the apparent conflict between what an egalitarian calls for and what is fair, there is more to be said about why we are so much more comfortable allowing the outcome of a human-constructed lottery to determine what should be done than leaving the outcome to the idiosyncrasies of nature. One explanation is that we know the chances only in lotteries we construct, and people have an aversion to ambiguity (Ellsberg 1961). Another explanation is that explicit lotteries, like the lottery at t_{-6}, can be consensual gambles. Those legitimately in charge of health policy may have had the authority to commit members of the population to accepting the results of the lottery at t_{-6}. The outcome of the explicit lottery is no more or less equal than what results from the natural lottery, but no one has made a commitment to accepting the results of the natural lottery. There is also a crucial expressive difference: Accepting the outcome of happenstance, unlike accepting the outcome of an explicit lottery, does not affirm the equality of the members of the population. To the contrary, it may fail to show baseline respect, appearing to be indifferent to the fate of those whose prospects are poor. They may never have had equal objective chances. In contrast, if at t_0 those needing one dose had been favored by a previous explicit lottery, there would be a good case for the fairness (as well as efficiency) of giving them the single dose of M they need.

Explicit lotteries *assign* chances rather than accepting outcomes of unknown chance mechanisms as they come. In this way, they acknowledge people's claims and show respect and concern for the claimants. I take this defense of holding a lottery as a powerful reason to prefer explicit to natural lotteries, even though the benefit claims of those who lose a natural lottery receive no less attention and are not worse satisfied than the claims of those who lose an explicit lottery.

Speaking of a natural lottery is metaphorical. What determines why some people are more susceptible to a disease is often unknown and can easily reflect unjust inequalities (as is true in COVID-19). One reason not to rely on natural lotteries is the risk that doing so will aggravate existing stigma and disadvantage. Although the outcome of an explicit lottery is as unequal as the outcome of a natural lottery, the fact that the outcome comes from an explicit lottery helps protect against unjust discrimination, and it overtly expresses respect.

A further wrinkle confirms what I have said about the reasons why it seems unfair to rely on the natural lottery that leads some to require two doses of M while

---

[11] For example, allocating infants at birth randomly to rich or poor families would not erase the inequalities between rich and poor. It would fairly satisfy the procedural but not the benefit claims of the infants.

others need only one dose. Suppose that there were a series of epidemics causing severe illness but not death, and in each case there are shortages of medications, with some people needing lower doses than others. There is no correlation between those needing a higher dose in one epidemic and those needing a higher dose in another. Giving everyone equal chances of being medicated in each epidemic results in virtually everyone being more seriously ill than if the medication had been reserved in each epidemic for those needing a lower dose. Shifting to a policy of reserving medication to those needing lower doses when medication is in short supply would appear in these circumstances to be both efficient and fair. It runs the risk that in the future this policy will disadvantage some substantial portion of the society, but it has the prospect of fairly benefitting them all. In this case, unlike the single case, there is reason to believe that the unknown factors responsible for the sensitivity to medication provide individuals with something like an equal chance and do not sacrifice some to benefit others.

6.7 Is It Fair to Give M Only to Those Who Need Only One Dose?

On Broome's theory, if the need for one or two doses does not stem from a previous fair lottery, it is unfair to satisfy only the claims of those who need one dose. This is true, even if the claims of those who need two doses are weaker than the claims of those who need only one dose. This conclusion might be challenged from the perspective of a different interpretation of impartial reciprocity that argues that providing M only to those who need one dose does not call for undue sacrifice or fail to show baseline respect.

Veil-of-ignorance defenses of c-e allocation have been considered and dismissed by authors such as Brock (1995, p. 173), Kamm (1993, pp. 241–242, 285–288; 2013, pp. 385–388), and Voorhoeve and Fleurbaey (2012) by adapting Rawls' (1970) critique of Harsanyi's implicit assumption that the losses of one person can be compensated by the gains to others. But in the Epidemic case, one minimizes the number of those who are worst off by giving all of M to those who need only one dose. The outcomes for the worse off are not diminished in order to benefit those who are better off. The worst off in the Epidemic case are those who die. A "maximin" strategy that aims to make the worst outcome as good as possible might be indifferent to how many die, but minimizing that number is surely consistent with a concern for those who are worst off.[12] There is no maximin argument here against maximizing benefits.

---

[12] Setting aside Taurek's (1977) view that there is no better reason to save more lives than to save fewer, which is discussed in Chapter 8.

Suppose that rather than a choice from behind a hypothetical veil of ignorance, there is an actual meeting of the population before it is ascertained who needs one dose of M and who needs two. Nature has provided, as it were, a partial veil of ignorance. It is known that if all those who need one dose are treated, none will be left for those who need two and that there is no correlation between needs for doses of M and other socially salient differences among individuals. In such a situation, rational individuals concerned to promote their own well-being—and indeed many other objectives—would favor using all the medication on those who need only one dose. This actual vote would presumably justify the policy, but it does not automatically show that the policy is fair. The vote in favor might have been due to the expected benefits, despite the policy's unfairness. But what can be unfair about a policy that offers everyone both equal expectations and outcomes that are no worse than any alternatives for those individuals who lose out, whose number is minimized? How can there be a failure to take seriously the separateness of persons when those who fare worst are at least as well off and at least as few in number as those who would fare worst with any alternative policy? How can a policy that equalizes and minimizes the sacrifices individuals make fail to be fair?

There remains an equal-respect argument in favor of explicit lotteries, and one should also take into account the consequences for members of the population of knowledge of lotteries and of their outcomes. The interim outcome of a decision process that as it were stamps "saved" or "lost" on everyone's foreheads is unavoidably unfair. Creating a distinction between "first-class" and "second-class citizens," however justifiably, impartially, and temporarily, is itself unfair. But then the fair chances objection morphs into an objection to creating a stigmatized or disadvantaged group—that is, into an objection to discrimination, which I discuss in Chapter 9.

6.8 Conclusion

Although an insistence on proportional satisfaction of claims expresses equal respect for individuals, it seems that c-e allocation can do so as well. Under conditions of scarcity, some will be treated, and others will not be, and whenever fairness overrules cost-effectiveness, fewer will be treated.

Unlike more humdrum allocations, the distribution of M is a life-and-death matter. Future allocations cannot make up for inequalities in this allocation, and few past differences in treatments are of a magnitude sufficient justifiably to influence who should now receive the doses of M that they need. If we set aside the lottery backstory, which makes it fair to give M exclusively to those who need only one dose, then, from Broome's perspective, if claims to M are equally strong, then giving everyone an equal one-third chance of receiving the doses of M that they need is fair. If those who need two doses have a weaker claim, they should have a lesser chance of being satisfied, but Broome's view of fairness would still condemn failing to satisfy claims to two doses altogether. Outweighing claims, rather than satisfying them or giving them chances in proportion to their strength, arguably fails to respect the individuals whose claims are outweighed. It does not treat those who need two doses as (in Kant's terminology) ends in themselves, whose claims must be acknowledged and to whom our concerns should extend. Even if the c-e allocation is, all things considered, the better choice, one might argue that the sacrifice it involves on the part of those who need two doses of M is unfair.

But this is not the only way to interpret Kant's view that we must never treat individuals merely as means. Showing to all baseline respect does not rule out any allocation where some do better and have better chances than others. The difficult question is determining when an unequal allocation treats individuals as equals. In the Epidemic case, giving all of M to those who need only one dose is impartial and makes those who are worst off as well off as are the worst off with any alternative, while also minimizing how many are worst off. Both impartiality and reciprocity would seem to find it fair to give M only to those who need only one dose.

Something has got to give. We have two reasonable claims about fairness that conflict. The conclusion I draw is that Broome's view that fairness requires chances proportional to strength of claims cannot be defended as always the best way to show equal baseline respect. Reserving M to those who need one dose requires a sacrifice, but there is no alternative that requires a lesser sacrifice, and the criterion that determines on whom the sacrifice falls does not imply any lesser respect for those who need two doses.

The conclusion that c-e allocation in the Epidemic case is fair[13] does not imply that c-e allocation is always fair. Unlike what one finds in this case, what is cost-effective may require wrongful sacrifice, particularly when the losers in one allocation lose out consistently in other allocations.

This chapter's consideration of the fair chances objection casts light on complications concerning c-e allocation. First, allocations should not be appraised in isolation. What principles does an allocation instantiate? What are the cumulative consequences? Second, although consistent with the conclusion drawn in Chapter 4, that whether a lottery is fair depends on whether it gives individuals the right objective chances, the Epidemic case shows us that subjective probabilities also matter, both with respect to whether people accept

---

[13] Frances Kamm suggested to me that the conclusion that it is fair to give all of M to those who need only one dose endorses the distribution that cost-effectiveness analysis also endorses, but that it does so on entirely different grounds and thus provides no support for the claim that c-e allocation is fair. I return to this question in Chapter 10.

lotteries as fair and respectful and, prior to the drawing, tangibly in terms of the ticket holders' expectations and the social consequences of those expectations. From an egalitarian perspective that focuses on the character of the relations among people, the consequences of the differences in expectations are of great importance.

Third, there are often many alternatives, especially when one considers the different ways the health care system may be structured, and different alternatives create other puzzles concerning fairness. For example, suppose that the society facing the epidemic had an ideally fair distribution of wealth and income. The health authority then issues a coupon to everyone that can be redeemed for one-half of a dose of M. At the same time, those in need of two doses are given a cash supplement to help them buy coupons. Those who are willing to face significant risks in exchange for greater wealth will sell their coupons. Family members will pool their coupons in order to protect some of their members at the cost of exposing others to an elevated risk. Whether more of those who need only one dose will survive the epidemic than those who need two doses depends on people's attitudes toward risk and wealth and on the size of the cash supplement given to those who need two doses. Because many individuals will be willing to pay virtually everything they have for coupons, those who part with their coupons and face a 1 in 10 chance of death will receive substantial compensation, which they can bequeath to others if they do not survive.

Is this market response to the Epidemic case fair? In real life, such a market would be repugnant because we do not have anything like an ideal distribution of wealth. What one should say about such a market in ideal conditions from Broome's perspective depends on what one maintains concerning the claims of the individuals facing the epidemic. If one takes the strength of claims of individuals to doses of M to be proportional to what they are willing to pay (which is determined by the strength of their desire to live, their attitude toward risk, the overall supply and demand for coupons, and the ideal distribution of wealth), then everyone's claims are satisfied in proportion to their strength, and the coupon market is fair. If, on the other hand, one maintains that everyone has an equal claim to the doses of M that they need, then one would criticize the market, on the grounds it may not give everyone an equal chance of getting the doses of M that they need. In addition, if, as I have argued, it is fair to provide M only to those who need one dose, then one might conclude that a market in coupons coupled with the subsidy for those who need two doses is unfair because some doses of M wind up going to those who need two doses. But, because this distribution is the result of voluntary choice made in just circumstances, the fact that there are excess deaths does not reflect any failure of equal respect.

Provided that everyone starts on an equal footing, the outcome reflects the values and relations among the members of the population. Could such an ideal market be fully respectful of the diverse circumstances and values of members of the population? Notice that there is no such thing as an objectively equal footing. Whether someone who needs just one dose of M and who starts off needing just one additional coupon to be protected from the epidemic is at an advantage compared to receiving a subsidy of $\$X$ and needing three coupons will vary from person to person and according to the state of the market. Presumably, there is some value of the subsidy, $\$X$, that *on average* makes individuals indifferent to whether they need one coupon or have a subsidy and need three coupons, even though it would be difficult to determine what X is. So one might argue that from the perspective of both impartial reciprocity and proportional satisfaction, an ideal market coupled with subsidies for those who need two doses of M could be fair. On the other hand, why does the average indifference between subsidies and coupons make the market fair? The pre-exchange situations of individuals will differ enormously. For some risk-takers, the subsidy is frosting on the cake, whereas for others who want to protect their lives, it is insufficient. What is fair about that?

The example of the coupon market serves a useful function, even if it is not a plausible contender for a fair distribution of M. It exposes the idealizations built into accounts of how principles guide allocations. Individuals have different interests in avoiding risks. They have different interests in protecting others from risk. They have different interests in prolonging or protecting their lives or the lives of others. Out of these interests, coupled with the principles governing the health care system, come their claims to health care, which cannot all be met.

Because Broome is also concerned to prevent deaths, I conjecture that he would favor giving all of M to those who need only one dose, even though he would regard that allocation as unfair. Impartial reciprocity agrees with the policy conclusion, and it takes the distribution of M to be fair as well as saving more lives. What allows impartial reciprocity to count the allocation as fair is that the allocation does not require more than the minimum sacrifice, and it thereby shows equal respect. If those who need two doses of M were members of a stigmatized minority or individuals who suffered previous disadvantage, the verdict would be different.

Carrying out an explicit lottery would also show equal respect. People have claims to be regarded as full participants, over whose prospects there is no socially imposed black cloud. These considerations weaken the case for the fairness of giving M only to those who need a single dose and give some force to the fair chances objection, but they do not show that it is unfair to give M only to those who need a single dose. A fair distribution should reduce the inequalities in expectations that flow from proposed allocations, especially when these are systematic. But then the fair chances objection morphs into an objection to creating a stigmatized or disadvantaged group—that is, into an objection to discrimination, to be discussed in Chapter 9. When there is no discrimination, then it is questionable whether there is any unfairness in outcomes that today serve some interests and neglect others and may do the opposite tomorrow.

Broome's theory is a plausible way of making concrete the fundamental view of fairness as equal respect, and it provides a grounding for the fair chances objection to c-e allocation. However, because Broome's theory does not tell us what claims individuals have, objections to allocations that are not proportional to the strength of claims may miss the mark, and in some cases impartial reciprocity does not require proportional satisfaction of claims or chances.

7
Does Cost-Effectiveness Fail to Give Sufficient Priority to Severity?

Chapter 6 examined the fair chances criticism of cost-effectiveness (c-e) allocation, which I interpreted as an objection to allowing claims to be outweighed rather than satisfied in proportion to their strength. This view takes for granted that individuals' claims are not limited to what cost-effectiveness allocates to them. C-e allocation is not guaranteed to express equal respect. But in the context of ongoing interactions, satisfaction of claims in proportion to their strength is not a better way to implement equal respect than alternatives such as taking turns. Moreover, outweighing may be defensible. The fair chances criticism is inconclusive, even though it rests on a plausible theory of fairness.

This chapter turns to a different objection: that c-e allocation fails to place sufficient weight on the severity of health problems. If treatments T and T' cost the same and are equally effective, then they are equally cost-effective. But if the recipients of treatment T would be worse off if untreated than the recipients of T', then many people surveyed across a number of countries believe that T should be funded before T', even though the improvement in health or well-being is just the same. A number of philosophers share this view, which I shall criticize. Indeed, they maintain that even if T' is "somewhat" more cost effective than T, T should still be funded before T'. In giving a greater priority to treating those who are worse off, providing T is allegedly fairer than providing T'. The criticism maintains that c-e allocation is unfair because it fails to prioritize severity sufficiently (Brock 2003a; Nord 1999).[1]

As stated so far, it is not clear whether the concern about severity is a criticism of how effectiveness is measured or of how measures of effectiveness are

---

[1] Effectiveness consists of the gain in quality-adjusted life years (QALYs) that a treatment provides. Consider an operation to relieve paralysis in the left arm. Although equally likely to be successful, whether it is carried out on Paul, who has previously lost his right arm, or Ludwig, whose right arm is fine, it can be expected to be more *effective* on Paul. There is a larger health-related quality of life (HRQoL) gain in Paul's acquiring the use of one arm (not having had the use of either) than in Ludwig's acquiring the use of both arms (having had the use of one). The success of the operation has nothing to do with Paul's right arm, but its effectiveness does. Although this may appear to be a case in which Paul should get priority because his health condition is more severe, it does not ground a criticism of the allocation, which already gives priority to treating Paul. I am indebted to Frances Kamm for this example.

used to guide the allocation of health care. As discussed in Chapter 3, I maintain that the effectiveness of health care is mismeasured, but I argue in this chapter that this mismeasurement is not a failure to prioritize severity and that the way in which effectiveness measures are used does not fail to prioritize severity sufficiently. When I speak of "prioritizing severity," I mean *general policies* that assign a greater priority to treating those who are badly off than cost-effectiveness supports. I am not concerned with whether the circumstances of individual patients should influence the choices of providers at their bedsides.

This chapter has six sections. Section 7.1 distinguishes two interpretations of severity, which I call "acute" and "chronic." This distinction should not be identified with the difference between criticizing the measure of effectiveness and criticizing how that measure is used. Whether concerned with acute or chronic severity, critics of c-e allocation have criticized both the way effectiveness has been measured and how that measure has been used. Section 7.2 presents data showing that survey respondents assign a higher priority to treatments of more severe health problems than cost-effectiveness gives them, and it illustrates ambiguities in prioritizing severity. Section 7.3 considers how to implement greater priority for severity in the assessment of health states, and it points to problems that undermine the intuitive appeal of prioritizing acute severity. Section 7.4 presents and criticizes the main arguments that are invoked to support the conclusion that fairness requires prioritizing what I am calling chronic severity. Section 7.5 argues that compassion and solidarity do not justify a policy of prioritizing either acute or chronic severity. Section 7.6 concludes with speculations concerning why so many people mistakenly maintain that c-e allocation fails to place sufficient priority on severity.

7.1 Measuring Severity: Who Is Worse Off?

Which individuals are worse off? Whose condition is more severe? There is no single answer. When insisting on the importance of prioritizing severity, critics of c-e allocation have made different complaints. The different conceptions of severity in the literature are variations on interpretations of severity as acute or chronic. Acute severity is medical and immediate: What matters is how ill individuals are right now, or how ill they will be in the immediate future if they are not treated.[2] Someone who is about to choke to death on a salmon bone has an acutely severe health problem. P's health condition at time *t* is acutely more

---

[2] As Audrey Powers pointed out to me, this is problematic in the case of diseases with deferred effects. How (acutely) severe is Oscar's health, if he has a narrow window for treatment of a disease he just contracted that will kill him in a decade with few symptoms until it kills him? This is a problem for defenders of prioritizing severity which, as a critic of prioritizing severity, I need not resolve.

severe than Q's if and only if P's health state or immediate expectation at *t* is worse than Q's.

The other interpretation of severity, which I call the chronic view, looks to the past as well as the future and it regards P's condition as more severe than Q's if P has been worse off than Q over extended periods and, if untreated, may be expected to be worse off in the future.³ How chronically severe P's condition is may depend on non-health factors such as economic deprivation or social exclusion. Chronic views might focus on lifetime health or well-being, or health or well-being in some shorter but still substantial period beginning before the health care allocation takes place. There are many possible variations on the acute and chronic views, which require somewhat different discussion (Nord 2013). I focus on what I take to be a typical formulation of each approach, but in Section 7.4, I briefly consider some other varieties.

Section 7.3 focuses on Erik Nord's approach to valuing health states, which prioritizes acute severity. Nord describes severity as "current impairments and expected future loss of quality of life and/or length of life due to the illness" (Nord et al. 2013, p. 67). This description is problematic. How is one to combine a measure of current impairments (e.g., current HRQoL) with a measure of "expected future loss of quality and/or length of life" or with a measure of expected future loss due specifically to the illness? The HRQoL of a health state can be terrible, but the spate of poor health may be so brief that it matters little. Current impairments (if untreated) must thus be supposed to last for some substantial period. What weights should be placed on current HRQoL understood as lasting in this way versus expected loss of QALYs, where HRQoL, in Nord's view, reflects the values of health states to individuals?

Taking into account expectations concerning the future creates a risk of confounding concerns with severity with concerns about age. Expected future loss of QALYs from permanent impairments, which is one of the criteria governing health care allocation in Norway (Ottersen et al. 2016), will be larger for those with a longer life expectancy, who will generally be younger. Note that greater priority for treating health deficiencies that are expected to last longer is already built into the definition of QALYs. Improving the HRQoL of an individual by 0.2 units results in an expected gain of 2 QALYs in someone whose life expectancy is 10 years and 6 QALYs in someone whose life expectancy is 30 years. To maintain that this dependence of the benefits of treatment on life expectancy

---

³ In a case in which Amanda's health and well-being have drastically improved and are now satisfactory, one might no longer judge that her treatment should be prioritized owing to the (chronic) severity of her health problems or her shortfall in well-being, but one might defend prioritizing her treatment as a compensation for her past hardship. Whether one should use health care in this way is controversial and a digression from the question of whether c-e allocation fails to sufficiently prioritize severity. I am indebted here to Audrey Xu.

fails to prioritize severity sufficiently is to maintain that health conditions are in some additional way worse if they last longer. Perhaps this makes sense for some health deficiencies, such as serious pain or depression. But intuitively, the same health condition is not more severe on account of the fact that those it afflicts are younger. Whether one health deficiency is more severe than another should not usually depend on age.

If instead of taking severity to be the expected total loss of future health, one takes it to be the expected proportional loss of future health, as has been the case in the Netherlands (Van de Wetering et al. 2016), then temporary health deficiencies will be more severe in older people than in younger, because they occupy a larger portion of the remaining life span.[4] But once again, except in special cases (in which, because of the characteristics of the health deficiency, severity depends on expectations of the duration of an illness), the measurement of severity should depend on the health state and prognosis, not on age.

As far as I can tell, there is no analysis of the acute notion of severity that satisfies the following three intuitive conditions. In formulating them, I shall for the moment accept Nord's view that HRQoL measures what I called in Chapter 3 the "personal value" of health states.

1. Severity depends indirectly on age only in the subclass of cases, such as pain, in which the length of a health condition affects its severity.
2. Severity is a decreasing function of HRQoL of health states if untreated (provided that the HRQoL persists for some substantial period).
3. Severity is proportional to the expected loss of QALYs if untreated rather than treated.

If one accepts condition 3, then one is committed to taking impairments that are expected to last longer to be more severe. No account of severity can satisfy both conditions 1 and 3. To resolve this conflict, one should jettison condition 3 because one cannot reasonably give up the thesis that the same health state is just as severe regardless of the age of the person afflicted.[5]

My solution to this conundrum is to take individuals to be more (acutely) severely ill if their health expectations for the *immediate* future are lower. This conforms to what Gu et al. (2015, p. 47) find to be the most popular definition of (acute) severity.[6] However, one must say more because, as noted above, the

---

[4] These difficulties are pointed out by Robberstad (2015), who canvasses seven different conceptions of severity—none of which appears adequately to capture the intuitive idea.

[5] I am indebted here to Bastian Steuwer.

[6] Gu et al. (2015) note that four of the studies of preferences for prioritizing severity operationalize severity as life expectancy if untreated. But Olsen (2013) presents evidence that what people care about is total length of life rather than how much remains. There are other notions of severity in

severity of health states such as serious pain depends on their duration. A health condition that involves a minute of terrible pain is not as severe as another health condition that is longer lasting, such as an extended bout of constipation. Moreover, one needs to count as severe health conditions that are as it were "time bombs" expected to explode in the near but not immediate future. A small tumor, which, if not removed promptly, will be fatal in a year, may have a negligible effect on HRQoL for the next few months. Rather than seeking a satisfactory general characterization of "severity," whose existence I doubt, I limit comparisons of acute severity to health states that persist for similar lengths of time and ignore dangerous symptomless conditions. This compromise is unsatisfactory, but because I am not defending greater prioritization of severity, I need not seek further for a precise characterization, unlike those who defend prioritizing severity, who have their work cut out for them.

So far, it appears that the concern to place more priority on severity is directed entirely to correcting the mismeasurement of the effectiveness of treatments as improvements in the personal values of HRQoL of health states. As I argued in Chapter 3, health care policy ought to be governed by the public rather than the personal values of health states, where both public and personal values of health states depend on the suffering and activity limitations those health states involve. What distinguishes them is that public values reflect the limitations poor health places on the range of things that humans value doing, whereas the private value depends on the limits poor health places on people's ability to accomplish their given aims.

On this view, the personal values of health states will sometimes be higher than their public values, and to the extent that this is the case, the distinction between personal and public values supports a critique of some standard cost-effectiveness studies as failing to prioritize severity sufficiently. But personal values will sometimes be lower as well as higher than public values. For example, I cannot see any reason why pain and distress should diminish public values more than private values. On my view, c-e allocation (as it is actually practiced) relies on the wrong set of values, rather than failing to place sufficient weight on severity.

7.2 Survey Results: Priority to Those Who Are More Severely Ill

If the costs of completely curing two ailments are the same, it will be more cost effective to cure the more severe ailment. Cost-effective allocation responds in

the literature. For example, to make questionnaires simpler for respondents, Van de Wetering et al. (2016) identify severity with quality of the initial health state.

this way to severity—that is, to how bad people's health would be if they were untreated. But it does so only because of a correlation between the severity of health problems and the size of the benefit from alleviating them. Once one has specified the cost and the health improvement (effectiveness)—which depends on the improvement in HRQoL and the duration of the change—the allocation of health care implied by cost-effectiveness is fixed; the severity of someone's health state if untreated has no further relevance. There is considerable evidence that many people object to this implication of cost-effective allocation. Many of those surveyed maintain that fairness requires that treatments of more severe conditions are more worth funding than treatments that provide similar-sized benefits to less severe conditions. This is a belief about how to make use of measures of how good or bad health states are, not a belief about whether those measures understate severity.

Let us begin with a classic Norwegian study, which Peter Ubel replicated and modified in a later study in the United States. In the Norwegian study, 150 "Norwegian politicians involved in healthcare decision making at a county level" (Nord 2001b, p. 87) were presented with a scenario that, translated into English (Ubel 1999), reads as follows:

> Imagine an illness A that gives severe health problems and an illness B that gives moderate problems. Treatment will help patients with illness A a little, while it will help patients with illness B considerably. The cost of treatment is the same in both cases. There is insufficient treatment capacity for both illnesses, and an increase in funding is suggested. Three different views are then conceivable. (1) Most of the increase should be allocated to treatment for illness B, since the effects of these are greater, (2) Most of the increase should be allocated to treatments for illness A, since these patients are more severely ill, (3) The increase should be divided evenly between the two groups. Which of these views comes closest to your own? (p. 896)

The study found that 11% favored option 1, 38% option 2, and 45% option 3. Only approximately one out of nine favored the most cost-effective policy. In Ubel's replication, which was carried out in Philadelphia, Pennsylvania, on prospective jurors waiting to be called to jury duty, an even smaller percentage—only 9% –favored policy 1; 64% chose to divide the increase equally, and 26% preferred to devote the increase entirely to those with the more severe illness A. An equal division, like a preference for treating illness A, rejects the most cost-effective allocation, presumably due to the greater severity of the illness A.

As Ubel (1999) notes, the Norwegian study and his replication are flawed. Respondents might have chosen the equal division option out of an unwillingness to make a choice between treating A and treating B. I would add that the responses might also be explained by a concern with fair chances, rather than severity. Respondents might prefer the equal division on the grounds that health policy should not ignore the claims of any portion of the population.

In addition to replicating the Norwegian survey, Ubel investigated how people respond if the questions are modified. In a follow-up study, Ubel (1999) clarified the wording of the surveys and eliminated the option of dividing the increase in health care resources between illnesses A and B. Of those completing these revised surveys, approximately 60% favored the cost-effective alternative of improving the health of the moderately ill "considerably," and approximately 40% favored improving the health of those who are more severely ill "a little" (1999, p. 897). The results of the Norwegian study and its American replication are fragile: The preferences of American respondents for prioritizing severity are not as widespread as the original study suggests. On the other hand, it is still the case that 40% of respondents in the modified experiment were willing to sacrifice improvements in health in order to prioritize severity.

As the results of this inquiry illustrate, many survey respondents favor providing health care first to those who are more acutely severely ill, even if the health benefit to them is somewhat smaller than the benefit that could be provided to those who are less severely ill. These results do not appear to challenge the accuracy of the measurement of health. In his 2009 literature review, Koonal Shah concludes, "Overall, the majority of studies suggest that *people are, on the whole, willing to sacrifice at least some aggregate health in order to give priority to the severely ill*" (Shah 2009, p. 82 [italics added]). Gu et al. maintain that "the empirical evidence is consistent with 16 (out of 19) studies suggesting that members of the general public are in general willing to give priority to a patient with more severe disease" (2015, p. 47; see also Nord 2012; Nord and Johansen 2014). Shah (2009) points out, however, that a sizeable minority in most studies disagree, and Gu et al. note three studies that found "small or no effects of severity on priority setting with the small effect favouring the less severely ill" (2015, p. 47).

Much of the evidence showing that people support prioritizing acute severity comes from comparing the personal values individuals place on health improvements to the values inferred from "person trade-off" questions. But it is ambiguous whether relying on person trade-offs supports weighting health state measures so as to prioritize severity or whether person trade-offs provide alternative health state measures. As explained in Chapter 1, individual values— the HRQoL of health states—are derived from techniques such as time trade-offs. Individuals are asked questions such as "Suppose you had 10 years to live in health state H. How many years in full health would be equally good?" In a person trade-off, in contrast, people are asked questions such as, "If you faced a choice between improving the health state of 100 people from 0.6 to 0.8 or improving the health of N other people from 0.8 to 1, for what value of N would you be indifferent?" Someone who seeks only to maximize QALYs would answer that $N = 100$. In fact, many people regard improving someone's HRQoL from 0.6 to 0.8 as more socially valuable than improving someone's HRQoL from 0.8 to 1 (Nord 2001b, pp. 87–89). In asking the person trade-off questions this way, it appears that people are being asked how they would *use* health state values rather than to determine what health state values ought to be. If asked instead to compare the benefit of curing 100 people of psoriasis to healing X broken legs or saving Y lives, there is no reason to believe that person trade-off health state values would be uniformly lower than personal values.

Consider, for example, the following results that Ubel et al. (2000) report:

> For example, in one study, people estimated the HRQoL of moderate knee pain as being 0.94, a value that would imply that curing this knee condition (thereby bringing an HRQoL improvement of 0.06) is about 1/16th as valuable as saving a person's life. Yet these people felt that greater than 1,000 people would need to be cured of moderate knee pain to equal the value of saving 1 person's life. (p. 894)

Are individuals judging the value of curing knee pain (and thus the difference between one's health state with or without knee pain) that is relevant to policy, or are people registering their views concerning how to take into account the given value of knee pain when lives are at stake?

Before one takes findings such as those discussed above as establishing that people prioritize severity, one should recognize that the person trade-off might have other explanations, such as a special concern for saving lives (Dolan 1998, p. 41). Nevertheless, the contrast between the ratios implied by the quality weights and the responses to person tradeoff questions is evidence that many people prioritize severity.

The contrast between the ratios implied by the quality weights and the responses to person trade-off questions might seem paradoxical, but the preferences from which the values of health states to individuals are inferred do not concern distribution. They express no view concerning trade-offs—that is, social choices—among different health improvements for *different* individuals. Nord puts the point as follows:

> Some may argue that the extent to which people have a concern for severity will be captured in their initial *personal* utility assessments of health states.... In utility assessments, ... subjects are not asked about distributive concerns or *societal* value. They are asked to quantify the disutility they personally would feel with different states of illness.... On the basis of responses to such questions it is possible only to say which of different programs provides the greater sum of

individual utility gains. *The respondents have not expressed any opinion about priority setting.* (1999, p. 28)

I would not put things in quite the way that Nord does, because I do not identify expressing quantitative preferences among health states with quantifying "the disutility they personally would feel with different states of illness." Whether preferences among health states match the feelings individuals expect to have in those health states requires argument.

But this disagreement is not what is at issue. The crucial point is that there is a difference between measuring how health states bear on single individuals and setting priorities for the care of different individuals (Nord 2001b). In discussing this point, Nord conflates two criticisms: that c-e allocation misuses the values of health states and that c-e allocation assigns the wrong values to health states. Consider in contrast how Dan Brock expresses the concern about the use of cost-effectiveness information:

Do people who assign the utility level of 0.95 to requiring equipment to see or hear or speak mean by that assignment that saving one healthy person's life is of equal importance to keeping 20 persons from having to use eyeglasses or a hearing aid (1998, p. 7)?

Brock is maintaining that c-e allocation is misusing health state measures rather than mismeasuring health states.

What should one conclude concerning popular attitudes toward prioritizing severity? The preferences respondents in Ubel's studies express might reflect mistaken beliefs that treating those with illness A will provide a larger health improvement because they are sicker. Another possibility is that individuals might believe that failing to prioritize severity constitutes a form of discrimination. Nevertheless, it appears that a great many people favor prioritizing acute severity and take the strength of an individual's claims to health care resources to depend in part on how bad the individual's health state is, not just how much it can be improved. When Ubel asked respondents to give their reasons, by far the most common response among those who favored providing the smaller health benefit to those who are more severely ill was that those who are more severely ill "deserve priority" (1999, p. 898).

Although there may be egalitarian considerations lurking in these attitudes toward severity, these studies do not address people's attitudes toward the distribution of health states after treatments have been allocated. Moreover, obviously, treating the individual whose health state is at the moment most acutely severe may benefit individuals whose health or well-being up to now has been excellent and whose future health expectations if treated are enviable. Prioritizing severity in such cases aggravates rather than moderates inequalities. The concern with acute severity should accordingly be distinguished from an egalitarian concern that allocation via cost-effectiveness leads to inegalitarian outcomes.

7.3 Implementing Priority for Severity

Before considering whether there is an ethical justification for giving the claims of those who are severely ill greater weight than a standard cost-effective allocation gives them, let us consider how to implement a policy of prioritizing acute severity. Questions about the significance of severity are often described as concerned with "the trade-off between health maximisation and pre-treatment severity" (Shah 2009, p. 82). Such a trade-off would not exist if one were to capture the significance of severity within the values of health states. I am also uncomfortable with Shah's formulation because, as I argued in Chapter 1, there is no such thing as a quantity or magnitude of health that can be maximized. What can be maximized is instead the value of health. What most health economists mean by "health maximization" is maximizing the extent to which people's health states satisfy their (health-related) preferences.

Although there are ambiguities in preference surveys and good reasons to doubt the accuracy of people's predictions about what they would prefer or would choose if, for example, they actually faced a time trade-off between longer life and a higher quality of life, it is reasonable to interpret the numbers that one infers from those surveys as rough measures of what I call the "personal" or "individual" value of health—that is, the value of health to a particular individual. Those who prioritize severity and also seek to enhance population health must find some way to capture severity in a corrected set of health-state values or to trade off enhancing the total of individual values against the distributional considerations that support prioritizing severity.

If the health authorities seek both to enhance health and to prioritize severity, then there are several ways to proceed. The best-known scheme for prioritizing severity while enhancing health is Erik Nord's proposal (Nord 1999, 2016; Nord and Johansen 2014; Nord et al. 1999) to encompass the priority of severity in assignments of a "social value" $SV(H_i)$ to a health state H_i. Nord's social values attempt to encompass distributive concerns *within the values assigned to health states*. Rather than offering a new construal of the values of health states from a social perspective, Nord applies a uniform concave transformation to the individual values of health states as a way of embedding concerns for fairness into health state values. If the social values properly capture the priority that more acutely severe health states should have, then maximizing the sum of the social value of each person's health (cost-effectiveness with increases in social value rather than increases in QALYs as the measure of effectiveness) will implement the proper prioritization of severity. This approach can be summarized as follows:

The value encompassing maximization strategy for prioritizing severity

$$\text{Maximize} \sum_j \text{SV}(H_j), \text{ where SV}(H_j) = f\left[U(H_j)\right]$$

H_j is the individual j's health state, $U(H_j)$—which is HRQoL—is the individual or personal value of H_j, SV(H_j) is the social value of H_j, and f is some concave function that derives the social values of health states from measures of the individual values. In lieu of specifying f and deriving SV(H_j) from $U(H_j)$, Nord suggests measuring SV(H_j) directly by means of person trade-offs. This scheme retains maximization and consequentialism but argues that the sum of unweighted QALYs is the wrong maximand.

The value-encompassing maximization strategy is attractive because it is apparently algorithmic. Once the social value of health states is known, then, *ceteris paribus*, policy is determined.[7] The trade-off between prioritizing acute severity and maximizing the individual value of health is implicit in the function f that transforms individual values into social values (or, less explicitly, in person trade-offs). By insisting that f be concave, Nord ensures that the same increase in individual value will be a larger increase in social value when an individual is in worse health. To determine *how* concave members of the population think that f should be, Nord relies on surveys of population preferences among different distributions of health improvements. As the results discussed above illustrate, there is no popular unanimity about whether f should be concave, let alone how concave it should be. To specify the transformation of individual values without themselves making very difficult and controversial value judgments, health economists can seek to minimize the extent of disagreement about the weight to be placed on severity by averaging the survey responses of individuals.

To operationalize the value-encompassing maximization strategy, Nord lays out a tentative set of social values like those shown in Table 7.1, on the assumption that the difference in individual value from every row to the row below is roughly the same.[8]

---

[7] Note the ceteris paribus clause: There are other considerations, not discussed here, that Nord takes to influence social value in addition to costs, severity, and HRQoL.

[8] Notice that the upper-end compression of the social values mitigates the discrimination that is implicit in cost-effective allocation, which is discussed in Chapter 9. If healing a broken leg brings the same improvement in personal value to Mary and Mortimer, healing Mortimer's broken leg will provide a greater improvement in social value if Mortimer has a disability such as a speech defect, and Mary is otherwise healthy. However, it is not obvious that Mortimer should have priority or that most people think he should.

Table 7.1 Severity Levels

Severity Level	Social Value
Healthy	1.0
Slight problem	0.9999
Moderate problem	0.99
Considerable problem	0.92
Severe problem	0.80
Very severe problem	0.65
Completely disabled	0.40
Dead	0

Source: Nord (1999, p. 119).

It is questionable whether the best way to respond to the diversity of views concerning the weight that should be placed on severity is via a transformation applied to individual values. Is it defensible to transform deontic questions concerning how those who are in different health states ought to be treated into telic questions concerning the social value of different health states?[9] If the right way to encompass ethical considerations such as acute severity were to treat them as constraints on policies rather than as factors influencing the values of policies, then concerns about severity could not be encompassed by maximizing the social value of health.

Suppose we set aside these doubts and assume that the right way to understand the ethical significance of the acute severity of health deficiencies is to take it as influencing the value of acutely severe health states. Does Nord's operationalization then capture what it is intended to? Severity is, in Nord's words, a matter of "current impairments and expected future loss of quality of life and/or length of life *due to the illness*" (2013b, p. 67 [italics added]). Although

---

[9] Although Broome prefers the term "teleology" to "consequentialism," he takes the defining feature to be treating moral considerations as having a certain weight that can be traded off against other moral considerations (1991, pp. 6–7). It is that feature of the value encompassing maximization strategy that I am objecting to. It could be that the outcome of providing an equal health improvement to either of two individuals is equal in *value* or *moral weightiness*, even though it would be unfair or in some other way unjust to treat the less severely ill person before the more severely ill. See Klonschinski (2014). Although such a possibility requires a different way of representing how fairness and justice bear on the ethical appraisal of health care allocations, it introduces no new ethical justification for prioritizing severity.

Table 7.2 Relevant Versus Irrelevant Severity

	Group 1	Group 2	Group 3
Pain if untreated	Severe	Moderate	Moderate
Pain after treatment	Moderate	None	None
Other independent disability	No	Yes	No
HRQoL if untreated	0.6	0.6	0.8
HRQoL if treated	0.8	0.8	1.0
Benefit from treatment	0.2	0.2	0.2

HRQoL, health-related quality of life.

this does not rule out prioritization owing to impairments or future QALY loses that are independent of "the illness," it suggests that they have a different relevance for health care allocation. However, the social values in Table 7.1 measure impairments without regard to their source.

For example, suppose that the health authorities are considering policies to allocate physical therapy for back pain, when resources are too limited to treat everyone in need. In Table 7.2, there are three groups in need. Nord's scheme makes no distinction between those whose condition is "relevantly" more severe, like those in group 1, and those whose health problems are more severe due to an independent disability, like those in group 2, who may, for example, have a severe speech impediment.[10] If one examines only the last three rows, which contain all the information that Nord takes to be relevant, groups 1 and 2 should have the same priority. Refusing to distinguish relevant from irrelevant severity makes ethical sense (and helps address the discrimination implicit in c-e allocation). However, at the same time, I suggest that drawing no distinction between the priority given to the claims of groups 1 and 2 greatly diminishes the intuitive appeal of prioritizing acute severity.

When most individuals think about prioritizing severity, I conjecture that they envision giving priority to group 1 over both groups 2 and 3 rather than giving the same priority to groups 1 and 2 or giving priority to group 2 over group 3.[11]

---

[10] Intuitively, "irrelevant" health states may bear on priority due to the interaction among comorbidities discussed in footnote 1 in this chapter.

[11] I have only informal evidence for this claim, including correspondence with Erik Nord. If this conjecture is correct, it would be further evidence of the difference between criticizing c-e allocation for failing to prioritize severity and criticizing it for its indifference to egalitarian values.

Prioritizing only "relevant" acute severity—that is, greater severity that is "due to the illness"—is inconsistent with Nord's proposal, and it is badly in need of ethical defense. Why assign different priority to two groups of individuals whose health state is equally bad and who can benefit equally? The intuition that calls for prioritizing only relevant severity is difficult to justify. Do we think that if both Lee and Lena need a kidney transplant, Lena should have priority because she has irritable bowel syndrome?

My hypothesis is that we are inclined to relativize "severity" to the health problem that treatment addresses. In this example, we aim to ameliorate back pain. A more severe health state is one with greater back pain. This hypothesis about our inclinations does not justify an exclusive concern with relevant severity or bridge the gap between the grounds for prioritizing acute severity and prioritizing chronic severity. If the severity criticism rejects any priority for group 1 over group 2 and prioritizes group 2 over group 3, it may no longer seem so intuitively appealing. And if the criticism does give group 1 priority over group 2 and gives no priority to group 2 over group 3, we are owed an explanation why.

7.4 Chronic Severity, Prioritarianism, and Egalitarianism

As previously noted, in Ubel's study, the most common answer to the question, "Why give additional weight to the claims of those who are more severely ill?" is that they "deserve priority." This reason merely shifts the question: *Why* do those who are more severely ill "deserve priority"? In addition to or apart from gut feelings and surveys, philosophers and health economists have provided the following reasons for prioritizing severity:

Adaptation: "People may think that patients and disabled people over time more readily adapt to moderate conditions than to severe ones" (Nord and Johansen 2014, p. 283).

Urgency: The needs of those who are more acutely severely ill may be more urgent; a decision not to assist them is more likely to be irreparable (Ubel 1999, p. 898).

Distributional equality: Justice requires lessening inequalities; treating those who are more (chronically) severely ill typically lessens health inequalities (Dolan 1998; Nord and Johansen 2014, p. 282).

Priority: Justice requires giving priority to those who are worse off (Nord 1999).

Compassion and solidarity: "One [reason] is a simple emotional one, namely that their feeling of obligation to help others increases with the intensity of other people's acute suffering and/or the badness of their prognosis" (Nord and Johansen 2014, p. 282).[12]

The first two reasons maintain that due to adaptation or urgency, the benefit of treating the more severely ill is larger than the benefit of treating the less severely ill. This justification applies more to acute severity than chronic severity. In any case, these arguments in favor of prioritizing the claims of the more severely ill do not challenge cost-effective allocation. Urgency and adaptation are instead reasons why the effectiveness of treating those who are more severely ill has been underestimated. If, as these two considerations allege, there are greater total health benefits from treating those who are more severely ill than health economists have realized, then defenders of prioritizing severity are objecting to a miscalculation of "effectiveness" rather than to a flaw in allocating health care by its cost-effectiveness.

Although misdirected, the first two arguments for prioritizing severity escape a problem facing the remaining arguments. Unlike the three remaining arguments, considerations of adaptation and urgency provide guidance concerning *how much* extra weight to place on addressing the health needs of those whose health is worse. In contrast, the remaining considerations—distributive egalitarianism, prioritarianism, and compassion or solidarity—say very little about how much priority should be given to those who are worse off.[13] Empirical investigations suggest that members of various populations disagree, and the prioritarian, egalitarian, and compassion/solidarity arguments provide little guidance concerning how to resolve those disagreements. Nor do they ground any reason to rely on the average of the differing weights people place on severity. Agreement on prioritizing severity may mask irreconcilable disagreement concerning how much.

Prioritarians and distributional egalitarians[14] may hold that prioritizing severity contributes to the value of allocations or, like Adler, that considerations

---

[12] Part of this compassion and solidarity may derive from a commitment to prioritarianism rather than serving as a ground for it. There is also an issue, to be discussed in Chapter 8, of prioritizing what is immediately before us. Those who are not prioritarians and who may be sympathetic to allocation via cost-effectiveness may change their minds when confronted with someone who is suffering.

[13] The best-known and virtually the only effort in this direction is Ronald Dworkin's (1981) exploration of a hypothetical insurance market that would ideally indicate how much well-being individuals would exchange for greater equality. As explained by Roemer (1985, p. 175), the proposal is flawed.

[14] Contemporary egalitarians fall into two main camps. The egalitarian argument in support of prioritizing severity considered here relies on "distributional egalitarianism," which is concerned about inequalities in resources, opportunities, and capabilities, regardless of whether individuals have social relations to one another. In contrast, "relational egalitarians" (Anderson 1999; Scheffler 2003) are concerned about matters such as subservience, stigma, respect, and voice—that is, aspects of the relations among individuals. In many cases, egalitarians from the two camps will agree, and Voorhoeve (2020b) argues that despite some conflicts, the two versions of egalitarianism complement each other. The policies distributional egalitarians support typically promote egalitarian relations among individuals, and relational egalitarians object to distributional inequalities that disrupt egalitarian relations among individuals. The motivations and ideals are not the same, however. I shall not consider whether prioritizing severity might contribute to more equal relationships, apart from

of justice require favoring the treatment of those who are chronically more severely ill. Either way, prioritarian views maintain that the benefits and burdens of the worse off should count more heavily,[15] whereas egalitarians favor eliminating inequalities in outcomes with respect to some "currency" (e.g., well-being) for which individuals are not responsible or which individuals do not deserve. On the assumption that those who are chronically more severely ill are not responsible for their poor health and that they are, all things considered, worse off, both the distributional egalitarian and the prioritarian apparently support placing greater weight on the health care needs of those who are worse off.

The prioritarian and the egalitarian are arguing for prioritizing chronic severity, not acute severity.[16] Those whose health at any given time is most acutely severe are a cross section of the population as a whole, although those who have experienced hardship and discrimination will be overrepresented. A policy of prioritizing the treatment of those whose health is acutely severe is an ineffective way to benefit those with low lifetime well-being. As several authors note (Kamm 2002a; Brock 2002; Cookson and Dolan 2000; Scanlon 2003; and especially Nord 2013b), a "special concern and priority for the worst off" does not justify singling out for special concern those whose untreated health state is at the moment especially bad. Neither prioritarianism nor distributional egalitarianism justify placing a priority beyond what c-e allocation already provides on treating those whose health is acutely severe. All that speaks in favor of prioritizing acute severity are the intuitions that support some priority for those whose ill-health is in some imprecise way relevantly more acutely severe.

Let us then focus on chronic severity, the prioritizing of which appears to be justified by prioritarianism and distributional egalitarianism. However, prioritarian and distributional egalitarian arguments for prioritizing chronic severity are problematic. If one supposes that health is a factor that contributes to well-being at least in part in the same ways that income, wealth, and education contribute, then diminishing marginal utility commits the utilitarian (and those who defend cost-effectiveness) to place a greater weight on the health of those whose health is worse quite apart from prioritarianism.[17] Furthermore, as already mentioned, prioritarianism itself says nothing about how *much* priority

---

the links between relational egalitarianism and solidarity touched on later. For classic statements of distributive egalitarianism, see Dworkin (1981) and Temkin (1993).

[15] (Parfit 1991), at least if individuals are worse off through no fault or choice of their own (Arneson 2000). I ignore questions concerning responsibility.

[16] This is true of those who are concerned with inequalities within life stages as well as lifetime inequalities.

[17] It is plausible to maintain that as an individual's income increases, so does that individual's overall well-being, albeit at a diminishing rate. Graphing well-being as a function of income, one gets a curve like that shown in Figure 7.1.

should be placed on benefits and burdens received by the worse off. Additional arguments are needed to support any particular weighting of their claims. Of course, any pluralist ethics faces a problem of trade-offs, but in this case, it is difficult to see what sort of arguments can be made for larger or smaller weights, and no one that I know of has ventured any specific suggestions.

Egalitarianism might appear to escape these problems because the degree of priority that would equalize well-being (to the extent to which equalizing is feasible) is in principle knowable. But equality is not plausible as the sole principle governing distribution. Egalitarians maintain instead that social policies should balance the demands of equality against other moral desiderata, such as satisfying claims and making people better off. Without any definite guidelines concerning how to trade off equality, claim satisfaction, and well-being, the egalitarian, like the prioritarian, leaves open the question of how much priority should be placed on the treatment of those who are worse off. Moreover, what matters to the distributional egalitarian is the post-treatment lifetime or life-stage distribution of health, not how much weight should be placed on pre-treatment hardship.

A further difficulty, which I can only sketch here, is that distributional egalitarianism and prioritarianism are far from obviously correct. In my view, what is right about both of these doctrines is that we should have a society without second-class citizens (apart from those who have forfeited their status by their vicious or insensitive behavior). In grossly unequal societies such as the United States, lessening inequalities in income and wealth, status, and education are all first priorities, as both a distributional egalitarian and a prioritarian would likely agree. However, in my view, the goal is not to maximize some distributionally weighted social value function or to achieve equality in well-being (apart from

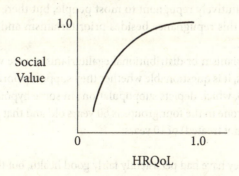

Figure 7.1 Diminishing Marginal Social Value

One might claim that the graph of well-being as a function of HRQoL has a similar shape and thereby recover the intuitions of those who want health care to favor those who are worse off by shifting the measure of effectiveness in cost-effectiveness analysis from HRQoL to well-being.

Table 7.3 Who Is Worst Off?

	Previous Well-Being	Previous Average HRQoL	Expected Lifetime Well-Being	Expected Lifetime QALYs	Expected HRQoL in the Next 10 Years
Indigent	Lowest	0.9	Lowest	62	0.8
Injured poor	Medium	0.8	Low	53 lowest	0.5
Rich disabled	Medium	0.78 lowest	Medium high	54.6	0.78
Newly afflicted	High	0.99	Medium high	62.9	0.35 lowest

HRQoL, health-related quality of life; QALYs, quality-adjusted life years.

that part of well-being for which individuals are responsible and which they deserve). A society of equals does not require equality in well-being: If Jim and Judy are both flourishing, the fact one is better off than the other is not by itself a reason for moral concern. If there is no causal connection between the greater benefits Judy receives and Jim's lesser benefits, and the two never interact, what is the ethical objection (Rowe 2019)?

The previous paragraph consists of assertions and a rhetorical question rather than arguments, and many well-known first-rate philosophers disagree, such as Matthew Adler, whose views I discussed in Chapter 4; Frances Kamm; and the late Dan Brock, whose formulation of the fairness objections to c-e allocation have structured this book. In my defense, it is noteworthy that there is very little argument in the literature in defense of distributional egalitarianism or prioritarianism. Instead, what one finds are appeals to intuition, like what we saw in the examination of Adler's theory in Section 4.8. Clearly, many inequalities are intuitively repugnant to most people, but there are many theories that explain this repugnance besides prioritarianism and distributional egalitarianism.

Even if prioritarianism or distributional egalitarianism were well-confirmed normative theories, it is questionable whether they support prioritizing severity. Consider Table 7.3, which depicts subpopulations in some hypothetical society. Suppose that everyone in the four groups is 60 years old and that everyone has a life expectancy (if not treated) of 10 years:

> *The indigent*: They have had persistently fairly good health, but they suffer from other deprivations such as poor living conditions, social exclusion, and stigma. Their lifetime well-being if untreated now is lower than that of any other group.
> *The injured poor*: They were healthy and otherwise their circumstances were so-so until, in their 40s, injury or disease left them with serious

impairments and a low HRQoL. Their lifetime QALY total if they are now untreated will be lower than that of any other group.

The rich disabled: They have been disabled for most of their lives, and their average HRQoL up to this time is the lowest of any group. However, owing to adaptation and their other resources, they can be expected to have a reasonably high level of lifetime well-being.

The newly afflicted: They have had a very high level of well-being, but now, owing to injury or disease, they are seriously ill. Without treatment, their circumstances are dire. If untreated, their health state now and in the future is the worst of any group.[18]

The first two columns in Table 7.3 concern past well-being and past health, whereas the last three columns state expectations of lifetime well-being, QALYs, and expected HRQoL for the next 10 years if there are no interventions to improve the health or well-being of members of any of the groups.

Which group is worst off? Depending on what kind of treatment is in question and how one understands "worst off," the prioritarian or egalitarian might favor giving a greater priority to members of any one of the four groups. Each group is worst off in at least one column. On one interpretation of prioritarianism or distributive egalitarianism, the indigent are worst off in virtue of how low their well-being has been up to now and in virtue of their low lifetime expected well-being. On the other hand, the current health problems of the newly afflicted are the most acutely severe. Their HRQoL is worst now and in the immediate future. If members of all four groups were in need of physical therapy for their backs (and could benefit equally from it at the same cost), the greatest social value (in Nord's sense) would lie in treating the newly afflicted, followed by the injured poor and the rich disabled.

Once one recognizes the different ways in which individuals may be advantaged or disadvantaged, neither prioritarianism nor distributional egalitarianism justifies the priority for severity that one finds in polling. Those who emphasize "separate spheres"[19] and urge health economists to focus exclusively on health would counsel ignoring the first and third columns. Doing so would undermine the indigent's claims, but it would not come close to providing a prioritarian or distributional egalitarian justification for prioritizing severity.

A defender of prioritizing severity might respond to this critique by arguing that the factors that diminish well-being tend to go together so that those whose

---

[18] These are not the only possible regards in which one might compare how badly off groups of individuals may be, but they suffice to make my point. This discussion borrows from and improves upon a comparison among health states in Hausman (2017a, p. 181).

[19] "Separate spheres" is, roughly, the view that health policy should concern itself exclusively with health conditions and consequences. See Brock (2003b).

immediate untreated health expectations are worse will usually be worse off overall. Or perhaps there are different prioritarianisms to address different ways of being worse off. But the premises in these responses are questionable. Many among the worst off in society are, at any given moment in time, in far better health than those approaching death who, regardless of their wealth and privilege, are often most severely ill. How are the different bases for priority related? If there is a case for prioritizing severity (in the sense of immediate health prospects if untreated), it must lie elsewhere than distributional egalitarianism or prioritarianism.

7.5 Compassion, Solidarity, and Severity

That brings us to the last of the five arguments in defense of prioritizing severity: that compassion or solidarity require prioritizing severity. Compassion is grounded in a vivid appreciation of the hardships of particular individuals or occasionally groups, and it may place too little weight on the consequences of policies for unidentified individuals—"statistical lives." Moreover, as Nord and Johansen (2014) mention, compassion tends to focus on suffering and prognosis, not on the whole range of hardships imposed by health deficiencies.

Unlike compassion, solidarity derives from a connection with a *group* with which one's identity is entwined. This bond gives rise to a commitment to fellow feeling and sharing burdens and risks (Prainsack and Buyx 2011; Zhao 2019). Unlike compassion, solidarity is in principle mutual. When students in Europe express solidarity with student protesters in Hong Kong, as opposed to mere concern for their plight, they imagine that they would find support were the tables turned. Whether or not it is possible to possess some minimal solidarity with the whole of humanity, solidarity grows weaker as groups grow larger and less proximate. Nevertheless, solidarity is of normative importance as a "glue" that stabilizes social life and makes it more rewarding. Solidarity is linked to relational egalitarianism as both a consequence and a cause of egalitarian relations among individuals within some group.

In contrast to allocating health resources by their cost-effectiveness, which reflects an impartial concern for everyone's health, compassion is grounded in a concern for particular individuals and solidarity is grounded in group or status identification. Accordingly, compassion and solidarity can lead to partiality that goes beyond what is morally permissible. Morality may require a compromise between the demands of compassion and solidarity and the impartial concerns of benevolence, justice, and fairness.

Compassion seems to have its place mainly at the bedside, not so much at the level of policy. Those charged with treating victims of a natural disaster may be directed to gird themselves *against* their compassion toward those at the front of the line seeking immediate help. Unlike the impartial benevolence that grounds both allocation by cost-effectiveness and triage in the case of disasters, personalized benevolence should play only a limited role in social policy and administrative ethics. At the bedside and in the shifting interstices of impartial policies, there is an urgent need for the moral sentiments that refuse to abandon comrades or those who are in desperate need. These sentiments should be cherished and nurtured, but their role in determining policy is rightly limited.

Solidarity, on the other hand, might reasonably have a significant role in the design of national health policies, which are inevitably more concerned with citizens and residents than with all of humanity.[20] However, the bearing of solidarity on the different construals of severity is obscure. Why should solidarity call for a greater concern with acute severity or with what I called in Section 7.3 "relevant" severity than with greater severity owing to independent health problems (or, for that matter, non-health problems)? As someone who cares about the health deficiencies of particular individuals or of those who are part of her community, why should Emma prioritize acute severity rather than, as egalitarianism and prioritarianism imply, focusing her attention on chronic severity—that is, those who are worst off more generally?

It thus seems that compassion and solidarity do not justify any systematic prioritization of severity. Although they demand that health policy show a human face, they support no principle of allocation that challenges cost-effectiveness. For the health system to show a human face means that occasionally there should be exceptions to cost-effective allocations in cases of particularly unfortunate individuals or groups. There should also be serious laments when desperate pleas are denied—as they often must be.

7.6 Conclusion

Assigning personal values to health states leaves open questions about how health-related resources should be distributed among people. Survey data show that many people favor placing greater weight on treating people whose health states are more acutely severe. Yet this chapter has questioned whether there is solid moral argument in defense of prioritizing severity.

First, it points out that there are two general notions of severity—chronic and acute—that imply different prioritizations. Acute severity is not well-defined, and

---

[20] For example, see Stuart (2001). He writes, "One way to understand Canada's health system is in terms of social solidarity. Canadians have chosen a universal approach to basic health services on the premise that we should all be in the same boat," and he asks, "Is social solidarity still the driving value in how we want to pay for and deliver health services?" (p. 6). Martin et al. (2018) view Canada's health care system as grounded in "the Canadian values of equity and solidarity" (p. 1718).

as Table 7.3 shows, what constitutes chronic severity is ambiguous. Measuring severity as immediate health expectations if untreated leads to absurd results unless one limits comparisons to health states that have the same duration. Measuring severity by absolute or proportional shortfalls in QALYs or life expectancy implies age weighting, which is foreign to the concerns about severity.

Second, neither egalitarianism nor prioritarianism supports prioritizing acute severity, as it is conceived in this chapter, let alone provides any guidance concerning how much priority severity ought to have. Whether there is any popular support or solid argument in defense of prioritizing chronic severity is questionable.

Third, as the discussion of Table 7.2 suggests, popular attitudes toward acute severity implicitly draw a morally arbitrary distinction between relevant differences in impairments, which result from salient health threats, and irrelevant differences in impairments, which result from differences in pre-existing or independent health states.

Finally, although compassion and solidarity lead to dissatisfaction with cost-effective health care allocation, they have no clear bearing on whether health care policy should prioritize severity.

Some might argue that health policy must be guided by popular attitudes, even if they have no moral defense and, like prioritizing severity, imply fewer aggregate health improvements. In a representative democracy, one would either expect health policy to conform to the popular consensus or find a compelling account of why the popular consensus is mistaken. In the case of prioritizing severity, there is, I believe, a compelling error theory that explains why so many people mistakenly support prioritizing severity. In my view, this mistake has five sources:

1. People mistakenly believe that treating those who are more acutely severely ill brings about a greater health improvement than treating those who are less severely ill.
2. People are confused about what acute severity is. As just mentioned, there is no clear characterization of it in the literature that does not involve favoring the old or the young or that takes into account "time bomb" states.
3. People mistakenly take the considerations of urgency and adaptation to be arguments for prioritizing severity rather than for correcting the measure of effectiveness.
4. Moved by compassion or solidarity, people do not approach the problem of allocating health care from a policy perspective.
5. People mistakenly accept prioritarianism or distributive egalitarianism and mistakenly take them to support prioritizing acute severity.

SUFFICIENT PRIORITY TO SEVERITY? 153

What about prioritizing chronic severity? It is questionable whether doing so enjoys any intuitive support. It might find some support in prioritarianism or in distributional egalitarianism, if those general normative positions were themselves well supported. As mentioned previously, placing a greater weight on improvements to worse health states does not automatically make one a prioritarian, because a utilitarian can maintain that the personal value of health states, like other particular goods such as income, may make a diminishing marginal contribution to well-being.

8
To Aggregate or Not to Aggregate

The third objection to (c-e) allocation presented in Chapter 3, "non-aggregation," resembles at first glance the severity objection, and I argue that it is also indefensible. "Non-aggregation" is a misleading name because many who make this objection have no general quarrel with aggregating benefits and harms. They agree that when there is a choice, health policy should save two lives rather than one or that it should prevent 1,000 elderly people from contracting Alzheimer disease rather than save one elderly person from death. What the objectors deny is that health policy should treat or prevent minor ailments when it might instead alleviate major illnesses, even if the treatment of minor ailments is more cost-effective. Giving more cost-effective treatments of minor health problems priority over less cost-effective treatments of major or life-threatening ailments strikes many people as heinous. For example, they are appalled that the original Oregon Medicaid rationing scheme gave a higher priority to capping teeth than performing appendectomies (Jacobs et al. 1999).

Like the severity objection, the non-aggregation criticism alleges that rationing by cost-effectiveness fails to place sufficient moral weight on satisfying the claims to health care of those whose health needs are serious. Whether or not it is more cost-effective to treat a minor health condition than to treat a serious problem, many think that it is *never* right to do so. In Frances Kamm's words, those who reject aggregation maintain that "there are [sic] no number of headaches such that we should prevent them rather than certainly save a few lives" (2002a, p. 691). Some minor health problems are not as it were "in the same ballpark" as serious health problems. Scanlon (1998) notes,

> If one harm is not only less serious than, but not even "relevant to," some greater one, then we do not need to take the number of people who would suffer these two harms into account in deciding which to prevent, but should always prevent the more serious harm. (pp. 239–240)

If a headache is not relevant to a loss of life, then no matter how many individuals a health care policy cures of their headaches or how cost-effective it may be to treat them, it is worse to treat them than to save one life.

Why should one reject aggregation? If the reason is that the values of some goods are incomparably greater than values of others, then the objection to aggregation has nothing to do with fairness. The objection would be instead that those who would aggregate the lesser goods assign mistaken values to health states. If the burden of a headache is truly infinitesimal compared to the loss from death or serious illness, then no finite number of headaches can be as bad as a death or serious injury. But the burden of a minor headache is not infinitesimal. For example, curing a large number of headaches might be of greater value than setting a broken leg. The allegation is that minor headaches are only negligible when something much more important is at stake, such as preventing a death. But if harms such as minor headaches are not infinitesimal, then it would seem that they can be added up, and enough headaches would constitute a greater harm than a death.

There are at least two ways to reconcile the fact that a headache has a finite value with the denial that one should ever treat a large number of headaches, when one could have saved a life. One possibility is to deny that harms can be added. Two cases of gout are not twice as bad as one.[1] According to a number of authors,[2] rather than aggregating competing claims of greatly different importance, one should make pairwise comparisons between them, and one should be governed by whichever individual claim is strongest. Alternatively, those who object to allowing aggregate value to determine policy can concede that harms add up but deny that the right thing to do is determined by what has the greatest value.

I reject both of these tacks. I assume that minor harms have finite values, and I criticize both the view that goods and harms cannot be added and the view that it is morally obligatory to alleviate major health deficiencies, even when one could do more good by treating minor ailments. The argument will proceed on two tracks. In addition to challenging the general view that small harms such as missing some portion of a sports event are not relevant to major harms such as losing one's life, I argue that minor health conditions, unlike small harms, pose risks of major harms, which makes ignoring them untenable.

Those who maintain that some small benefits or burdens are relevant to the allocation of care to those who are seriously ill and that some are not, must explain what makes the aggregative perspective appropriate to some cases and the pairwise comparison perspective appropriate to others. One answer relies on the thesis that if policy is governed by aggregating benefits when instead it should

---

[1] I shall not discuss a third way to capture the intuition that alleviating headaches can ever be of more value than saving a life, no matter how many headaches one alleviates. That way is to suggest that claims to treatments of minor problems add in a nonlinear way so that n headaches are worse than $n - 1$, but the value of curing an additional headache grows smaller and smaller so that the alleviation of any finite number of headaches never constitutes a stronger claim than the prevention of a death. Such a view runs into trouble when comparing headaches to other lesser health problems.

[2] Including Kamm (2002b, p. 348), Kelleher (2014), Nagel (1979, p. 123), Scanlon (1998, p. 241), and Voorhoeve (2014).

be governed by pairwise comparison, then it fails to show proper respect for the individual or individuals with stronger claims. Allowing a number of small benefits to take precedence over some major health gain, such as saving a life or preventing quadriplegia, allegedly fails to show baseline respect, and for this reason, it is unfair.

In this chapter, Section 8.1 presents the case against ever aggregating. That case faces serious objections and, in addition, is not pertinent to questions concerning the allocation of health care. Section 8.2 presents what I believe to be the most plausible development of a partial aggregation view. Section 8.3 points out difficulties that require some refinement of the partial aggregation view, and Section 8.4 then offers three serious criticisms of the view. Section 8.5 responds to the position that despite its drawbacks, partial aggregation is superior to the aggregation implicit in c-e allocation. Section 8.6 concludes by drawing out the implications for c-e allocation.

8.1 Why Not Aggregate?

How should the number of individuals affected by different health care policies influence which policies are chosen? If a blood pressure screening program in some nation can be expected to prevent 1,000 strokes, 3,000 heart attacks, and 300 deaths, while for the same cost an advertising campaign for a healthier diet can be expected to prevent 500 strokes, 2,000 heart attacks, and 100 deaths, and neither has any other significant consequences, then the blood pressure screening program appears to be the obvious choice because it is expected to result in fewer strokes, fewer heart attacks, and fewer deaths. In this case, most people prefer the more cost-effective policy. Of course, it might turn out that the actual number of strokes, heart attacks, and deaths prevented by the screening is not as great as expected, and in that case policymakers may suspect that they selected the worse option. But that unfortunate possibility does not impugn the basic idea that the larger the number who are expected to be helped, the better.

Some philosophers have challenged the basic idea that helping a larger group people is better than helping a distinct smaller group. If one has a choice between saving one life and saving five others, it is, in John Taurek's (1977) view, other things being equal, no better to save the five people from death than to save the one.[3] One of his central arguments can be formulated as follows:

---

[3] This is Taurek's view when the choice is between saving separate groups of people. Taurek does not deny that it is good to save additional people. There is moral reason to save each individual. I am indebted to Frances Kamm for clarifying this point. Note that Taurek's view commits him to the

1. The death of five individuals is, other things being equal, no worse *for any individual* than is the death of another single individual.
2. If a harm is not worse for any individual than any alternative, then, other things being equal, it is not worse than any alternative.[4]
3. Thus, other things being equal, the death of five is not worse than the death of a separate single individual.
4. If the death of five is not worse than the death of a separate single individual, then, other things being equal, permitting the death of five and saving the one is no worse than permitting the death of one and saving five, when these are the only alternatives.
5. Other things being equal, permitting the death of five and saving one is no worse than permitting the death of one and saving five, when these are the only alternatives.

Clearly, this argument can be extended to show that saving the lives of those in a smaller group is no worse than saving the lives of those in a larger group, regardless of the exact numbers, and the same goes for causing harms. If one accepts the premises of this argument, then there is, other things being equal, nothing better about restoring vision in a larger group of individuals rather than restoring vision in a disjoint smaller set. The other-things-being-equal clause rules out complications such as moral commitments the allocator may have to individuals; causal consequences of how many are saved, such as effects on economic growth and on third parties generally; or prior duties and rights (Taurek 1977, p. 306).

In Taurek's view, the supposed additional good in saving five lives rather than one is not (other things being equal) a good *for* anyone. The good of saving 5 or 5,000 lives consists of the good for each of those saved. That good for one individual, Linda, is not made better if the lives of others are also saved. The fact that the blood pressure screening is expected to prevent more strokes, heart attacks, and deaths than the diet campaign is no reason at all to judge that it brings about more good than the diet campaign. The numbers are irrelevant to the good that is done to those who benefit.

Premise 2 is crucial to this argument. It identifies the harm or badness in a state of affairs with the harm to each individual in that state of affairs. The purported

---

intransitivity of the values of the outcomes of action. Saving A & B is better than saving A. Saving A is of the same value as saving C. But saving A & B is not better than saving C.

[4] "Five individuals each losing his life does not add up to anyone's experiencing a loss five times greater than the loss suffered by any one of the five" (Taurek 1977, p. 307). "In such a trade-off situation as this we are to compare your pain or your loss, not to our collective or total pain, whatever exactly that is supposed to be, but to what will be suffered or lost by any given single one of us" (Taurek 1977, p. 308).

badness of five dying that one might think makes the death of five worse than the death of one is not a harm to anyone and hence not a harm at all. In this way, Taurek rules out adding harms (or goods) across people. How good or bad a state of affairs is (or how much better or worse one state of affairs may be than another) is how good or bad it is for each individual. Thinking about the sum of harms is confused; the sum corresponds to nothing of any ethical relevance. Sums are not harms or benefits for anyone.

I have three replies. First, the ceteris paribus condition is often not satisfied in the most egregious cases in which the numbers ought to count. For example, vaccinating more people rather than fewer may lead to herd immunity, which will enable individuals, including many who are unvaccinated, to interact with one another more freely. Second, if one countenances impersonal goods and bads—that is, goods and bads that are not benefits and burdens for individuals—then one can claim, plausibly, that from an impersonal perspective, the harm to more people constitutes a greater impersonal harm than harm to fewer. As Parfit states, "If more people are in pain, there is more pain" (1978, p. 297). An impartial sympathetic observer will feel both pains and hence more pain. Of course, one cannot simply assert that there are impersonal goods, and because this book is not aimed at academic philosophers, I will not pursue this criticism of Taurek's argument further, although I believe it has merit.

Instead, my insistence that the numbers count in health care rests on a different consideration, which Taurek himself raises. He considers a case in which a Coast Guard captain faces a choice of going to the north or south end of an island with an active volcano, thereby saving a larger or smaller number of people. What makes this case different from others in which Taurek rejects aggregation is that the Coast Guard is governed by the policies imposed by the population that funds it, and the captain is not free to do whatever she may judge to be better. Regardless of whether it is better to rescue the larger number of people than the smaller number (provided that it is morally permissible to do so), the captain may be required to rescue the larger number. Without making any judgment concerning which action does the most good, "such a policy [of maximizing the number saved] might be found acceptable to all these people simply on the ground that such a policy maximizes each individual's chances of benefiting from the resource" (Taurek 1977, pp. 312–313). Regulators face constraints in making ethical policy choices.

Although one can in this way justify deciding to fund the blood pressure screening rather than the diet campaign without having to challenge Taurek's claim that the blood pressure screening is no better than the diet campaign, I believe that there is also reason to question Taurek's view that actions that help more people are, other things being equal, no better than actions that help fewer. This foray into what might initially appear to be an absurd philosophical discussion will prove valuable when we consider a more modest objection to letting the numbers count.

8.2 Partial Aggregation

So far, we have considered only cases in which one choice relieves a greater number of individuals from the same harms that an alternative addresses. But what about problems where the harms prevented by alternative health care interventions differ? Consider the following case:[5]

> **Dialysis Versus Strep Throat Screening**
>
> Health policymakers face a choice between (a) purchasing a dialysis machine to keep alive three individuals in their 50s—Ann, Alan, and Albert—and (b) screening 1 million children for strep throat and providing antibiotic treatment where indicated. Dialysis can be expected to enable the three individuals to live for some additional years, albeit with a diminished quality of life. By saving their lives now, it also improves their prospect of having a kidney transplant, which could be expected to lengthen their lives considerably and restore its quality. Strep throat screening, on the other hand, usually provides no direct health benefit at all to the children who are screened, because most of them do not have strep or would easily fight it off themselves. But there is a 3 in 1,000 chance that those who have strep throat will get rheumatic fever, which can in turn cause serious heart damage or even death.

Which should be funded? Cost-effectiveness provides one way to find an answer. If the incremental cost-effectiveness of dialysis or of strep throat screening is within the threshold, then it should be made available. If not, it should not be provided. Depending on how the numbers work out, it could be that the strep throat screening is cost-effective, whereas dialysis is not. Suppose that with the funds freed up by not providing dialysis, which results in three preventable deaths, 1 million children can be screened for strep throat. The good that the

---

[5] I constructed this case, because sore throats are used as examples of irrelevant harms, but it introduces the complication of screening as well as treatment. One can instead compare dialysis for a small number of people to vaccinating a large number of young healthy individuals against COVID-19. The expected benefit of each vaccination is very small, but for the cost of an additional dialysis machine, a large number of people can be vaccinated, and a great deal of suffering and mortality can be avoided. What is crucial to the case is that the small benefit involves a small probability of a very large benefit, which when conferred on many individuals translates into many major benefits.

screening actually provides to each child screened varies from zero (or even a negative value) to possibly life-saving. The expected value to each child is miniscule compared to the expected value that dialysis provides to those who will die without it. Because screening is so much cheaper and available to so many more, cost-effectiveness may favor providing the screening and not the dialysis.

The result may appear perverse. As already mentioned, in an early and imperfect attempt to apply cost-effectiveness to the allocation of health care, an Oregon commission concluded that if funding was extremely limited, tooth capping should be funded in preference to surgical treatment of appendicitis. This particular implication horrified many, who went on to question whether many very inexpensive small benefits could ever justify withholding a major benefit, such as saving a life. Recall Frances Kamm's remarks, quoted in Chapter 3:

> It is a mistake in what is called "moral mathematics" to aggregate in an additive fashion small losses to many people, . . . There is no one person who suffers the loss of 40 million years of life. . . . This kind of "interpersonal aggregation" is morally misguided. (2020c, pp. 2–3)

This sounds as if it invokes Taurek's view that harms and benefits are personal and do not add. One might similarly say that there is no one person who suffers the loss of five lives. But Kamm wants to defend something very much like aggregation when the harms and benefits of alternative policies are of a similar magnitude and thus "relevant" to one another. In her view, it is when the harms are vastly different that additive aggregation is unacceptable.

The question of whether small harms can be "relevant" to large harms does not only come up with respect to health care. Consider the following example of T. M. Scanlon (1998):

> (*Jones and the World Cup*) Suppose that Jones has suffered an accident in the transmitter room of a television station. Electrical equipment has fallen on his arm, and we cannot rescue him without turning off the transmitter for fifteen minutes. A World Cup match is in progress, watched by many people, and it will not be over for an hour. Jones's injury will not get any worse if we wait, but his hand has been mashed and he is receiving extremely painful electrical shocks. Should we rescue him now or wait until the match is over? Does the right thing to do depend on how many people are watching . . . ? It seems to me that we should not wait, no matter how many viewers there are. (p. 235)

Scanlon's case is so persuasive that the doctrine that minor benefits or harms are not relevant to major harms or benefits may seem obvious. Regarding someone's life, agony, or bodily integrity as worth exchanging for minor benefits to many others arguably fails to show the level of respect and concern for people's lives that should be manifest in fair treatment.

This objection to the unfairness of allowing many minor expected benefits to take priority over a small number of major expected benefits is less open and shut than it may appear. Scanlon's case is potentially misleading in four ways. First, what is at stake in turning off the transmitter is a game. Although no doubt of great importance to many fans, the state has a much stronger obligation to protect the health of its residents than their enjoyment. Second, the collective harm of many people missing 15 minutes of the World Cup probably has few further consequences or risks beyond the chagrin of the fans, unlike the harm of failing to vaccinate thousands, which may be much greater than thousands of times the harm of failing to vaccinate a single person.

Third, witnessing extreme suffering has an emotional impact that is out of proportion to the severity of a health state. For example, suppose that turning off the current would spoil a kidney at a nearby hospital, whose transplantation into Smith would save her life. Alleviating Jones' agony would in that case come at the cost of a life. There is no question here of balancing minor benefits against the major benefit of alleviating Jones' suffering, yet I conjecture that most people would still be reluctant to let Jones' agony continue. Without the salience of immediate suffering, reactions would differ. I conjecture that many would find it less disturbing to allow the World Cup transmission to continue when the current is needed for 15 minutes instead by a nearby hospital to preserve a donated kidney and thereby to save a life.

Fourth, Scanlon's example concerns a microallocation problem: whether to let Jones suffer for 15 minutes or to frustrate millions of fans. But this book is concerned with health care *policy*—with a sort of administrative ethics—the rules and institutions that govern allocation across the board. Suppose that the broadcasts were from a state-operated television station. What policies should govern its behavior in the case of an accident? Even if, as is plausible, ignoring accidents that might interfere with popular spectacles such as the World Cup resulted in far greater well-being, state policy need not be determined by what maximizes well-being, and it might mandate protecting Jones. If, on the other hand, what was being shown was a hurricane warning, whose benefit to each individual is small, the station's policy might rule out rescuing Jones. Whether to turn off the current to spare Jones would be determined by the policy of the broadcaster, although not, of course, without ethical constraints. Depending on the character and consequences of the general application of the policy, it might mandate preventing harm to employees and visitors, or it might not allow the staff to interfere with certain broadcasts.

In addition, the focus in health care is on the satisfaction of claims, not on benefits and harms. The bottom line is that Scanlon's case provides much weaker support for the view that claims to the treatment of minor health problems are irrelevant when much stronger claims to the treatment of major health issues are in question than it appears to. Our intuitive response might reflect the exaggerated salience of manifest suffering, our sense of what the state ought to protect, or principles concerned with "bedside" ethics rather than health care policy.

A further argument in defense of distinguishing among weaker claims that are relevant and that are irrelevant is that the distinction explains some of our purported intuitions in cases that do not involve aggregating large numbers of small benefits or harms. Frances Kamm considers a case in which we can prevent C or D from dying and give one of them 10 additional years of life. We cannot save both. As it happens, if we save D's life, we also cure E's sore throat (2002a, p. 689). Our intuition, Kamm maintains, is that it should make no difference to whether we should save C of D that saving D cures E's sore throat. What purportedly explains Kamm's intuition is that a claim to a cure of a sore throat is not relevant to a claim to prevent a death.[6]

It is not easy to present a precise and plausible statement of limited aggregation. The most successful formulation that I know of appears in a paper by Bastian Steuwer. He supports what he calls a hybrid "balance" of relevant claims (2021a, p. 18). His position rests on three main ethical premises. First, following Voorhoeve (2014), Steuwer regards claims c_1, c_2, etc. as relevant to some given claim, C, if they are of similar strength or, if weaker, individuals can reasonably invoke a personal prerogative and refuse to defer to the stronger claims. In that case, there is a conflict that can be resolved by the weighing and aggregating of the competing claims.[7] Voorhoeve specifies that an individual's claims are stronger the worse off the individual is and the more the individual can benefit from aid. In the case of claims that are much weaker than other claims, deference to the stronger claims is required even from a personal perspective. There is only so far one can go in promoting one's own interests. Reasonable individuals will abandon far weaker claims. Consequently, when the competing claims are much weaker, there is no moral conflict, and the strongest individual claims should be satisfied, regardless of how many weak claims are unsatisfied. This framework apparently implies that the reason why a sore throat is not relevant to life-saving is that no one could justifiably hold out for treatment of their sore throat at the cost of causing or allowing someone to lose their life.

---

[6] What may explain the intuition is the belief that the benefits of life extension to C and D are on par rather than precisely equal. So adding the small benefit of curing a sore throat leaves C and D still on par. In that case, Kamm's example does not support the assertion that claims to the cure of sore throats are not relevant to claims to life saving.

[7] Voorhoeve and Steuwer are not committed to Broome's view that claims should be satisfied in proportion to their strength, and accordingly one should not identify the claims that Voorhoeve and Steuwer discuss with the claims that Broome discusses. I shall in any case move freely between talking about satisfying claims and providing treatments.

Second, when there are competing claims that are relevant to one another, one should be governed by whatever claims remain after equivalently strong claims have been "balanced." Although framed in terms of balancing, the treatment of relevant claims is more or less equivalent to aggregating them.

Third, Steuwer maintains that what is wrong with allowing a much weaker claim to count against satisfying a strong claim is that it is disrespectful. It fails to show what I have called "baseline respect." Steuwer states,

> To consider the headaches as a reason not to save the person from death would trivialize her situation. . . . It is disrespectful and impermissible to fail to save a person with a strong claim for the sake of persons whose claims are irrelevant to this strong claim. (2021a, p. 24)

Someone who, as it were, says, "Sorry about your arms and legs, but my throat is uncomfortable" fails to acknowledge the moral significance of others and to show the baseline respect that is owed them.[8]

To provide some grasp of Steuwer's theory, without going into all the details, consider the following example, which closely follows one of Steuwer's (2021a, p. 26):

Sequential Balancing

Suppose that policy A would satisfy 100 claims to the cure of severe (likely fatal) illnesses (100 S) and 100 claims to the cure of moderate illnesses (100 MOD). Policy B would satisfy 1,000 claims to the cure of moderate illnesses (1,000 MOD) and 1,100 claims to the cure of mild illnesses (1,100 MILD). For purpose of illustration, suppose that 10 MOD balance 1 S, and 10 MILD balance 1 MOD. Finally, suppose that MILD (a claim to the treatment of a mild illness) is not relevant to S (a claim to the cure a severe illness). We start with severe illness and consider whether there are any claims that balance 100 S. There are: The 1,000 MOD of policy B do that. We then consider the 100 MOD that policy A would also cure. Those are balanced by 1,000 of the 1,100 MILD that policy B cures. We are left with an additional 100 MILD that policy B cures. So one might be tempted to favor policy B. But because it would be disrespectful to the 100 with severe illnesses not to treat them in order to cure mild illnesses, which are (as we assumed) not relevant, we should ignore the

---

[8] Steuwer's view can be questioned. Is it disrespectful to say, "We regret not saving your arms and legs, but if we had done so, the health care system would have been unable to treat hundreds of thousands of minor complaints."

fact that policy B cures additional mild illness and favor policy A. The balancing is portrayed in Table 8.1:

Table 8.1 Sequential Balancing

Stage	Policy A	Policy B	Outcome
0	100 S 100 MOD	1,000 MOD 1,100 MILD	
1	100 S	1,000 MOD	Balanced
2	100 MOD	1,100 MILD	100 MOD balances 1,000 MILD
3	Selected	~~100 MILD~~	MILD remainder canceled: An irrelevant benefit cannot prevent S.

MILD, mild illness; MOD, moderate illness; S, severe.

Notice that it is less obviously disrespectful to the 100 who are seriously ill in this example to choose policy B. Rather than saying to them, "We chose not to satisfy your claims to treatment in order to satisfy a larger number of weaker claims to the treatment of mild ailments," we can truthfully say, "We chose not to treat you because we balanced satisfying each claim to treatment of severe ailments by satisfying 10 claims to treatment of moderate ailments, which then allowed us to balance claims to the treatment of moderate and mild ailments." Is that more disrespectful than saying to the 1,000 moderately ill and the 1,100 mildly ill who policy B would treat, "Even though your claims balance the claims of the 100 who are severely ill that policy A would treat and outbalance the claims of the 100 mildly ill that policy A would also treat, the claims of those of you who are mildly ill don't count in this context."

Although I have not defined Steuwer's views precisely, I have, I hope, provided the reader with enough understanding that I can now turn to criticism of his views and of partial aggregation in general.

8.3 Some Surmountable Challenges for Partial Aggregation

In this section, I discuss three criticisms of partial aggregation that are disquieting, but which can be answered, before turning in Section 8.4 to three criticisms that should be more troubling to those who criticize cost-effectiveness on the grounds that small health benefits should not be additively aggregated. Section 8.5 will then respond to what one might call "the best-of-a-bad-lot" argument in defense of partial aggregation: However problematic partial aggregation may be, it is a whole lot more plausible than either Taurek's complete rejection of aggregation or the total aggregation that permits tooth capping to take priority over appendicitis surgery. I hope in Section 8.5 to remove the sting from the view that all benefits and harms, no matter how small, are relevant.

The first of the three answerable objections concerns the apparent intransitivities implied by the thesis that claims to small benefits are relevant to somewhat stronger claims but not to claims to really major benefits such as lifesaving. If ">" represents "more choiceworthy than," 120 MILD > 11 MOD; 11 MOD > 1 S; and 1 S > 120 MILD. This intransitivity is, however, arguably merely apparent. For a defender of partial aggregation, 120 MILD is a different alternative when one is comparing it with 11 MOD than when one is comparing it with 1 S. 120 MILD (relevant), which is what more than balances 11 MOD, is a different alternative than 120 MILD (not relevant), which is undercut by the one severe condition. By thus building more detail into the alternatives, the intransitivity can be made to disappear.

Of course, the theory needs to reach a judgment when presented simultaneously with all three of the alternatives among which the pairwise comparisons are intransitive. On some formulations of partial aggregation (but not in Steuwer's), it is indeterminate what to choose when there are three alternatives such as 120 MILD, 11 MOD, and 1 S. For example, Victor Tadros cannot decide what his "localized" partial aggregation implies about such multi-alternative choices (2019, p. 187). Steuwer's view, in contrast, would treat the 11 moderate problems. As a result, his view violates so-called contraction consistency: From the set of alternatives {1 S, 11 MOD, 120 MILD}, his theory chooses 11 MOD, whereas from the subset {11 MOD, 120 MILD}, his theory chooses 120 MILD. There is, however, a ready explanation once one builds into the options a specification of the alternatives. Critics of partial aggregation deny that 11 MOD and 120 MILD are different alternatives, depending on whether 1 S is available, but there is no non-question-begging refutation here.

The second problem demands some change in partial aggregation views. It concerns the cutoff between those weaker claims that are nevertheless relevant and those that are not relevant. To put it crudely, if a claim to prevent the loss of a finger is not relevant when one could otherwise prevent a death and a claim to prevent the loss of both arms is relevant, where is the boundary? Defenders of partial aggregation need not specify a precise point, but they must tell us, for example, if a claim to prevent the loss of a hand or of a whole arm is relevant to a claim to prevent a death. Voorhoeve suggests, plausibly, that a claim to avoid loss of a hand is relevant to a claim to prevent a death if it would be reasonable for an individual to refuse to sacrifice a hand when doing so would save a life. Although this account does not identify a cutoff, it helps with the trade-off.

Suppose, for the purposes of argument, we judge that a claim to prevent the loss of a whole arm is relevant to preventing a death, but a claim to the loss of a hand is not. That means that in the context of considering whether to devote resources to preventing death, arms are infinitely more valuable than hands. Preventing the loss of some number of arms, perhaps 1,000, is more valuable than preventing a death, whereas the loss of millions of hands is never worse than the loss of a life. To make partial aggregation useful in practice, there needs to be a relatively narrow gap between those relatively weak claims that are relevant and those that are irrelevant to some stronger claim, but a radical difference in significance between claims to the avoidance of harms that are quite similar is implausible.[9]

Alec Walen notices this difficulty, and his account of "weak" as opposed to "partial" aggregation proposes a solution:

> Weak aggregation adds the thought [to partial aggregation] that as we move from somewhat weaker to much weaker claims, their ability to aggregate to outweigh stronger claims fades away before it ultimately blinks out. In more mathematical terms, their [weak claims'] ability to aggregate falls off in a faster than linear manner. (2020, p. 66)

> The reason I introduce the idea of weak aggregation is that it picks up the appeal of limited aggregation without the sort of normative cliff entailed by the simple distinction between relevant and irrelevant claims. (2020, p. 67)

Walen's proposal is somewhat ad hoc, apparently motivated solely by a concern to moot this objection. Moreover, while lessening the height of the cliff, there is still a chasm where the progressively weaker relevance of progressively weaker claims finally "blinks out." But this modification of partial aggregation greatly diminishes the force of the criticism.[10]

A third curable difficulty for views denying the relevance of claims to small benefits lies in the details of recent developments of partial aggregation views. Tomlin (2017) shows that in comparisons of policies involving multiple competing claims of different strengths, simple formulations of partial aggregation

---

[9] This argument was suggested to me by Lefkowitz (2008, p. 413), who makes the different point that if one understands all claims as falling into two classes of relevant or irrelevant, then the weakest of the relevant claims to the avoidance of harms would be infinitely stronger than the claims to the prevention of slightly lesser harms. I am not making the mistaken claim that Lefkowitz is criticizing.

[10] Walen's proposal is in effect operationalized in the Dutch health care system, in which the cost-effectiveness of a treatment of an ailment receives progressively less weight when the ailments are less serious, with the weight diminishing to zero when the health burden is less than 0.1 disability-adjusted life year, which in this context is equivalent to a burden of less than 0.1 QALY (Voorhoeve 2020a).

run into trouble. Should one assess the relevance of claims from the perspective of the strongest claims with which they compete or with respect to the strongest claims that the policies under consideration would satisfy? If one adopts the first view, then weak claims may be relevant in some groups and not in others so that adding the same number of treatments for mild ailments to sets of treatments T and T^* can change their ranking. If instead one adopts the second view (that whether a weak claim is relevant depends on what is the strongest claim, whether or not the weak claim competes with it), then starting with a situation in which T is more choiceworthy than T^*, *strengthening T* (so that it provides additional treatments) can reverse the ranking and make T less choiceworthy.

The sequential balancing that Steuwer defends (largely following Tadros 2019) solves these problems. As shown in Table 8.1, the requirement that forbids weak claims from ever contributing to frustrating stronger claims to which they are not relevant prevents Steuwer's balancing from ruling in favor of policy B (like the views of Tadros [2019] and van Gils and Tomlin [2020]).

If one follows the logic of starting with the strongest claims and then acting on those claims that are not balanced, then in Kamm's example, one will take curing E's sore throat to be a reason to favor saving D's life rather than C's life. As Tadros states,

> C's claim to be cured from the lethal illness is exactly counterbalanced by D's identical claim. Therefore, there is nothing left for E's claim [to a cure to her sore throat] to outweigh. Therefore, Local Relevance implies that I ought to cure D and E rather than flipping a coin, which seems wrong. (2019, p. 184)[11]

Is this implication so obviously wrong? Tadros considers living with it, although he also discusses some ways of avoiding it. van Gils and Tomlin, in contrast, argue, "It may be that our intuitions about tie-break cases can be vindicated via some other route,[12] but, we will argue, this cannot be based upon the best understanding of when claims are relevant" (2020, p. 225). Steuwer's proposal refutes van Gils and Tomlin's pessimism.

8.4 Against Partial Aggregation of Health Care: All Claims to Health Care Are Relevant

Partial aggregation views run into trouble when one recognizes that the consequences of treatments of individuals are chancey. A treatment may have a

---

[11] In the quotation, I have changed the letter names given to the individual to match the names I have been using in the text.
[12] See footnote 6 for one possibility.

very small probability of benefitting an individual, but, if given to large numbers of individuals, it may save many lives. Moreover, increasing funding for major benefits may only increase the probability of receiving them by a small amount.

8.4.1 Small Probabilities of Large Benefits

Recall the example of screening for strep throat versus dialysis. Screening provides children with a very small probability of a very large benefit. The expected value of screening a single child for strep throat is smaller than the cure of a minor headache and thus, according to partial aggregation views, claims to screening are apparently not relevant to claims to dialysis. But the expected value of screening a million children is far larger than the value of providing dialysis to Ann, Alan, and Albert. If a million children are screened, the screening will pick up roughly 3,000 cases of rheumatic fever, prevent hundreds of serious injuries, and save several children from death. Given how much more valuable the aggregate consequences are of using the resources to provide the screening, how could claims to screening fail to be relevant to Ann's, Alan's, and Albert's claims to dialysis? However slight the risk of strep throat from an individual's perspective, those in charge of allocating health care must be concerned about the expected aggregate outcomes of the policies.

These two ways of thinking about the benefits of screening and treating—in terms of the expected value to single individuals versus the expected aggregate outcome—are described in the literature as the ex ante versus ex post perspectives on the significance of risks. The terminology is misleading because both perspectives are concerned with expectations. If one were to allow aggregation and regard all benefits and harms, no matter how small, as "relevant," then the total benefit of the screening ex ante would be the sum of the expected individual benefits, which equals the ex post expected aggregate benefit.

From the ex ante perspective, the choice between dialysis and screening for strep throat is a no-brainer. The expected benefit screening provides is far too small for claims to screening to be relevant to the Ann's, Alan's, and Albert's claims to dialysis.[13] However, from the ex post perspective, the choice is between extending the lives of three older adults and preventing serious illness in scores of children and saving the lives of several. Responsible policymakers cannot ignore the ex post perspective. Although screening provides only a tiny expected benefit to any individual, scarcely a benefit at all, claims to screening must be

---

[13] In Johan Frick's view (2015b), fairness requires that the strength of a claim to some life-saving intervention be discounted by its probability of success and that policy should satisfy the strongest claim. Consequently, it is fair to save with certainty one life at the cost of failing to protect millions

relevant to claims to life-saving because as the number screened increases, the case for funding screening rather than dialysis grows stronger.

Defenders of partial aggregation thus apparently find themselves committed to the following inconsistent set of assertions.

1. Satisfying a claim to the relief of a minor headache or a claim to any smaller expected benefit is not relevant to satisfying a claim to dialysis of an individual with failing kidneys.
2. Screening a child for strep throat (and treating those who need it) provides a smaller expected benefit to an individual than does curing a minor headache.
3. A child's claim to screening for strep throat (and to treatment if indicated) is relevant to a claim to dialysis of an individual with failing kidneys.

At least one of these claims must be mistaken. Defenders of partial aggregation cannot give up statement 1 without giving up their position. It seems that the truth of the second proposition can be stipulated in the example. However, Steuwer (2021b) argues that if it is determined which children will develop serious complications, then statement 2 is false because those fated to be seriously ill will suffer very significant harms. Rather than contesting this claim, let us assume that it is not determined which of those screened will develop serious complications. In that case, the only way for defenders of partial aggregation to respond to this criticism is to reject statement 3 and deny that claims to screening for strep throat are relevant to claims to dialysis. There is no individual child who we are failing to respect by providing dialysis rather than screening for strep; stated differently, there are no already determined beneficiaries of the screening whose interests or claims we can cite in explaining to Ann, Alan, and Albert why we are letting them die.

Although defenders of partial aggregation can in this way avoid inconsistency, I doubt that many would want to defend providing dialysis rather than the screening. Moreover, there is a significant argument for the truth of statement 3—that is, for the relevance of claims to strep throat screening to claims to dialysis:

4. The case for screening children for strep throat (and treating those who need it) rather than providing dialysis to Ann, Alan, and Albert grows stronger with the number of children to be screened.

from a small chance of dying. Frick recognizes this implication and agrees that it would be wrong to leave a multitude exposed to a risk like this in order to save one life. He maintains that this is a case in which benevolence trumps fairness. In his view, saving with certainty the single life and allowing thousands to die is fair.

5. If the case for screening children for strep throat (and treating those who need it) rather than providing dialysis to Ann, Alan, and Albert grows stronger with the number of children to be screened, then claims to screening children for strep throat (and treating those who need it) are relevant to Ann's, Alan's, and Albert's claims to dialysis.
6. Thus, statement 3 is true: Claims to screening children for strep throat (and treating those who need it) are relevant to Ann's, Alan's, and Albert's claims to dialysis.

One might challenge statement 4 on the grounds that there may be some children fated to be seriously ill with strep even in a small sample. But if it is undetermined in advance whether those children one happens to screen will become seriously ill, then statement 4 is difficult to deny. Those who would deny the relevance of claims to screening to claims to dialysis have to challenge statement 5. The best way to do that is to maintain that statement 5 is ambiguous. There is an all-things-considered stronger reason to carry out the screening when more children can be screened, but it is no fairer to satisfy claims to screening rather than claims to dialysis when there are more claims to screening. Although screening a million children for strep throat rather than providing dialysis to Ann, Alan, and Albert leads to a greater health improvement, defenders of relevance might maintain that it remains unfair. To assert that screening for sore throats is not relevant to providing dialysis to someone with kidney failure is to assert precisely that although the right thing to do is to use resources to satisfy weak claims for strep throat screening and to treat those who have strep, when those resources could satisfy Ann's, Alan's, and Albert's claims to dialysis, it is not fair to do so.

We have arrived at a consistent position, but is it plausible? The defender of the relevance thesis denies that claims to screening are relevant to claims to dialysis on the grounds that although screening a million children is more beneficial than providing dialysis to three people, it is never fair to favor screening over dialysis, no matter how many we screen. If we shut our eyes to the expected consequences of the screening policy and focus exclusively on the benefits to individuals discounted by their probabilities, then it seems plausible to maintain that favoring screening would be unfair: There is something profoundly disrespectful in letting three people die in order to give a throat swab to some individual 6-year-old.

But it is difficult to defend the premise that it is never fair to favor screening for strep throat and treating the cases of strep throat the screening identifies over providing dialysis to Ann, Alan, and Albert. Suppose a reliable soothsayer has a sealed envelope in which she has written the names of 10 children whose lives will be saved by screening a million children for strep and treating those found to have strep. It may not be entirely clear how the health care system should balance the claims of these 10 children against Ann's, Alan's, and Albert's claims, but it is not unfair to place a significant weight on the children's claims. We do not know the names of the children, but if the soothsayer is reliable, those children are already marked for death by strep—"doomed," in Frick's (2015a, p. 183), Rüger's (2018, p. 242), and Steuwer's terminology (2021b, p. 124)—if we do not embark on this mass screening.

I conclude that it is fair to withhold dialysis from three adults in order to screen a million children for strep throat. Steuwer would agree when it is determined which children will die, but not when it is undetermined. It is very difficult to accept the conclusion that if deaths and serious harms are undetermined, then it is unfair for claims to avoid risks of death and serious harm to have any relevance to claims to avoid known major harms. Even those who would place a lesser weight on saving the lives of unknown or as-yet-undetermined individuals do not maintain that with respect to fairness, known or determined victims are infinitely more important with respect to fairness—which is what the defender of the irrelevance of claims to the avoidance of small objective chances of major harms needs to maintain.

To maintain that unknown or undetermined casualties are less important from the perspective of fairness than known casualties has implausible implications. Consider the following:

> **Annabella and Radioactive Waste**
>
> Suppose I can dispose of radioactive waste in two ways. I can bury it on Annabella's property, which will cause her death, or I can put it in a rocket that will take it to a high altitude before exploding. Placing the waste in the rocket has a 1 in 10,000 objective chance of killing any particular individual on earth, which means that the radioactive material dispersed from the rocket's explosion can be expected to kill at least three-quarters of a million people.

Unless one is prepared to conclude that it is fair to use the rocket, either those who are not determined to be harmed must have a serious claim against behavior that may harm them or one needs to allow the consequences to override one's account of what is fair (Frick 2015a, pp. 195-196; Steuwer 2021b p. 142). It is not plausible to maintain that it is fair to launch the rocket, even if one concedes that it is for other reasons ethically impermissible, all things considered.

This discussion of the significance of small risks purports to provide a counterexample to the proposition that claims to the prevention of very small harms or to small benefits are not relevant to claims to major benefits or the prevention of major harms, when the small benefit is a small probability of a large benefit. A claim to the very small expected benefit of screening an individual for strep throat must be regarded as relevant to a claim to prevent a death. It is wrong to use resources to avert the immanent deaths of Ann, Alan, and Albert, when instead one can provide a large number of small expected benefits in the form of screenings for strep throat. I conclude that if the expected benefits from alleviating minor headaches are larger than the benefits from screening, then claims to alleviating minor headache are, after all, also relevant to claims to saving a life. But one might disagree if curing headaches, unlike screening for strep, has no chance of providing a major benefit.

This last thought suggests another way that the defender of the relevance view might deflect the criticisms arising from small probabilistic benefits. The relevance theorist might maintain that the benefit of screening an individual child for strep throat is not the expected benefit of the screening but its actual benefit, which is often zero, sometimes negative (in virtue of calling for unneeded treatment with harmful side effects), and sometimes huge. Rather than focusing on the small average expected benefit to the children, the policymaker needs to attend to the very large harm to a small number of children that will result from not screening them. Unlike the many small benefits of providing aspirin to those who have headaches, what is at issue in the screening example are the huge benefits to a small number of individuals. In a small percentage of the screenings, there are substantial benefits and hence strong claims.

Can one defend the aggregation objection to c-e allocation by maintaining that claims to treatments with small expected values are relevant to major benefits, when the small expected values reflect a small probability of a large benefits? Although there are still grounds to deny the relevance of claims to small benefits that do not have some chance of providing a major benefit, most treatments with small expected values, such as vaccination against COVID-19 or bandaging a wound, have some probability of preventing a major health problem. So very few treatments will fail in the pertinent sense to be "relevant," and the aggregation objection collapses, at least in practice. To be sure, these small benefits will be relevant because of the large benefit they will likely provide, not owing to the summing of the small expectations of benefit. But it will still be the case that most small benefits will be relevant to major benefits, including life-saving.

This defense of partial aggregation implies implausibly that whether someone's claim to a treatment that has a small chance of providing a large benefit is relevant depends on how many others have the same claim. If, owing to shortages of swabs, only 50 children can be screened for strep throat this month, the probability of a major benefit resulting from the screening is too small to justify counting screening as relevant to the provision of dialysis. Sometimes, as in the case of herd immunity, the effects of a treatment depend on how many are treated. But that is not the case here. A strep throat screening on an individual has just the same benefits, regardless of how many are screened. But there is only significant value ex post in screening if large numbers are screened.

8.4.2 Small Benefits and Risks of Major Harms

Consider again the aspirin* versus ambulance example from Chapter 3:

> **Aspirin* or Ambulance**
>
> Some money is left in a state's health budget. There are two ways to spend the money. Either (a) it can be spent on building a factory to produce millions of doses of aspirin*, a new more effective treatment for minor pains, or (b) the funds can be used to install new defibrillators in ambulances, which will almost certainly save a few lives. Adding up all the small contributions that aspirin* makes to the HRQoL of many individuals, the health policymaker may conclude that it is more cost-effective to build the aspirin* factory. Critics of aggregation maintain that it is unfair to favor a large number of small benefits over a large benefit such as saving a life.

Unlike Dialysis Versus Screening, which argued for the relevance of claims to *small chances* of large benefit to claims to large benefits, Aspirin* or Ambulance argues for the relevance of claims to small *benefits* to claims to *chances of large benefits*.

Suppose that the odds of needing the new defibrillator are so low that almost everyone finds it to be more in their interest to have access to aspirin* than to have the new defibrillators. It is rational to accept small benefits that increase the risk of death if the increased risk is small. We do that all the time. In both public policy and individual decision-making, people are constantly trading off risks of serious injury or death against small inconveniences. When I drive to the store, I risk killing pedestrians, and when I walk there, I risk my own life, yet I do so anyway to save myself the expense of having my groceries delivered. If we limited highway speeds more stringently or required that all vehicles carry first-aid kits, we would save lives. If the small benefits of not having to keep a first-aid kit in one's vehicle are worth some excess deaths every year and hence relevant to whether injured people live or die, why aren't claims to the relief of minor pains also relevant to the claims of injured people in ambulances?[14]

This argument shows only that claims to small benefits (relief of various minor pains) are relevant to claims to small decreases in the risks of death. A defender of partial aggregation might reply that claims to small benefits can be relevant to claims to the avoidance of small risks of death without being relevant to claims to the certain or near certain avoidance of a large risk of death. Although a small risk of death is relevant to death, relevance is not transitive, and it does not follow that it could ever be morally permissible or fair to satisfy a claim to the relief of minor pains when one could instead with high probability save a life. Such a defense of the relevance of small benefits is strained, and in any case it is incompatible with the argument in Section 8.4.1 for the relevance of strep throat screening, which defended the relevance of claims to screening by looking to the small number of serious harms that screening averts.

The defender of partial aggregation may point out that if we imagine ourselves on the way to a hospital facing death for the lack of a new defibrillator in the ambulance, we will lament its absence. At that moment, minimally humane people would surrender their protection against minor aches and pains in order to save a life. However, it is perfectly possible for individuals who would lament the absence of the defibrillator when they need one to continue to favor building the aspirin* factory when they are not facing death for the lack of a defibrillator. The bedside lament does not impugn the policy because it does not challenge the relevance of claims to minor benefits to claims to the avoidance of risks of serious harms. Moreover, to defend the relevance of claims to small benefits to the decision-making of health care administrators, one need only show that many small benefits can justify increasing or not diminishing the risks of serious harms. From a policy perspective, as opposed to a bedside perspective, what is at issue are expectations and risks; and the possibility that building the aspirin* factory may be a better health care choice than installing updated defibrillators shows that claims to small benefits are relevant to policies that affect how many people will die. Refusing to allow small benefits to justify increasing or not diminishing the risks of serious harms is scarcely imaginable.

8.4.3 Implausible Implications for Health Care

Finally, can one accept the practical implications of partial aggregation for the allocation of health care? On the assumption that it is always possible for a

---

[14] If one allows full aggregation, then there is nothing puzzling about the example: If the small benefit for each individual more than compensates for the increased risk, then the total of the small benefits compensates for the harms that result.

health system to do something to reduce the expected number of deaths, only treatments of claims that are relevant to the prevention of death will be funded. If there is a low bar for relevance, then this result is not too worrying: Partial aggregation will look like total aggregation, and concerns about "relevance" will rarely be germane. Just about every claim will be relevant. Treating large numbers of minor cuts and scrapes will avert many infections and save some lives.

If, on the other hand, the defender of partial aggregation sets a high bar for relevance so that only claims to treatments of at least moderately serious conditions count as relevant to prevention of death, then, as John Broome points out (2002a), partial aggregation has radical implications, condemning the practices of existing health systems, all of which devote considerable resources to minor ailments such as headaches or hospital amenities rather than using health care resources exclusively to treat or prevent serious and life-threatening conditions. Most of the efforts of primary care doctors and nurse practitioners and a nontrivial proportion of health care resources are devoted to minor problems. I have argued that this is fair on the grounds that claims to minor health benefits and the avoidance of minor harms are relevant and that minor health problems typically have some chance of major consequences.

Moreover, as Nir Eyal noted in a discussion of this chapter, various palliative treatments may mask serious conditions and thus *lower* the probability of identifying and treating serious conditions. Claims to treatments that marginally increase people's comfort will not be relevant to treatments that avert or cure serious ailments. Partial aggregation condemns most palliative care as an unfair diversion of resources that should be devoted to the prevention or cure of serious health problems.[15]

8.5 Aggregation Without Aggravation

Defenders of the partial aggregation view are surely not overjoyed at the implausible features of their views and the contortions they go through to explain away the problems. It is uncomfortable to have to draw a line between those claims that are relevant to some strong claim and those that are not, particularly because items that are near the line and very similar in importance have radically different bearings on what should be done. There is more discomfort in recognizing that the consequences of many trivial treatments, such as screening for strep throat, deemed not to be "relevant" may turn out to matter more than saving a

---

[15] In response, Voorhoeve (2020a, p. 287) has argued that the provision of such care may result in a greater willingness to fund health care and thus not divert resources away from the treatment of serious illness. Moreover, individuals may want to forgo treatment in favor of palliation, and the health care system should allow this choice.

life. Moreover, even if the refusal to aggregate small benefits and harms were justifiable in bedside, microallocation decisions, it is unacceptable when (as in the Aspirin* or Ambulance case) assessing policies that increase or diminish risks of serious harms. Finally, the consequences in practice for health care of partial aggregation are either empty or unlike actual health care practices.

Defenders of partial aggregation might ruefully respond that however implausible its consequences, partial aggregation is nevertheless better than either total aggregation or a complete rejection of aggregation. Do we really want to conclude that if capping teeth were more cost-effective than an appendicitis operation, then capping teeth should take priority over life-saving surgeries? Should we not say that the cost-effectiveness calculation is beside the point, because claims to capping teeth are not relevant to saving lives?

In defending the view that capping teeth should never take priority over a life-saving procedure such as an appendectomy, defenders of relevance argue that we should look at the question as whether a single case of tooth capping could be preferred over saving someone else's life by a reasonable person, who is allowed some bias on their own behalf. I suggest that this is not the question that those designing or administering the health care system should be asking. The administrator should be concerned to distribute treatments fairly to lessen pain and lessen activity limitations. A large enough number of tooth cappings will accomplish these ends better than an appendectomy. People have claims to capping teeth when they are in pain, at risk of infection, and facing the likelihood of losing teeth. Capping teeth can save lives by preventing infections. I have no idea whether, given current costs, it is more cost-effective to cap teeth than to perform appendectomies. But I do not believe that the possibility that it is constitutes a criticism of allocation via cost-effectiveness. *In my view, all claims are relevant to the assessment of health care policy.*

Whatever the merits of the partial aggregation view, I conjecture that it is probably not the source of the layperson's outrage at prioritizing capping teeth over appendectomies. A more plausible explanation of the reactions traces them to a compassionate outrage at the thought that a life is sacrificed that could easily be saved. As in the case of the severity objection, I think that compassion or a highly localized benevolence, rather than a theory of fairness, motivates the anti-aggregation objection to rationing via cost-effectiveness. If, as argued in the previous section, there is no way to deny the relevance to life-and-death decisions of a small chance of detecting and treating serious consequences of strep throat or relieving minor pains, then partial aggregation is not the right way to allocate health care, and one can turn one's back on its unresolved difficulties. It is, of course, horrible to say to someone who is denied dialysis that the resources were better spent on screening children for strep throat. Nor would we be happy explaining to someone dying for the lack of an updated defibrillator that the resources were used to manufacture aspirin*. Partly for that reason, we want a general rule, such as c-e allocation, that compares the cost-effectiveness of dialysis to the cost-effectiveness of many interventions of varying significance rather than, as it were, slapping individuals in the face with a bedside comparison of dialysis with a single strep throat screening.

8.6 Conclusion

In designing health care policies, claims to treatments for minor as well as major ailments must be considered. This is unavoidable. One reason is that minor health conditions, unlike missing part of a World Cup transmission, can transform into major health problems. Life is full of small benefits and burdens, and in the case of health, these usually include chances of major harms. The cumulative effect of these minor problems can be huge. Lots of discomfort and disability from ailments such as arthritic knees should not be ignored, even when lives are at stake. It will not do to say that claims to treatment of these ailments count in virtue of their relevance to other claims to moderately severe health conditions because the possibility of addressing the most severe ailments is always on the table, leaving claims to the treatment of mildly arthritic knees, like those currently annoying the author, not "relevant" to health care policymaking.

From the perspective of overall health care policy, partial aggregation is a nonstarter. When we are caring for individual patients, we can sometimes pretend to reject aggregation and even make some gestures toward doing so. But the non-aggregation objection to c-e allocation collapses, at least for claims to small benefits that involve small changes in probabilities of major harms or gains. Is it so obviously inconsistent with baseline respect to say to those whom we refuse to help (given the resources available for health care) that we have chosen policies that provide the largest aggregate health benefits?

The most potent objection to c-e allocation remains. Does it discriminate against those who are badly off and those who are disabled? Chapter 9 addresses that objection.

9
Discrimination

The remaining objection to cost-effectiveness in terms of discrimination is, I maintain, the most serious. Section 9.1 distinguishes three different discrimination complaints that might be lodged against (c-e) allocation, and it distinguishes these criticisms from the fair chances and severity objections. It argues that the discrimination derives both from the way in which health measurement systems assign values to morbidity and mortality and from the way that c-e allocation makes use of those values. Section 9.2 discusses what makes some kinds of discrimination acceptable and even desirable, while other instances are intolerable. Section 9.3 considers an alternative way of valuing health improvements that assigns equal value to life-saving and thereby avoids the most egregious discrimination that is implicit in measures of the effectiveness of health care. However, Section 9.4 points to flaws in the alternative and argues that the discrimination criticism of cost-effectiveness cannot be resolved by changing the measure of effectiveness. Section 9.5 concludes with a way to avoid the wrongful discrimination c-e allocation may involve.

9.1 C-E Allocation and Three Kinds of Objectionable Discrimination

Recall the discussion of discrimination from Chapter 3: Saving the lives of those whose health-related quality of life (HRQoL) is lower or who can be expected if saved to live for fewer years makes a smaller contribution to population health and is less cost-effective than saving the lives of those in better health and who can expect, if saved, to live longer. The examples might make it appear that what explains why it is wrong to put those with disabilities at the back of the line is simply the fact that one is taking their disabilities into account when deciding whether they will be treated. That is not the correct explanation of what is wrong. Suppose that the only way to save many thousands from death and suffering in a pandemic would be to earmark a scarce vaccine to those who can carry out certain tasks that are impossible for the blind. In that case, it might be morally permissible—perhaps even morally obligatory—to refuse to use any of the scarce vaccine to protect the blind. But the reason would not be that saving their lives is of less intrinsic value than saving the lives of those who are sighted. What is wrong with the disability discrimination is its *devaluing* of the lives of those who are disabled.

Let us accordingly define what I call "disability discrimination" as follows:

> *Disability discrimination* consists in assigning a lesser non-instrumental value to saving the lives of the disabled than one assigns to saving the lives of those without disabilities.

To avoid disability discrimination, it is not enough that there is a social purpose served by placing a lesser priority on extending the lives of the disabled. Janitors are less economically productive than schoolteachers, but to allow economic productivity to justify placing a lower priority on extending the lives of janitors devalues their lives. It is wrong for the same reason that not vaccinating those with post-traumatic stress disorder (PTSD) is wrong.

"Devaluing" the lives of those with disabilities consists of allowing their diminished health to justify placing less importance on saving their lives; it is not merely judging (correctly) that their health is worse than that of those who are free of disabilities, or that a population without PTSD or emphysema is healthier than a similar population with them. To speak of "devaluing their lives" is evocative, but what is at issue is not whether their lives are equally good.

The claim that everyone's life is of equal value is ambiguous and, in many of the ways of resolving the ambiguity, it is false. There is nothing morally objectionable in recognizing that people's lives are better and worse in many respects. Much of what motivates talk of whether some policy devalues the lives of some people has, I believe, nothing to do with the value of people's lives but is instead a matter of the consideration or baseline respect that is due to all those who have not forfeited those attitudes by despicable behavior. Whether or not life has intrinsic value, most people expect of any legitimate state that its institutions secure to everyone both basic rights and the respect owed to those who possess such rights. The prioritization of COVID-19 vaccine recipients would have violated people's rights if it had rested on the view that some people are more worthy of continued life than others. There is no inconsistency between insisting on placing equal non-instrumental weight on saving everyone's lives from the ravages of COVID-19 and giving priority to those who are at greatest risk of harm or to those who are more likely to transmit the disease. Nor is there any inconsistency in assigning everyone the same non-instrumental priority while at the same time recognizing that one person's life is going better than another's or that one person is healthier, more productive, or more valuable to friends and family than another. Only an equivocation on the notion of value should lead one to conclude that there is a conflict between placing equal non-instrumental priority on saving lives, largely without regard to what those lives are like, and recognizing that people's lives have different values of various kinds. Judging how well people's lives are going, whether as a result of their health or for any other reason, is not judging what claims individuals should have on the consideration of others.

In addition to what I have defined as disability discrimination, health problems and other disadvantages people have incurred may make it more costly and hence less cost-effective to treat them. For example, those who have been excluded from education may not be able to read or understand instructions for their care and may consequently need more time and attention from caretakers. It may be difficult and expensive for health care providers to reach those who live in impoverished remote areas. In this second sort of discrimination, which I call "cost discrimination," the lives and health of the disabled or disadvantaged are not treated as of any lesser value than the lives of those without health deficiencies or other disadvantages. What leads to the lower treatment priority is the greater cost of treatment.

Although cost discrimination has a different source, like disability discrimination, cost discrimination seems to involve a sort of "double jeopardy" (Harris 1987; Singer et al. 1995). Disadvantage serves to justify further disadvantage. If one believes, as I do, that fairness requires that health policies should aim not to aggravate and indeed to ameliorate inequalities, then cost discrimination may often be unjust. As Brock states,

> We should not use a person's undeserved or unjustified disadvantages as the grounds or basis for choosing to impose a further disadvantage on them. Social policies under our control should not compound further an already existing undeserved or unjustified disadvantage.[1]

Brock makes two claims here. He maintains that a person's unjustified disadvantages should not serve as the *grounds* for actions that policymakers expect to aggravate that person's disadvantages (as is the case in disability discrimination), and he asserts that regardless of the grounds, policies should avoid compounding existing discrimination (as is often the case in cost discrimination). Rationing by cost-effectiveness can result in discriminatory exclusion of the disadvantaged, and it often finds its rationale in their already existing disadvantages.

---

[1] Brock (2009, p. 35). Kamm (2004) calls this "the non-linkage principle." She does not endorse it as a general condition on health policy. Hellman (2018) argues that compounding—exacerbating or magnifying—a previous *injustice* is itself unjust, but adding to a disadvantage that is not an injustice may be perfectly permissible. For example, hiring and training a skilled worker may blamelessly compound the disadvantage of a less skilled worker.

A third way in which disabilities and disadvantages may lower the expected value of treatments is by rendering them riskier, less reliable, and less beneficial. Let us call this "effectiveness discrimination." Owing to malnourishment, an individual may be seriously injured by a surgery or medication that otherwise would have cured some health problem. Individuals with cognitive limitations may be unable to follow postoperative instructions and for that reason may be poor candidates for certain treatments. For these reasons, the treatment of individuals with other disadvantages or with health problems that are separate from the problems whose treatment is under consideration may have a lower priority.

Cost and effectiveness discrimination, unlike disability discrimination, are not ethical objections to using cost-effectiveness to allocate health care. They object instead to some of the possible outcomes of c-e allocation. They point out that policymakers face a trade-off between enhancing health and promoting equality. The greater costs or lesser efficiency of treating the disabled call for constraints on cost-effectiveness rather than for its modification or abandonment.

9.2 When Is Discrimination Wrong?

Instances of cost and effectiveness discrimination are not always morally impermissible. Discrimination, in the generic sense of drawing distinctions or applying some criterion to favor some and disfavor others, is not always wrong. There is nothing wrong with using a swab test to discriminate between cases of the flu and cases of COVID-19, even though doing so may require some to be quarantined while others need not isolate themselves. Disabilities and all sorts of other traits may in some cases justifiably diminish someone's eligibility for jobs, admission to universities, and other social positions and benefits. On the other hand, obviously, discrimination is sometimes seriously morally wrong. When discrimination is wrong, what makes it wrong?

Disability discrimination is wrong because it assigns a lower non-instrumental value to extending the lives of the disabled than to extending the lives of those without disabilities. To say to someone that it is more important to save someone else's life, not for instrumental reasons but because you place a greater value on their life, is as deep a violation of baseline respect as one can imagine. When drawing and employing distinctions is inconsistent with baseline respect, it is wrongful discrimination.[2]

---

[2] In failing to show baseline respect, discrimination may also have the consequences of excluding, stigmatizing, and oppressing. These consequences magnify the wrong. Although locating the wrongfulness of some discrimination in the violation of baseline respect, this account is consistent with Hellman's view that wrongful discrimination is *demeaning* (2008). However, I place more emphasis than does Hellman on consequences of demeaning individuals, such as exclusion and oppression.

Cost and effectiveness discrimination need not show any disrespect, and they are sometimes morally permissible. For example, it is not unfair to discriminate in the provision of cosmetic surgery against hemophiliacs, who face increased risks of bleeding, even though doing so involves the double jeopardy discussed above. Placing an equally high priority on treating those whose health cannot be greatly improved or who are especially expensive to treat would diminish the health system's capacity to promote health. As the example illustrates, that fact sometimes justifies discrimination. On the other hand, it appears to be unfair to discriminate in the provision of cosmetic surgery against deaf patients owing to difficulties they may have in communicating with doctors. There is no general principle to the effect that past disadvantage should not be the ground for further disadvantage. Double jeopardy is particularly troubling when it relies on or amplifies not merely past disadvantage but also past wrongs.

I suggest that what explains why discrimination in the provision of cosmetic surgery against hemophiliacs appears to be fair, whereas discrimination against deaf surgical candidates is unfair, is its disrespectfully stigmatizing or demeaning individuals, which causes or exacerbates their exclusion and sometimes oppression. Compare this discrimination to the discrimination in hiring or college admissions against African Americans that used to be ubiquitous in the United States (and has not yet disappeared). What makes that discrimination wrong is not the mere fact that it distributes benefits on the basis of race. What is wrong with discrimination against African Americans is that it stigmatizes, excludes, and oppresses, whereas so-called reverse discrimination, which is wrongly conflated with it, does none of these. For example, the provision of separate restrooms for "whites" and "colored" that used to exist in the South was an appalling public insult to those with dark skin, despite the pretense of symmetry.

Assigning a lesser value to saving the lives of the disabled excludes, stigmatizes, and can easily not only oppress but also kill the disabled. It is clearly wrongful discrimination. Cost discrimination is more difficult to judge and is in any case not an objection to c-e allocation per se. In many cases, it stigmatizes, excludes, and oppresses, as when, for example, poor transportation to a remote area inhabited by Indigenous peoples is the reason why only those who live in the city are treated. If, on the other hand, those who are expensive to treat have randomly distributed allergies that preclude the use of cheaper medicines, then the cost discrimination does not stigmatize any groups. The same applies to the case of George and Georgina, in which Georgina's need for an expensive antibiotic subjects her to cost discrimination without any stigma attached.

Similarly, effectiveness discrimination, assigning a lower priority to treating those who are less likely to benefit from treatment, is sometimes benign, whereas in other instances, it presupposes or aggravates the stigmatizing and exclusion of some group of disadvantaged individuals. For example, suppose that due to a health condition, such as an allergy, the most effective analgesic for persistent back pain cannot be used on group B. Should group B members' lesser capacity to benefit from treatment lower their priority? Nord et al. argue,

> However, it may be seen as unfair to hold against patients in group B that they happen to have a lesser degree of treatability than group C. Their potential for health improvement is still substantial and important to themselves, and they are just as ill as patients in group C....
>
> One may ask why those with a lesser outcome should give up their chances of receiving something valuable to them just because somebody else can benefit even more. (1999, pp. 27–28)[3]

As Nord et al. note, the concern here resembles the fair chances objection, which was discussed in Chapter 6. In fact, if the view Nord sketches were defensible, it would enlarge that objection, suggesting that even very large differences in capacity to benefit should have little importance. Contrary to Nord, I see nothing unfair in "holding the lesser degree of treatability against individuals." Whether it is permissible to deny treatment to members of B while treating members of C (which by assumption provides a greater health improvement) depends on the circumstances. It might be unjust discrimination of the sort I have just described, or it may be, in effect, C's turn to benefit. To favor health care policies that improve health and promote well-being is unobjectionable as one important evaluative criterion. It is not the only one, and adopting the most cost-effective policy may result in objectionable discriminatory outcomes. But merely favoring some treatments over others that contribute less to health and well-being is not in itself unfair or otherwise objectionable. There is no ethical objection here to the use of cost-effectiveness information. When the differing capacities to benefit map on to salient groups, some of whose members are excluded and stigmatized or at risk of becoming so due to the treatment prioritization, then discrimination in terms of capacity to benefit becomes wrongful. For example, prioritizing the treatment of group C would be a different matter, if what distinguished group B from group C, instead of an allergy, was the ethnic ancestry of its members.

Differing capacities to benefit from health-improving treatments do not typically lead cost-effectiveness to favor policies that stigmatize and exclude. Indeed, insofar as we expect scarce medications and procedures to be distributed in part on the basis of who is most likely to benefit, we welcome effectiveness discrimination, as in the case of cosmetic surgery for hemophiliacs. There is nothing demeaning attached to being denied treatment because one is not a good match for a transplant or because a medication is known not to work well for individuals

---

[3] The back pain example is mine.

with one's blood type. Like any assignment of priorities, these assignments will disadvantage some individuals. Even when they disadvantage those who have already been disadvantaged by poor health or other misfortune, it is not obvious that any change in cost-effectiveness is called for. Those prior misfortunes often call for social redress, but a further argument is needed to establish that the proper way to provide that redress is via the allocation of health-related resources.

To begin the task of specifying how to eliminate or limit wrongful discrimination in the allocation of health care, the next section focuses on disability discrimination, which, unlike cost and effectiveness discrimination, identifies a flaw in cost-effectiveness itself. Section 9.4 returns to cost and effectiveness discrimination.

9.3 Valuing Life Extension

As noted in the discussion of severity in Chapter 7, health economists such as Erik Nord have hoped to address fairness objections to c-e allocation by incorporating concerns about fairness into the values assigned to health improvements. Thus, Nord argues that the worry that c-e allocation unfairly fails to prioritize the treatment of severe health conditions can be addressed by measuring the effectiveness of treatments by how much and for how long they increase the social value of health states rather than by how many QALYs they provide. Measuring effectiveness by improvement in social value rather than QALYs lessens the difference between the value of extending the life of someone in poor health and extending the life of someone in good health. But there is still a difference, which strikes most people, including Nord, as unfair. Accordingly, Nord proposes that regardless of an individual's health state (provided that it is not worse than death), every year of life extension should count as a full social value–adjusted life year. That implies that extending someone's life and at the same time eliminating their disabling back pain counts for no more than saving their life and leaving them in agonizing pain. The valuation of health states and improvements is caught in "the QALY trap" (Ubel 2000, p. 163): Either one has to assign lower values to extending the lives of those whose health conditions are worse or one cannot assign lower values to worse health conditions.

One response that Nord has defended is to use different values in different contexts. When comparing policies involving life extension, treat each additional year of life provided for individuals of the same age as equally valuable.[4]

---

[4] As Nord points out elsewhere (2018, p. 270), one might allow the value of life extension to differ depending on the age of the individual whose life in being extended, whereas the value of health improvements is, arguably, independent of age.

When, on the other hand, comparing policies involving health improvements, rely on social value. Such a proposal leaves us with no principled guidelines for appraising policies that affect both morbidity and longevity.

There are other ways to proceed. Here is one recent proposal.[5] A treatment can affect an individual's health in two ways: It can affect the value of health states, which Basu et al. identify with Q (HRQoL), and it can affect how much longer an individual will live (L). Suppose one treats the value of a treatment as the *sum* of the values of its contribution to longevity and its contribution to HRQoL, and that one treats a change in longevity as having the same value regardless of an individual's HRQoL, provided that Q is high enough that life is worth living. Let the expected QALYs of an individual if untreated be $Q.L$ and the expected QALYs if treated be $Q'.L'$, where Q and Q' are HRQoLs and L and L' are longevities. For simplicity, I assume that $Q' > Q$ and $L' > L$, and that Q' and Q are expected not to change during the future.

To avoid disability discrimination, the value of the change in longevity ($L' - L$) should be just the same, regardless of Q and Q', so one needs to specify some constant level of HRQoL to capture the value of longevity. Following Nord, Basu et al. take the level to be full health (1.0). So the uniform value of life extension will be simply $L' - L$. Basu et al. suggest that the value of the improvement in the quality of one's health that treatment provides is $L'(Q' - Q)$. To understand their reasoning, consider Figure 9.1. HRQoL is measured on the vertical axis and longevity on the horizontal axis. The rectangle with three vertical divisions, which is shown to the right of the graph, is the value of the increase in longevity, $L' - L$, multiplied by $Q = 1$. The square labeled QL shows the expected QALYs if untreated. Expected QALYs if treated is the square with the four divisions labeled QL, $Q(L' - L)$, $L(Q' - Q)$, and $(L' - L).(Q' - Q)$.

In considering the contribution that the treatment makes to the quality of life, clearly one needs to subtract from the total QALYs if treated both the QALYs if untreated (the square at the left bottom corner of Figure 9.1 and also the small rectangle in the lower right corner), which represents $Q(L' - L)$; I am here taking this to be the QALYs the individual would have had during the period $L' - L$ if, contrary to fact, the untreated individual would have been alive. So health years in total (HYT) consists of the vertical rectangle ($L' - L$) plus the horizontal rectangle $L'(Q' - Q)$ (which is $L'Q' - LQ) - Q(L' - L)$. One might wonder why the effect of treatment on the quality of health is $L'(Q' - Q)$ rather than $L(Q' - Q)$. Doesn't $L'(Q' - Q)$ double count $(Q' - Q).(L' - L)$? No because $(Q' - Q).(L' - L)$ is both a portion of the increase in longevity and a period of life with a greater HRQoL.[6] The yearly contribution of a life-extending treatment measured in

---

[5] Basu, Carlson, and Veenstra (2020). I have simplified their proposal, which is more general.

[6] When there are more than two treatments under consideration, the quality difference in the first term is multiplied by the largest increase in life span provided by any of the treatments.

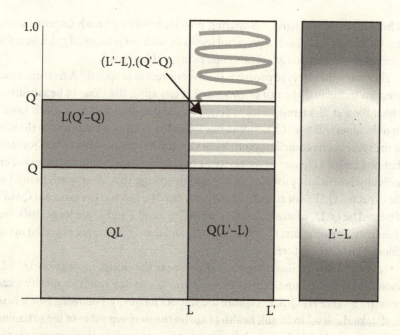

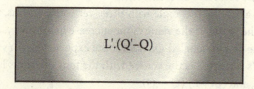

Figure 9.1 Health years in total.

HYT ranges between 0 (when $Q = 1$ and $Q' = 0$) and 2 (when $Q' = 1$ and $Q = 0$). What distinguishes HYT from QALYs or from analogous measure of social value–adjusted life years or public value–adjusted life years is not the measure of the value of health states but, rather, the valuing of health interventions separately by their improvement in health states and by the extension of life they provide.[7] HYT cannot replace QALYs or "social values" or "public values" because differences in HYT depend on the life expectancy of the alternative with the longest life expectancy and measure only changes in longevity and HRQoL.

---

[7] Although this proposal borrows from Erik Nord and co-authors (Nord 1999; Nord et al. 1999), it ignores his insistence, discussed in Chapter 7, that the social assessment of health policies should depend on their social value rather than on the QALYs they produce.

Clearly, the HYT assigns the same value to saving the lives of individuals, regardless of their health (provided that their health is not so bad that it is not worth continuing to live). If the longevity after treatment is fixed at L^*, then the contribution that an increase in the quality of health to the value of the treatment is $L^* . \Delta Q$, regardless of whether ΔQ boosts HRQoL from 0.4 to 0.6 or from 0.7 to 0.9. However, it is possible to substitute Nord's social values of health states for their quality weights to accommodate a concern to prioritize severity.

HYT may assign a higher value to one treatment, T, than to T', even though T' provides individuals with more QALYs. For example, suppose there is a group G of individuals, all of whom have an HRQoL of 0.5. They will die soon without treatment. There is a choice among two life-saving treatments. Treatment T gives members of G 20 years of life and improves their HRQoL to 0.8. Treatment T' does not improve HRQoL, but it gives members of G 30 rather than 20 years to live. T provides each person with $20 \times 0.8 = 16$ QALYs; T' provides each person with 30×0.5 QALYs or 15 QALYs total. On the other hand, T provides $20 + 20.(0.3) = 26$ HYT, whereas T' provides 30 HYT. When evaluated in terms of HYT, T' is superior, whereas when evaluated in QALYs, T comes out on top.

Which of these rankings should guide our assessment of the two treatments? One might favor the ranking by HYT on the grounds that in other contexts this measure avoids disability discrimination. However, note that the implicit time trade-offs in the HRQoL values conform to the QALY rankings, not to the HYT ranking. The time trade-off between the HRQoL values with T and T' implies that individuals prefer X years at $Q = 0.8$ to Y years at $Q = 0.5$ if and only if Y is, as in this case, less than $8X/5$. The ranking in terms of HYT differs because measures of HYT place more weight on longevity in the evaluation of treatments than, on average, do the survey respondents from whom the HRQoL values are elicited.

As previously noted, HYT cannot replace QALYs or "social values" or "public values" because the HYT of a health state is defined only relative to the alternative with the greatest life expectancy. This means that HYTs cannot serve as summary measures of health levels or health inequalities. Because HYT depends on the increase in longevity and weights the contribution to HYT of an improvement in the quality of life by the greatest longevity of the alternatives, treatments of ailments of the aged will have low HYTs. Whether this constitutes an ethically objectionable form of discrimination is debatable.

The conflict between evaluation in terms of HYTs and average time trade-offs highlights two aspects of the problem of disability discrimination. First, as Nord emphasizes, the evaluation of health states for the purposes of guiding health policy need not conform to the evaluation of health states by individuals to guide their own choices and their interactions with others. Which health state over which interval I prefer for myself or my children is a different question than which health state over which interval should be favored by health policy. Second, the QALY is not an obvious, albeit simplified, measure of the value of health. It depends on evaluative choices. One could instead define a QALY* as $Q.\sqrt{L}$ or as $Q.L^3$. A measure such as HYT could be defined as $L'(Q' - Q) + \sqrt{(L' - L)}$ or as $L'(Q' - Q) + 2(L' - L)$. In evaluating population health or the health of an individual, how much weight should be placed on quality versus length of life? In finding a "cure" for what I have called "disability discrimination," the HYT is committed to a particular weighting of the value of increasing longevity versus diminishing morbidity, without any argument for this weighting. The QALY is in no stronger position in this regard.

How important to the appraisal of health is longevity compared to morbidity? Put this way, the question is not well posed. People differ in their priorities; the personal weightings are diverse. From a public perspective, there could be a single correct answer, but it is difficult to imagine how public deliberation could settle on it. As argued in Chapter 3, the public value of health states or life extension does not coincide with the average of private values. The trade-off between the length and quality of life that should govern health care policy cannot be determined by polling individuals concerning the trade-offs they would make in their own health decisions, because the objectives of individuals and the health care system are not the same.

How should the policy assessment of population health weigh length versus quality of life? Why should the trade-off between a 0.1 improvement in HRQoL and 10 years of life be the same if one's initial HRQoL is 0.2 or 0.9? Both in QALYs and in HYT, these must be equal, and it is convenient to treat them as the same. Is that a sufficient justification? Is there any other? I do not know how health care policies should weigh life extension against improvements in the quality of life. But I do not see any argument here against HYT, which can, in any case, be modified so as to diminish or increase the weight it places on longevity.

Despite the solution it provides to the problem of disability discrimination, allocation guided by HYTs has implausible implications concerning the value of extending lives. Consider the following case, which I borrow and adapt from Frances Kamm (2013b). Suppose that Florence, Gail, and Henrietta all have a disease that will kill them immediately if they are not treated. We can treat only one of the three. If treated, each would have a life expectancy of 10 years. Florence and Gail are paraplegics with a HRQoL of 0.8, whereas Henrietta has no disability. If Florence receives the treatment, it will also cure her paraplegia. This is not the case for Gail, who if saved would remain a paraplegic. According to QALY maximization, we should save either Florence or Henrietta. In either case, we minimize the disabilities in the population. According to HYT, in contrast, we should save Florence. In defense of the implausible implication that it

Table 9.1 QALYs, HYTs, and Intuitions

	Q	Q'	QALYs	HYT	Intuition: $Pr_F(S) = Pr_G(S) = Pr_H(S) = 0.33$
F	0.8	1.0	10; Pr(S) = 0.5	12 (save)	Save F from {F,G}; indifferent re: {F, H}
G	0.8	0.8	8; (dies)	10 (dies)	Dies if choice from {F,G}; indifferent re: {G, H}
H	1.0	1.0	10 Pr(S) = 0.5	10 (dies)	Indifferent who is saved from {F,H} and {G, H}

HYTs, health years in total; QALYs, quality-adjusted life years.

is ethically preferable to save Florence rather than Henrietta, one might argue that there is more lifetime equality if Henrietta dies and Florence lives, because the extension of her life compensates for the worse health she has experienced previously. Alternatively, one might argue that the prioritarian injunction to favor those who are worse off supports saving Florence. But HYT gives a higher value to saving her life regardless of anything other than her current health state. She might have already had a much longer, healthier, and flourishing life than Henrietta, despite her current disability.

Table 9.1 summarizes the contrasts. F, G, and H stand for Florence, Gail, and Henrietta, respectively. "S" is an abbreviation for saving the individual's life. Notice that the intuitive pairwise ranking of the three alternatives is intransitive and inconsistent with indifference among the three alternatives. The pairwise comparisons are indifference between saving Florence and saving Henrietta and between saving Gail and saving Henrietta, but saving Florence if the alternative is saving Gail. These intuitions cannot be explained by the values of the health of the individuals during the additional 10 years of life they will have if their lives are saved. That value is, as calculated in QALYs, equal for Florence and Henrietta and less for Gail. What explains the indifference between saving Florence and Henrietta is not what most enhances health.

9.4 Avoiding Wrongful Discrimination

The conclusion I draw is that it is impossible to avoid disability discrimination by fiddling with the measure of effectiveness. Insofar as the objective is to maximize the value that health provides in terms of avoiding pain and limitations on activities, the value of life-saving depends exclusively on how little pain and how few activity limitations there are in those whose lives are saved. Given the HRQoL and life expectancy after someone is saved, facts about their previous health are irrelevant to the contribution that life-saving makes to the value of the health of a population.

If one's objective were exclusively to limit the burdens of health deficiencies of all sorts, then there is more value in saving Florence's or Henrietta's life than in saving Gails' life. Rather than denying this, as Basu et al.'s HYT and possibly Nord's work do, the way to address disability discrimination is to insist that the moral importance of saving lives does not lie mainly in the effect on overall population health. What matters more is the value of continued life to the individuals facing death, and that value is much the same, regardless of most common disabilities. There may be exceptions in the case of some cognitive disabilities or when there is chronic pain or emotional distress. But rather than modifying cost-effectiveness, decision-makers must be prepared to set it aside in those rare cases in which the incremental cost-effectiveness of a treatment depends on assigning a lower value to saving the life of someone who is disabled than to saving the life of someone in better health. Treatments are rightly constrained by the rights of individuals, including their rights to equal recognition as agents committed to their own projects and to the value of their own lives.

Standard c-e allocation will rarely endorse policies that discriminate against the disabled, because c-e allocation assesses the average effects of treatments rather than their efficacy for particular individuals, and it only compares treatments for the same health conditions. In practice, disability discrimination is an expressive problem that derives from conflating the value of health and the value of life rather than from any actual stigmatization or oppression (Nord 2001a). The *fact* that average health of the U.S. population was lower owing to Helen Keller's disabilities does not mean that her death was a good thing or that her life was inferior to the life of her teacher, Anne Sullivan. Assuming similar life expectancy, we should be as concerned to save Helen Keller's life as the life of the professional tennis player, Serena Williams, even though the population is healthier if we save Serena Williams.

From a public policy perspective, the same value should generally be attached to extending the lives of individuals of the same age, whether or not it makes the same contribution to health. The way to escape the QALY trap is to recognize that individuals have rights to the recognition of their equal attachments to their lives and that accordingly c-e allocation faces ethical constraints.

As suggested above, there are two other kinds of discrimination, which, when wrongful, must be avoided. Allowing differences in effectiveness and in costs to affect the allocation of health care, unlike allowing disability to affect the value of life-saving, is not in itself morally objectionable. The objection is instead to distributions that may result from choosing the most cost-effective health care policies. What these kinds of discrimination call for instead is a recognition that distinctions among treatments in terms of their cost-effectiveness create the *possibility* of wrongful discrimination. When the most cost-effective allocation would result in wrongful discrimination, there is a reason to reject it in favor of an alternative that is not wrongfully discriminatory. How strong that reason may be depends on how serious is the demeaning, exclusion, stigmatization, and harm that the discrimination causes and whether there are other ways of addressing these objectionable outcomes than by changing the allocation of health care.

Avoiding discrimination requires vigilance concerning the consequences of policies for salient groups of individuals who may be facing exclusion and stigma. Which groups these are differ in different societies. The more that the cost-effective policy aggravates these disadvantages and the smaller the loss in aggregate health in rejecting the policy, the stronger the reason to diverge from it. I doubt that there is any general algorithm governing such trade-offs between improving health and diminishing discrimination. The loss in the value of health required to avoid discrimination might be large, or it might be small. The discrimination might be serious or minor; and there might be other ways to lessen the inequalities that give rise to the discrimination. Rather than regarding any wrongful discrimination that allocation guided by cost-effectiveness may cause as reason to jettison cost-effectiveness altogether, cost or effectiveness discrimination should be addressed by a case-by-case weighing of the benefits of lessening discrimination against the costs of diminishing the contribution to overall health.

9.5 Conclusion

Regardless of whether the effectiveness of health care is measured in QALYs, disability-adjusted life years, or as social value–adjusted or public value–adjusted life years, it might appear that one must choose between assigning equal value to the loss of health in each death, which apparently rules out assigning different values to different treatments of nonfatal health conditions or, on the other hand, assigning lesser value to extending the lives of those in diminished health. Neither of these horns of the dilemma is tolerable. Measuring changes in effectiveness in HYT rather than QALYs apparently avoids both horns, but it mistakenly assigns different values to life-saving that results in the same level of population health. The way out of the conundrum is to recognize that the imperative not to allow the quality of one's health state to limit one's claim to life-saving does not rest upon any views concerning the quality of health states (other than that they are not so bad that life is not worth living). To have the same non-instrumental priority for life-saving is a matter of respect, not of health enhancement.

Disabilities are among the factors that determine the costs and the effectiveness of the provision of health care. The fact by itself represents no moral failing of c-e allocation. There is nothing disrespectful in recognizing that health is worse in a society with a larger percentage of individuals with disabilities, so long as one does not confuse this with the conclusion that that society is worse. The greater cost involved in treating some individuals, like the lesser efficacy of certain treatments, is relevant to the allocation of health care. There is often nothing objectionable about taking into account the greater costs or lesser efficacy of treating some people compared to others. In refusing to treat some individuals who are very expensive to treat, as in the case of George and Georgina, the health authority may be behaving properly. If, however, those whose treatment is more expensive or less efficacious belong to some recognized disadvantaged social group, then the health authority no longer has the luxury of focusing almost exclusively on enhancing health. The subsidiary aims of health care to reduce inequalities, stigma, and exclusion and to ensure that all are treated with the same respect and concern then move to the forefront.

10
Health Care
Respectful, Cost-Effective, and Fair

After clarifying in the Introduction and Chapter 1 what health is, why it matters, and how its value is measured, Chapter 2 laid out the structure of cost-effectiveness analyses and Chapter 3 discussed some of the difficulties in making cost-effectiveness precise and implementable. Chapter 3 laid out conceptual issues that must be resolved in order to employ cost-effectiveness analysis, and it presented four charges of unfairness against cost-effective (c-e) allocation, which were discussed at length in Chapters 6–9; these chapters also drew on the discussion of fairness in general and fairness in the allocation of health care in Chapters 4 and 5.

In this chapter, I draw on the discussion of the value of health and health care and of what constitutes a fair distribution of health care to reach some conclusions concerning how health care ought to be arranged. This discussion does not get into the nitty-gritty of exactly what conditions health insurance policies ought to cover, but it does defend the application of cost-effectiveness studies to provide a broad rubric to answer these questions. Section 10.1 argues in defense of universal health care (UHC) on the grounds of efficiency, fairness, freedom, and solidarity. Section 10.2 discusses how UHC should be structured. Section 10.3 argues that for reasons of efficiency, freedom, and solidarity, cost-effectiveness should be one of the main considerations governing UHC. Section 10.4 examines how the four criticisms alleging that c-e allocation can be unfair apply in practice to two examples of actual cost-effectiveness analyses. Section 10.5 draws more general conclusions concerning what can be said about fair health care allocations, and Section 10.6 offers a concluding assessment of the use and limits of cost-effectiveness as a guide to the allocation of health-related resources.

10.1 The Structure of the Health Care System: Universal Health Care

By universal health care (UHC) for a country, I mean a health care system in which everyone has the same access to "a suitably extensive" or "a decent minimum" array of health care, without loss of financial security. What counts as financial security differs across nations and so does what counts as a suitably extensive array of health care. As explained in the Introduction, I shall not attempt to specify how much of the budget should go to health care, but I shall assume that the health care systems in most affluent countries make available an array of treatments that meets the "suitably extensive" or "decent minimum" standard. Extremely poor countries cannot provide satisfactory UHC, but middle-income countries, such as Thailand, can (Sumriddetchkajorn et al. 2019).

Although not beyond all controversy, I believe that the evidence shows conclusively that UHC improves health and financial security compared to unregulated or only lightly regulated health care and health insurance markets, without remotely comparable costs to well-being.[1] The only serious (but in my view unpersuasive) arguments challenging this claim maintain that UHC stifles medical innovation or collapses in bureaucratic incompetence and corruption (Cannon and Tanner 2007; Turner et al. 2011). A strong utilitarian argument rests on these empirical claims about the benefits of UHC. Unlike utilitarians, I do not regard maximizing well-being as the sole moral criterion. To the contrary, I place a great deal of weight on fairness, freedom, and the egalitarian character of the relations among individuals within nations. All of these, I suggest, only strengthen the case for UHC.

This book is concerned with fairness, and so the central question here is whether UHC is fair. Is it fair to require that everyone contribute to the health care of those who need it? What about the libertarian view that individuals have rights to their income and wealth and that they should be free to insure themselves against injury and illness or to refuse to insure themselves, however they wish (Lomasky 1981; Nozick 1974)?

To allow individuals to go without health insurance if they choose not to purchase any runs into serious problems. In the case of infectious diseases, choices not to be treated or vaccinated may pose risks for others, as COVID-19 has made only too obvious. In addition, what are the rest of us supposed to do when uninsured libertarians without wealthy uncles or sufficient funds to pay for their care show up at the emergency room with heart attacks or potentially fatal gunshot wounds? Are they to be escorted out, to die on the doorstep, or, to spare us that distressing view, removed to a discrete temporary lodging in the basement of the morgue? Should we go in search of contributions among wealthy and good-hearted strangers? If one supposes, as suggested in Section 5.1, that everyone has stringent but sharply limited imperfect duties of beneficence, which we enlist the state to fulfill, then we must save the lives of these would-be John Galts or Howard Roarks, unless resources are too limited to do so without major

---

[1] For evidence, see Organisation for Economic Co-operation and Development (2013).

sacrifice. That means that the uninsured are insured after all.[2] Whether they intend to or not, those who refuse to be insured may easily free ride on our benevolence. Many of us are prisoners of our decency. This unpurchased insurance is minimal but real, and it must be paid for.

Some measure of universal health insurance recommends itself as a fair and efficient way for people to discharge a large part of their imperfect duty to aid others. Otherwise, the hospitals and providers where the uninsured show up would have to pass the costs along to paying patients, which is not a fair way to distribute the costs. These duties of beneficence do not stop at national borders, and they are not only concerned with health. However, I shall not discuss duties to the rest of the world or what the duty of beneficence requires outside of health.

In addition, justice and benevolence arguably require that people have extensive freedoms and opportunities. These freedoms are not limited to the absence of interferences from others. For example, Norman Daniels (1985, 2007) argues that subject to resource constraints, a broadening of Rawls' requirement of fair equality of opportunity supports providing everyone within a country with health care that will restore them to full health. Daniels reinterprets fair equality of opportunity to require that all those who have the same talents and exert the same effort have access to the same share of the normal range of opportunities in that society. Health deficiencies deprive individuals of some portion of their share. Thus, Daniels concludes, (remediable) health deficiencies are unjust.

This argument is problematic. It relies on a tenuous distinction between limited "effort" or "talents," which delineate the individual's fair share of the normal opportunity range, and health deficiencies, which prevent individuals from accessing their fair share. Moreover, Daniels' argument supports eliminating inequalities in health, rather than rights to the health care that restores individuals to full health.

Nevertheless, Daniels is on to something important and true: A concern for freedom and opportunity supports UHC. When combined with a benevolent concern for suffering, the interest we have in securing freedom and opportunity grounds a strong case. The requirement of universality is grounded in both impartiality and reciprocity. The financial protection UHC provides, although not directly a matter of health, is justified by considerations of justice as well as by how strongly it bears on well-being and freedom.

It is not enough to point out the benefits of UHC without giving some thought to the fact that the resources that go to health care could be used for policing, transportation, housing, nutrition, education, national defense, or private

---

[2] As Frances Kamm pointed out to me, if these suffering libertarians are conscious and refuse treatment or have provided an affidavit specifying such a refusal, then we have reason not to treat them, but in the circumstances sketched in the text, treatment will not be a violation of autonomy.

consumption. Moreover, a portion of the resources applied to addressing health care needs comes from private consumption choices. Whereas individuals do not purchase shares of national defense, most of the resources going to housing and nutrition come from private expenditures. Health care is a mix, funded everywhere (although in different proportions) by both individual expenditures and government programs. This complicates the specification of the health care budget, which depends in part on how individuals decide to spend their incomes.

Whether administered by the government or provided by a strongly regulated health insurance market, UHC is far superior to an unregulated or only lightly regulated health care system. Much of this argument for this assertion consists of criticisms of alternatives to UHC. The fact that almost every affluent country provides UHC also provides some evidence that it is advantageous. In supposing that there is a meaningful question to be asked concerning how health care should be allocated among the members of the population, both the defense of c-e allocation and all of the objections to it presuppose that everyone has some access to the health care whose allocation is under ethical scrutiny.

10.2 Health Care and Health Insurance: Problems with Markets

The case for UHC rests largely on the peculiar demands and constraints on health care provision. I touched on these issues at the beginning of Chapter 1 to motivate the inquiry into the fairness of the principles governing health care allocation. But the principles that govern how the health care system allocates resources do not tell us how the health care system should be structured to implement the principles. What role should markets play? Should health care providers be paid on a fee-for-service basis or via a capitation fee? Should private health insurance beyond the minimum required by beneficence be available? If these structural questions were independent of the questions about how to allocate health care, then I might be able to ignore them here. But they are not independent. For example, if providers are paid a capitation fee, unlike a fee per service, they have an incentive to undertreat, and the effect would be stronger for health care that has minor benefits. The undertreatment bias of capitation fees could thus lessen the concerns about aggregation of small benefits addressed in Chapter 8.

We want the structure of a health care system, coupled with the principles governing it, to have many virtues. We want it to be efficient, fair, compassionate, caring, responsive to individual values, and opportunity- and autonomy-enhancing. How successfully a health care system manifests these values (which will sometimes conflict with one another) does not depend only on its structure: The principles governing allocation obviously also matter. Nevertheless, the focus in this section is on the structure.

An unregulated market, even if supplemented with vouchers for those who are poor, is inefficient, unfair, and destructive of social solidarity. Such a bald assertion may strike the reader as not only tendentious but also absurd. After all, markets for many services are remarkably efficient. Ron Johnson, a senator from Wisconsin, spoke for many when he wrote the following in an op-ed in *The New York Times* (Johnson 2017):

> The primary goals of any health care reform should be to restrain (if not lower) costs while improving quality, access and innovation. This is exactly what consumer-driven, free-market competition does in other areas of our economy.... Once again, a simple solution is obvious. Loosen up regulations and mandates, so that Americans can choose to purchase insurance that suits their needs and that they can afford.

Knowing just enough economics to understand that markets are remarkably flexible and efficient ways of allocating many goods and services, many are tempted to suppose that markets are the best way to structure every sector of society that allocates benefits and burdens.[3]

Health care is unlike most other services. It is typically needed for only a small portion of one's life, but when it is needed, it may be needed urgently, and it may be extremely expensive. Moreover, the need for health care is often unpredictable and thus difficult to prepare for. Whereas states can leave the provision of food and shelter to the market, supplemented with vouchers for those who cannot pay for themselves, vouchers for health care would either be unneeded, in the case of individuals who remain healthy, or grossly inadequate, in the case of someone who suddenly needs heart surgery.

The only sensible way to address an unpredictable risk such as the risk of urgently needing expensive health care is for individuals to insure themselves, whether the insurance be public or private. In all affluent societies, insurance pays the hefty health bills. Otherwise, only a wealthy minority could afford expensive treatments. One might imagine that individuals could instead save and borrow to finance their health care. But this alternative would require massive saving, which often would be inadequate or excessive.

---

[3] They should read Kenneth Arrow's "Uncertainty and the Welfare Economics of Health Care" (1963) and some of the literature it spawned. Even without understanding the limitations on markets, one ought to be suspicious of Johnson's "simple solution." After all, despite heavy reliance on markets to distribute other benefits and burdens, no affluent nation has put into practice this simple method of allocating health care.

Although insurance is necessary and attractive, due to its virtues in enabling people to smooth their health care expenditures and pool their financial risks, insurance creates problems. First, there is moral hazard (Finkelstein et al. 2015). Possessing insurance that will pay for chemotherapy if one contracts lung cancer or for the treatment of a broken leg will change people's behavior in two ways. First, because it lessens the incentives to avoid getting lung cancer or to avoid breaking one's leg, people will smoke and ski more, and there will be more cases of lung cancer and more broken legs. One suspects that this effect will be small, especially in the case of lung cancer. Free chemotherapy does little to make the prospect of lung cancer alluring. Second, if insurance is paying for treatment, individuals will have no incentive to economize in their choice of treatments. To cope with moral hazard, insurance policies contain deductibles, co-pays, and co-insurance, all of which restore some financial incentives to economize on care. These have large administrative costs for providers, patients, and insurance companies, and it is difficult to find incentives that are large enough to be effective yet small enough that they do not undermine the value of the insurance, especially for the poor. Another way to limit moral hazard is to specify coverage limits that rule out reimbursements for expensive treatments, especially if there are more affordable alternatives. Addressing moral hazard already takes us far from Senator Johnson's vision of individuals choosing insurance that suits their needs. With the complications of coverage limits, deductibles, and co-pays, it will be very difficult for individuals to choose among insurance policies, and what those policies pay for may not be what individuals anticipate wanting.

Another problem, adverse selection, makes it impossible for individuals to purchase insurance that exactly "suits their needs." Insurance that pays for a specific treatment will be a better bargain for those who expect to need that treatment. If individuals are able to purchase insurance that "suits their needs," then, for example, those who have a family history of diabetes or some early signs of the disease will be more eager to purchase insurance that covers treatment for diabetes than those without any reason to believe themselves at risk. Among those purchasing this insurance, there will, consequently, be many more claims than the frequency of diabetes in the population. Premiums must be higher than the average expected cost of treatment per person, and these high premiums will drive away many who would otherwise have insured themselves.

Similarly, insurance for the costs of pregnancy and child birth will attract only those expecting to be pregnant. Its premiums would have to be so high that families would be better off paying out of pocket. The result is adverse selection: Health insurance attracts exactly the customers that insurance companies do not want—which are those who are most likely to make claims. Adverse selection can cause the insurance market to break down altogether. A less dramatic but also unfortunate outcome may be that only a fraction of those who need insurance and who, in the absence of adverse selection, would purchase insurance wind up insured. To protect themselves from adverse selection, insurance companies selling insurance to individuals need to be sure that their policies do *not* precisely suit their customer's needs. If a policy zeros in on exactly the individuals whom the insurance best suits—that is, those who are most likely to make claims—then in order to cover overhead and profits, the premiums will have to be so high that individuals are better off paying out of pocket.

Companies selling private individual insurance on a "free" insurance market must screen out those who most need insurance against specific risks by refusing to insure those with preexisting conditions or charging them higher premiums. Offering such "risk-adjusted" insurance requires costly inquiries into whether individuals have preexisting conditions, and, in the limit, risk-adjusted insurance undermines the risk pooling that makes health insurance socially beneficial. Apart from risk adjustment, the only cures for adverse selection are substantial purchasing pools, such as the mostly healthy employees of large companies, or getting everyone to purchase the same insurance, in which case there is no selection, adverse or not.

In an ideal market for commodities or services, approximated by the markets for stockings or shoe repairs, purchasers have the same knowledge of the characteristics of the commodities and services offered by sellers that the sellers have, and sellers know the preferences and purchasing power of the purchasers. But health care and health insurance are not like that. They are instead characterized by massive asymmetries in information (Akerlof 1970). Individuals may withhold information about their health from the providers and, more commonly, from insurers. Providers frequently know more about the medical needs of patients and the efficacy and side effects of possible treatments than patients or insurers do. Providers thus have an opportunity to exploit patients and insurers by providing unneeded tests or treatments. Patients have an opportunity to exploit insurers by concealing preexisting conditions.

The asymmetry of information between providers and patients calls for some method of licensing or certification, both to lessen the risks that providers will exploit patients and to provide patients with some assurance of their provider's competence. Licensing and certification could be provided by private firms, such as those that provide bond ratings, but without the coercive power of the state, the advantages of licensing are more tenuous. Whether certification is state-provided or private, the need for it introduces an element of regulation that is absent from markets in shoe repair or stockings. Under these circumstances, unregulated markets in health care will not be efficient.

Interferences with markets for health care and health insurance have to be understood against the background of the difficulties posed by free riding, asymmetric information, adverse selection, and moral hazard. These problems demand responses, in the form of market regulation or direct government control. The bottom line is that the inefficiency of unregulated markets rules them out of consideration as acceptable structures within which to allocate health care.

The problems with markets may lead one to jump to the conclusion that even with regulation, private insurance is inefficient and ethically questionable, and direct government provision of health insurance and superintendence of health care is the only attractive alternative. But that is not the case. Consider, for example, the health care system in the Netherlands.[4] Everyone is required to purchase the same comprehensive basic health insurance from one of several competing private health insurance companies. Purchasers have a choice concerning the deductible in the policy, which varies between 375 and 875 euros. Insurance companies compete for customers by the price they charge for the basic insurance package and by the quality of care provided by the health care providers with whom the insurance company contracts. Individuals pay a nominal premium to the insurance company they choose. The revenue of the insurance company is then supplemented from a fund to which all residents contribute. The supplement paid to the insurance companies is adjusted for the risks different individuals pose. Subsidies for the premiums individuals are charged are available to individuals who have low incomes. In addition, insurance companies offer private additional insurance, which most of the Dutch purchase. Because everyone must purchase the same basic insurance, there is no adverse selection for basic insurance. There will be adverse selection for the private add-on insurance, which could be a serious issue if the basic insurance package were not so comprehensive. At the same time, the existence of supplementary insurance lessens the pressure to expand the basic insurance package. Because individuals freely choose among insurance companies, individual choices provide incentives for insurance companies to economize and to improve quality, and the choices of individuals and insurance companies determine a trade-off between the partly conflicting goals of quality and economy. By relying on the choices of individuals, private insurance companies, and mostly private providers to drive the system, within the parameters of the rules I have sketched, decision-making can be decentralized and improved.

A UHC system like the one in the Netherlands is a long way from a simple "Leave it to the market" view. Rather than relying on the market to avoid centralized decisions about the allocation of health care resources, the system in the Netherlands uses the market to implement such decisions.

---

[4] See the National Health Care Institute, "The Dutch Health Care System." https://english.zorginstituutnederland.nl/about-us/healthcare-in-the-netherlands (accessed December 17, 2020); the document, "Health Care in the Netherlands" available at https://english.zorginstituutnederland.nl/about-us/publications/publications/2016/01/31/healthcare-in-the-netherlands and Daley and Grubb (2013).

Neither government provision of insurance nor a tightly regulated market such as that in the Netherlands is without flaws. Unless there are no choices among health insurance policies, adverse selection is always lurking as a problem for markets in private individual health insurance. Moreover, there is strong evidence that people on average make poor choices among insurance policies, increasingly so if they are less wealthy and less well educated (Handel et al. 2020; McWilliams et al. 2011; Bhargava et al. 2017). On the other hand, government control submits the provision of health insurance to the turbulence of political debate and to the sclerosis of bureaucratic management. We can look to the relative performance of existing health care systems that are government administered or guided by choices on heavily regulated markets, but those data do not take us far, owing to the small number of data points, the short intervals in which to observe the success of sophisticated regulated markets, and the influence of differences in culture and mores. For whatever it is worth, the European Health Consumer Index has rated the Dutch system highly.[5]

Unregulated markets for health insurance and health care are unfair because they condition the receipt of health care on the ability to pay, which is not distributed fairly. Although the previous chapters do not lay out a theory of fair access to health care, they find allocation by wealth to be unfair because it conditions the allocation on facts concerning wealth, which are not relevant to claims to treatment. There may be exceptions, where conditioning treatment on ability to pay is fair. Making extremely expensive and experimental procedures available only to those who can afford them may be an efficient and not unfair way of building the capacity to provide such treatment more widely at a lower cost (Deaton 2013). It is debatable whether this rationale for providing some treatments only to those who can afford them makes the practice fair, but it may make it permissible. Be such cases as they may, it would be unfair for an affluent society to allow some individuals who have Lyme disease to suffer because they cannot afford a course of doxycycline.

The unfairness caused by the expense of health insurance can be addressed without appreciable interference with the market by providing vouchers to the poor, with which they can purchase insurance. Preexisting conditions pose a knottier problem. The most market-friendly solution is to set up so-called high-risk pools to provide subsidized insurance to those who cannot purchase insurance privately, owing to the anticipated magnitude of their claims. Although high-risk pools are in principle a solution to the problem of adverse selection that is fair to those with preexisting conditions, in reality they are never funded sufficiently. Those with preexisting conditions never have enough political clout.

---

[5] Ministry of Health, Welfare and Sport. "Healthcare in the Netherlands." https://ses.sp.bvs.br/wp-content/uploads/2016/09/Ministry-of-Health-Welfare-Sports-Daphne-Dernison_13.pdf.

Although not immediately an issue of fairness, high-risk pools also add another layer of inefficiency, in addition to the huge costs risk-adjusted insurance imposes to investigate whether claims involve preexisting conditions.

Although unregulated markets are inefficient and unfair, the large role that markets give to individual choice is an attractive feature. It is of great importance that individuals have a say in their treatment (Engelhardt 1997; Lomasky 1981). Health care decisions are often not purely technical, even though they are often guided by the advice of professionals. Cost-effectiveness aims to determine the menu and not, as it were, the dinner. It is an important input into health care allocation, but it is not the only relevant consideration, especially in individual treatment choices. Treatments will have different risks, and individuals may reasonably have different attitudes toward these risks. Treatments have different short-term side effects, and they may lead to different long-term impairments. The importance of these differs across individuals. A decision about which (if any) chemotherapy to employ may depend on many factors apart from its efficacy, cost-effectiveness, and the severity of its side effects. Some individuals dread nausea, or they may have a horror of being unable to take care of themselves. Some would take huge risks to extend their lives, whereas others are more concerned about the quality of their remaining life. Health care decisions express attitudes toward the human body and mind and the significance of human lives.

Relying on cost-effectiveness as the main consideration determining which treatments will be available free or at low cost is not meant to belittle any of these important aspects of health care. Choices among treatments are not just matters of individual taste: Individuals have moral and religious commitments that rule out some treatments. Because of the importance of choice and self-determination, health care decisions should be responsive to individual values, but that responsiveness must be limited by costs and information about efficacy. Health care in liberal societies is voluntary. Even when seeking care affects the well-being of others, health care systems are reluctant to intervene—as is evident in the tolerance health care systems are currently showing toward those who refuse to be vaccinated against COVID-19. But for the sake of both efficacy and economy, health care systems will not pay for treatments that are inefficacious or only slightly efficacious and at the same time extremely expensive.

Centrally managed UHC can be reasonably responsive. A centralized government-run UHC system can make room for patient input concerning treatments and providers. But the inability to dismiss one's provider and to seek others who are more sympathetic to one's values and biases, no matter how far out of the mainstream they may be, is both a virtue and a drawback of UHC and an argument for allowing a significant role for individual choices via a market for health care. Choice of treatment and provider is a crucial desideratum for health care that may compete with efficiency and fairness. For example, vaccinating children against measles may be cost-effective, but requiring it limits the choices of parents who may object to vaccination. Such limitations may be, as in this case, justified, but the potential conflicts between choice, fairness, and efficiency are evident.

Freedom is important, and unregulated markets in health insurance and health care allow for extensive choice, free of coercion from the government and other individuals. Community-rated insurance with guaranteed issue is not possible without limiting people's choices and forcing people to purchase health insurance that meets minimum standards. Subsidizing health insurance for the poor and for those with preexisting conditions requires substantial taxes, which necessarily limit other choices. However, unregulated private health insurance also limits choices. Individuals whose health history makes it difficult to purchase health care on the open market may be locked into their current jobs or even into marriages. These are serious problems, even if one focuses exclusively on freedom, and they are not easy to cure. There is no health care institution that does not limit freedom.

Negative freedom—the absence of constraints imposed by other people, and especially by the state—is not the only kind of morally significant freedom. There is also *self-determination*—the ability to make one's own choices and successfully execute them—and *opportunity* or *choice*—the range of alternatives that is open to an individual (see Berlin 1969; MacCallum 1967; Hausman *et al.* 2017, Chap. 10). Even if an unregulated market in health care best protects negative freedom, it greatly constrains the range of alternatives that are available to those who are not affluent, and it thus limits the extent to which they can determine their own lives.

Solidarity is an additional important value that weighs in favor of UHC. People need health care when they are vulnerable; and in addition to prophylaxis and cure, health care is, crucially, *care*. In the way we as a society treat those who are vulnerable, we reveal either the bonds that bring us together or the fences surrounding individuals, families, or other groups. Community-rated insurance, whereby everyone of the same age pays the same premium (assisted by vouchers if needed), makes obvious the sharing of risks, unlike risk-adjusted insurance with its illusion (and possibly its aspiration) that insurance serve only to smooth out the risks within each separate individual's life. Community-rated insurance expresses solidarity; risk-adjusted insurance ignores it. Although an unregulated market health care system would surely make insurance available to a large portion of the population, it would celebrate this as the outcome of prudent individual choice rather than as a collective achievement driven by a commitment to caring for one another.

I do not know whether a market system like the one in the Netherlands or some centrally controlled health system like that found in the United Kingdom or Canada is a better way to implement UHC; and at a finer level of details, there are thousands of alternatives, which I shall not discuss. All that this section hopes to have established is that efficiency, fairness, self-determination, opportunity, relational egalitarianism, and solidarity all speak in favor of some form of UHC.

10.3 What Principles Should Determine Which Treatments Universal Health Care Covers?

Consider some UHC system in an affluent country. In a poor country, it may be impossible to provide anything like a decent minimum of health care. No doubt ethical questions remain concerning how to distribute the pittance that is available, but I focus on the coverage decisions that determine the decent minimum. The health care system might rely on regulated markets, like the system in the Netherlands, or it might be government administered, like the systems in the United Kingdom and Canada. These systems provide everyone with access to "basic health care" at little or no out-of-pocket expense. This access is unconditional. It is provided to all residents. Those who engage in activities that pose serious risks to their health may be taxed to cover some of the expected costs, but, for example, chemotherapy for lung cancer that is included in basic health care will be available equally to smokers and nonsmokers. Some UHC systems, such as the Dutch and the English, permit individuals to purchase supplementary insurance to cover health care that is not included in the basic package, whereas others, such as the Canadian, do not.

This section asks what principles should determine which treatments are included in the basic package. Recall that I am using the word "treatments" broadly to include palliative care, diagnostic tests, and preventatives such as vaccinations. Providing everyone with the basic package must not cost more than the health care budget, which I take to be determined by some political process that weighs the importance of different rights to and uses for national income. Moreover, very inexpensive treatments such as aspirin, antacids, band aids, and toothpaste may be left out because it is more efficient and not unfair to leave their provision to individuals, who as residents of a reasonably affluent country should be able to purchase these for themselves.

These features of UHC do not take us far toward specifying which treatments should be covered. Recall the ethical desiderata: The basic health care package should be efficient, fair, and compassionate, and it should enhance freedom and solidarity. Regardless of the institutional form, the provision of health care will be efficient to the extent to which it is cost-effective. With the exception of those low-cost items that are more efficiently paid for out of pocket, an efficient basic universal health insurance package will cover health services that are at least as cost-effective as those health services that are not covered. There are alternative algorithms that can be employed. One might instead look to benefit–cost analysis or willingness to pay for different kinds of health care. One will not reach exactly the same answers because benefit–cost analysis takes non-health effects of policies into account explicitly rather than focusing exclusively on health consequences (Cookson 2003). But for the purposes of determining which principles should govern health care allocation, we can set aside the comparative evaluation of cost-effectiveness and cost–benefit analysis.

It is no surprise that something like cost-effectiveness (with some adjustment for non-health costs and benefits) can be expected to be the most efficient way of allocating health resources—provided that determining what is most cost-effective does not itself demand too many resources. But efficiency is only one value among several. I think that both compassion and solidarity would count against allowing cost-effectiveness by itself to determine the allocation of health-related resources. If one took cost-effectiveness as the sole determining factor, then there would be no "wiggle room" for accommodating unusual circumstances in which compassion or solidarity demands exceptions. However, I do not think that either solidarity or compassion is likely to count either for or against employing cost-effectiveness to serve as a general guide, subject to exceptions and other moral considerations.

Judging whether to rely on cost-effectiveness to allocate health care from the perspective either of well-being or of freedom is complicated. Although I see no conflict between c-e allocation and valuing autonomy, opportunity, or the absence of coercion as well as enhancing well-being, the derivation of effectiveness from preference surveys means that c-e allocation is responsive to off-the-cuff preferences rather than rigorous inquiries into the extent to which treatments enlarge opportunities and limit suffering. Although this is, in my view, a serious flaw in current applications of cost-effectiveness information, the fault lies in the way in which health states and treatments are valued, not in the reliance on cost-effectiveness reasoning.

What role should compassion and solidarity play in allocating health care? I suggest that compassion is impossibly demanding. It will never be content with health care systems that must unavoidably sometimes say "no" to the provision of health care that can be expected to be beneficial. The principles governing a health care system must determine what health care will *not* be provided. The result will inevitably appear to be cold-hearted or even heartless: When Grandpa is denied coverage, we do not see those who are treated with the resources that would have done much less for Grandpa.

Compassion is insatiable: It rebels against every "no" the health system declares. Its demands cannot be met. The most that can be done, after making sure that the decisions to withhold treatment are justified, is to listen to the laments and to honor them as expressing an admirable concern for the suffering and limitations of others. The health system should also leave a space for voluntary charitable interventions, and it should allow some small set of exceptions in especially distressing circumstances. These efforts are likely to bring about unjust results, with those who make a more compelling appeal on GoFundMe getting treatments that are not available to others. But compassion sometimes trumps fairness. Even as the health care system must usually reject the demands of compassion, it should recognize their worth.

How the health care system treats those who are ill is a matter of how we as members of some group—whether it be humanity as a whole or some much more salient smaller groups—care for one another. Solidarity is especially relevant to whether one conceives of health insurance as a way to share the risks and costs of disease and disability or as enabling individuals separately to promote their own health and financial security more efficiently. This difference in how one thinks about health and health care is particularly salient in the disgruntlement currently expressed toward wearing face masks.

10.4 Is C-E Allocation Unfair?

The previous discussion brings us to the main complaint against c-e allocation—that it is unfair—which is the subject of this book. I argued in Chapters 6–9 that apart from discrimination, the complaints against c-e allocation are not justified. But I have not considered how these complaints and the responses to them apply to the actual practice of determining incremental cost-effectiveness and using that information to guide policy.

When one looks more carefully at actual determinations of cost-effectiveness, the criticisms of its unfairness are no more apt. To defend this conclusion, I discuss two examples. Two examples prove nothing, but they put some flesh on the abstract skeletons provided by the arguments in previous chapters.

The first example is discussed in the article "Cost-Effectiveness of Facilitated Access to a Self-Management Website, Compared to Usual Care, for Patients with Type 2 Diabetes (HeLP-Diabetes): Randomized Controlled Trial." In this essay, Li et al. (2018) investigate experimentally whether HeLP-Diabetes—a Web-based self-management program for people with type 2 diabetes—is incrementally cost-effective compared to usual care, which in the experimental investigation included access to a website with useful information. In this investigation, information about effectiveness derives from the self-reporting of health-related quality of life (HRQoL) in a randomized controlled study of 374 participants, half of whom used the HeLP-Diabetes program. During the 12-month trial period, the intervention and control groups had mean HRQoLs of 0.802 and 0.764 with standard errors of 0.016 and 0.023, respectively. The unadjusted difference was 0.038, and after adjusting for the baseline HRQoL of the two groups and other baseline variables, the adjusted difference in HRQoL was 0.020, and the 95% confidence interval stretched from −0.001 to 0.044. The effectiveness in quality-adjusted life years (QALYs) was calculated only for the 1-year period of the trial, abstracting from any lasting effects, including possible differences in life expectancy. The costs within the trial of employing HeLP-Diabetes were used to estimate costs of the non-experimental implementation. Li et al. found that the incremental cost-effectiveness of HeLP-Diabetes compared to usual care was £5550/QALY, which puts it well below the National Institute for Health and Care Excellence (NICE) threshold value for the United Kingdom. Indeed, because it is inexpensive to scale up the use of HeLP-Diabetes, the per capita costs of the program are less than the costs of usual care if more than 363 individuals are enrolled. As is typical in cost-effectiveness analyses, the authors tested the sensitivity of their cost-effectiveness estimates to the various assumptions that the study relies on.

However, the incremental cost-effectiveness depends on the overly precise values of the HRQoL values assigned to health states (e.g., the 243 health states distinguished by the EQ-5D health state classification). Errors and exaggerated precision in those values introduce a great deal of possible error in addition to the standard errors reported.[6] Because HeLP-Diabetes is cheaper than the alternatives when used on a sufficient scale and is unlikely to be less effective, there seems to be good reason to support its use, even if one is skeptical about the calculated incremental cost-effectiveness.

The second study concerns the value of regular screening for lung cancer with CT scans compared to X-rays or no screening at all. Black et al. (2014a) report on the results of a 5-year trial (the National Lung Screening Trial [NLST]) involving more than 5,000 individuals older than age 50 who had smoked for at least 30 years. Each was screened three times a year either with X-rays or with CT scans. Because the cost-effectiveness study was not concerned exclusively with the consequences during the 5-year period of the study, the authors needed to make assumptions about life expectancy and future HRQoL for those screened in one of these two ways or not screened regularly. Relying on these assumptions (and many others)[7] and

---

[6] For evidence of unease about spurious precision within NICE Appraisals Committees, see Bryan et al. (2007). Moreover, relying on self-reported HRQoL introduces the possibility that the HeLP-Diabetes made individuals feel better about the disease without improving their health at all.

[7] Among other things, the authors assumed the following:
- Screening with low-dose CT did not decrease non-lung cancer deaths.
- All excess cases of lung cancer in the CT-scanned group were due to overdiagnosis.
- Radiographic screening compared to no screening would have had no effect on lung cancer mortality.
- Reporting the results of screening exams did not affect quality of life.

self-reported HRQoL derived from the SF36-6D,[8] Black et al. found an incremental cost-effectiveness of CT scans compared to X-rays of $81,000/QALY with a 95% confidence interval stretching from $52,000/QALY to $186,000/QALY. However, as the authors emphasize, this result is highly sensitive to the assumptions listed in footnote 7.

Before considering which criticisms of c-e allocation are pertinent to the practice of comparing the cost-effectiveness of alternative treatments, notice that the use of some method resembling cost-effectiveness studies seems to be unavoidable unless one is willing to tolerate arbitrary and wasteful decisions. Consider the question of whether to screen individuals at risk of lung cancer regularly with CT scans, X-rays, or not at all. Studies had already shown that CT scan screening saves lives, at least within the 5-year horizon of the NLST study. So there is a reason to institute regular screening via CT scans. They are "effective" (life extending), but are they cost-effective? Resources are not unlimited, and they can be used for other purposes than CT-scans of lifetime smokers. Without knowing how much the screening will cost and some quantitative measure of what the benefits will be in additional years of life and lessened morbidity, how could one choose? Proposing to leave it to some political process is no solution because those engaged in the political process are in need of the same information that the ideal health system administrator requires. This is an argument for making some sort of rational comparison of the benefits and costs of alternative treatments, not a defense specifically of cost-effectiveness analysis. Benefit–cost analysis might be employed instead, or one might tote up the costs and list the various benefits of CT scans versus X-rays and, as it were, eyeball the magnitude of the benefit. Moreover, nothing in this argument rules out tempering the pursuit of greater benefits with other ethical considerations or making exceptions on other ethical grounds.

Let us then examine how the four general criticisms of c-e allocation discussed in Chapters 6–9 bear on these examples.

- There was no overdiagnosis of lung cancer in the group screened with X-rays.
- NLST participants have average age, sex adjusted smoker mortality following the trial.
- Costs unrelated to lung cancer were excluded (Black et al. 2014b, pp. 5–6).

---

[8] The SF-36 is a 36-question health survey that was originally designed to provide a qualitative overview of patient health (Brazier et al. 2004). Later Brazier et al. (2002) derived a quantitative measure, the SF36-6D from the SF-36. The SF36-6D has six dimensions of health—physical functioning, role limitations, social functioning, pain, mental health, and vitality—with up to six levels on each dimension, defining 18,000 health states—far more than the 243 health states distinguished by the EQ-5D. A sample of these 18,000 health states was then scored by means of preference surveys, and values for the remaining health states were derived from the values from the preference surveys. The values of the cancer screening methods are computed from the trajectory of individuals through these health states and from mortality data.

10.4.1 Fair Chances

Both examples, like incremental cost-effectiveness studies in general, take for granted an incremental cost-effectiveness threshold and thus implicitly presuppose a distinction between those conditions that are cost-effective to treat and those that are not. This distinction in turn implies that the health needs of some individuals will be met, whereas the needs of others, which may be more urgent, are not met. Fifty-year-old long-term smokers may get CT scan screenings, while colon cancer screening, which also saves lives, is cut back. This would appear to provoke the fair chances objection.

I argued in Chapter 6 that not treating those with weaker claims, even though unfair on Broome's account of fairness, is not per se ethically objectionable. If resources are limited, there may be nothing wrong in treating George with an inexpensive antibiotic and not treating Georgina, who requires a much more expensive antibiotic, even though their needs are similar and equally urgent. The mere fact that cost-effectiveness implies that some claims will be satisfied and others will not be satisfied does not ground an ethical objection to its use, let alone to the details of studies of cost-effectiveness such as the two examples here.

10.4.2 Severity

Those who believe that cost-effectiveness insufficiently prioritizes severity might object to relying on changes in QALYs rather than on a measure such as Nord's social values, which places greater weight on more severe health states. The two examples do not add much to Chapter 7's criticisms of the severity objection. In the NLST and HeLP-Diabetes studies, prioritizing severity would have similar effects on the effectiveness of the alternative treatments being compared and would probably not significantly affect incremental cost-effectiveness. This is not the case in general, but, as argued in Chapter 7, there is no good case for giving a greater priority to the treatment of those whose health condition is more severe than the priority implied by cost-effectiveness (if it were to employ a measure of effectiveness reflecting the public rather than the personal value of health improvements).

As studies devoted to determining cost-effectiveness, it is not surprising that these two do not bear on whether to prioritize severity, which, depending on the interpretation of "severity," may concern the treatment of individual patients more than policies. Those concerned to prioritize severity would seek additional information concerning how "severe" untreated health conditions are, rather than objecting to the measurement of QALY benefits in studies such as the two presented here.

10.4.3 Aggregation

Both of the studies discussed here illustrate one of the central responses I made to the objection to aggregating small benefits or harms when resources could instead be used to provide major benefits or to avert major harms. The improvements in health that HeLP-Diabetes provides are small, as is the benefit of a small increase in the probability of an early detection of lung cancer. Moreover, the resources devoted to studies like these could instead have been used to expand and modernize intensive care units, which, let us suppose, would save more lives.

A health care system justifies providing software for managing diabetes when instead its intensive care units could be expanded and modernized by adding up the small good that the software provides to each of many individuals and finding that sum to be larger than the life-saving benefits to be derived by devoting similar resources to intensive care. The partial aggregation view that grounds the objection to aggregation denies that small benefits are relevant when large enough benefits compete with them for resources. But with respect to treatments such as those studied in these two examples and health conditions in general, small benefits ramify, and the rejection of aggregation is either irrelevant (because the benefits are not really "small") or mistaken.

Although lung cancer is an extremely serious disease, each CT scan provides a small expected benefit—a small probability of detecting developing lung cancer, which itself may turn out to be no benefit at all. On a partial aggregation view, screening with a CT scan and screening with an X-ray are relevant to each other, and a comparison may provide reason not to carry out one or the other screening methods; however, the comparison tells one nothing about whether to do any screening at all until one knows whether there are major health care benefits that could be provided with the resources required by the CT scans and whether those major benefits are balanced by other intermediate-sized health care benefits that are relevant to them. It is difficult to see how any practical method of distributing health care could be defended by those who accept partial aggregation, apart from devoting all of it to the cure of conditions that have a high probability of causing death or a very serious morbidity if not treated.

10.4.4 Discrimination

Chapter 9 identified three different kinds of discrimination, which I called disability discrimination, cost discrimination, and effectiveness discrimination. The most troubling of the three and the only one that offers a general criticism of cost-effectiveness analysis is the first, which assigns a lesser value to saving the lives of those in a worse health state. I sketched a formal technique, health years in total, that avoids this implication, but at the cost of implausibly maintaining that there is more value in saving Florence's life and at the same time curing her disability than in saving otherwise healthy Henrietta's life.

One crucial point, which is illustrated in both the examples, is that incremental cost-effectiveness compares treatments, not individuals. Although the participants in the HeLP-Diabetes study had diminished health, that was not germane to the comparison between information platforms. Nor was the overall health of smokers germane to the decision whether to rely on CT scans or X-rays. Unless there is a correlation between HRQoL of individuals if untreated and particular treatments for the same health conditions—which is unlikely—disability will have little effect on the values of life-saving treatments.

Although none of the three varieties of discrimination discussed in Chapter 9 appears to arise in the NLST or HeLP-Diabetes studies, another sort of discrimination does lurk in these examples, owing to racial and class disparities in the incidence and treatment of both diabetes and lung cancer. Rates of diabetes are far higher among African Americans, Latinos, and Native Americans than among those of European ancestry, and there are also strong (negative) correlations with education (see Centers for Disease Control and Prevention [https://www.cdc.gov/diabetes/disparities.html]). There are also significant differences in treatment, which increase the disparities between the outcomes for Americans of European ancestry and the outcomes for those with other racial or ethnic backgrounds (Heisler et al. 2003). Lung cancer is more prevalent among African Americans than Whites (Schabath, Cress, and Munoz-Antonia 2016) and among the poor than among the wealthy (Sidorchuk et al. 2009). Treatment appears to be more successful among those who are White and affluent (Dalton et al. 2015; but see Aldrich et al. 2013). Measurements of the incremental cost-effectiveness of HeLP-Diabetes and regular screening with CT scans are averages that take no account of race, education, or income, and there is no racial or class difference calculated into their incremental cost-effectiveness.

Because treatment of those who are White and affluent is more effective than treatment of the disadvantaged and the costs are no higher, the cost-effectiveness of treating diabetes and screening for cancer will be better on average than the cost-effectiveness among the disadvantaged. That is to the advantage of the disadvantaged, unless they suffer from other obstacles to treatment. This small advantage does not bear on the comparison between alternative screening or treatment methods.

More relevant might be differences in the response of the health care system to the race and class of those whom they treat and the response by race and class to the HeLP-Diabetes software or to the willingness to show up for lung cancer screening. If, however, the differences in effectiveness of alternative strategies are similar among the disadvantaged as among affluent Whites, then more effective screening and treatment will tend to help proportionately larger numbers of the disadvantaged than of affluent Whites because a larger percentage of the disadvantaged are diabetic and at risk of lung cancer.

These complications, like those involving cost discrimination and effectiveness discrimination, caution those administering the health care system to be on the lookout for disparities across socially salient lines and to address them explicitly, diverging from the cost-effective allocation when it would cause or aggravate unfair discrimination. Exactly how to diverge and how far depends on the details of the case. For example, diabetes is such a major problem among Native Americans that one may want to allot resources specifically to that subpopulation. Perhaps, for example, there is some way to rewrite the HeLP-Diabetes software so that it is more effective with members of this group.

10.4.5 Other Qualms about Cost-Effectiveness

The fair chances, severity, and non-aggregation critiques of c-e allocation have been answered, and the discrimination objections have little bearing on practice. Vigilance with respect to discrimination, coupled with ad hoc modifications where needed, is the best course. This book is thus a defense of c-e allocation *against these four objections*. But it is not a defense of c-e allocation as it is currently practiced because there are other objections mentioned in the Introduction and the first three chapters, and this book does not attempt to compare cost-effective allocation to allocation via benefit–cost analysis. Some of the other objections that were mentioned in Chapters 2 and 3 are technical: Should future health benefits be discounted, as they are in the cost-effectiveness study of cancer screening? And if they are discounted, at what rate? Because incremental cost-effectiveness depends crucially on assumptions about discounting, one has not defended any particular c-e allocation until one specifies whether health benefits should be discounted and at what rate. I argued against discounting the benefits of health care but in favor of discounting the costs.

In my view, a more important problem concerns the classification of health states, the assignment of values to health states, and the commensurability between improvement of health and extension of life. These problems do not point to any flaw in the logic of cost-effectiveness. The difficulties lie in taking QALYs to measure effectiveness and attributing an unjustified precision to the quality weights assigned to health states. The current practice of cost-effectiveness relies on a measure of effectiveness that is somewhat misconceived and whose precision is spurious. Because of these problems, I suspect that formal studies of cost-effectiveness such as the two examples in this chapter will be persuasive only when their conclusions could be reached without calculating incremental cost-effectiveness ratios. When the cost-effectiveness differences are not that large, they are unlikely to be meaningful, even if still useful as a method of reaching agreement, however arbitrary it may be. It seems to me that the argument in favor of HeLP-Diabetes is strong, whereas the argument in defense of CT scan screening is not.

10.5 Conclusions on Fairness in Health Care

It is very difficult to specify what constitutes a fair allocation of health care within some country (let alone throughout the world). First, the allocation of national income across health care, individual consumption, and many other governmental functions, such as defense, education, transportation, housing, and so forth, needs to be fair. Determining how to address these very different individual and collective interests fairly is a major problem. The only practical formal technique is benefit–cost analysis, but there are some theoretical alternatives in social welfare theory (Adler 2012) and work on capabilities (Sen 1985, 1993; Nussbaum 2000; Robeyns 2017). I have not tackled the difficult problem of judging the fairness of cross-sectoral allocation. It is difficult enough to assess the fairness of the allocation of a predetermined and fixed health care budget, which is not sufficient to pay for all potentially beneficial treatments. It is difficult to specify what constitutes a fair allocation of the health budget because needs for health care and properties of treatments are extremely heterogeneous: They differ in strength, quantity, kind, cost, unpleasantness, inconvenience, and the probabilities of outcomes, with or without different treatments.

One can assess the fairness of the distribution of health care from at least three perspectives: a procedural perspective; an ex ante perspective, assessing whether health expectations are fairly distributed; and an *ex post* perspective, assessing the fairness of the distribution of health care by examining the expected distribution of health outcomes. From each of these perspectives, one can say some things that are relevant to evaluating how fair or unfair the distribution of health care is, even though none of these perspectives enables one to define a fair distribution of health care.

Procedurally, access to health care should depend mainly on needs for health care, the efficacies of available treatments, and costs of treatments. Crucial to procedural fairness is treating each individual with equal baseline respect. Equal consideration and respect should ultimately determine which factors should be relevant to the distribution of health care. Exactly what constitutes "equal consideration and respect" is controversial and uncertain. Other contingencies of individual cases, such as special claims due to past injuries caused by harmful health care or for which individuals are themselves responsible, play a subsidiary role. I have not specified exactly what fairness demands concerning how to balance concerns about health care needs, costs, and treatment efficacy. This book has argued that c-e allocation is one procedurally fair method. This shows only that c-e allocation is not ruled out by procedural fairness, not that it is an entirely fair method of allocating health care or fairer than other procedurally fair methods.

Ex ante, fairness in health care is concerned with the availability and coverage of insurance and the probability distributions of risks and consequences of illness and of their treatment. Due to contingencies that there are no known ways of altering, there is no way to equalize expectations among equal claimants nor to proportion health or well-being expectations to the strength of individuals' claims to health or well-being. Because individuals have extremely heterogeneous health complaints and claims to radically different treatments of very different efficacies to address those complaints, there is no simple metric by which to compare the strength of individuals' claims to health care. From an ex ante perspective, the best that can be done is to adopt a procedurally fair process that places weights on claims to health care that depend on costs and expectations of the consequences of treatments for QALYs or some other measure of the value of health outcomes, such as Nord's social values or the public values that I espouse. It is impossible to provide an expectation of health improvement that is proportional to the strength of the claims of individuals to health care. There is no satisfactory algorithm that derives some measure of the strength of claims to health care from information about expected costs and expected QALYs with and without that health care.

With respect to ex post fairness: it is not to be had this side of the grave. There is no distribution of health care that makes any plausible array of health outcomes, considered in itself, fair.[9] Enormous arbitrariness, both biological and social, is overlaid on the pattern of health outcomes determined by individual choices and health care policies, and it is by no means obvious that one can assess the fairness of the proceedings, expectations, or outcomes of a health system in isolation from other relations among a country's populace. An unequal set of health outcomes may be less unfair if its inequalities counteract rather than exaggerate other inequalities. Many health deficiencies arise from chance factors that are morally arbitrary or from causes that are unfair, such as the lead poisoning of those who live in dangerous housing or drink unsafe water. One child grows up with abusive and neglectful parents; another has a loving home; a third experiments unwisely with drugs. One of two children from similar homes has leukemia; the other is healthy. The health care and public health system can

---

[9] If one were to define a fair outcome as the result, whatever it may be, of a fair procedure, then there are fair outcomes if there are fair procedures. But in that case, outcomes provide no information concerning fairness beyond what procedures specify.

lessen these inequalities, but there are limits to what health care can accomplish, especially when resources are scarce. As the result of chance, nature, research, and decisions about what treatments will be available, the distribution of health *outcomes* will not be fair.[10]

If the cost of treatment is not one of the factors determining the strength of claims, then Broome's view that claims to divisible goods should be satisfied in proportion to their strength is irrelevant to the assessment of health care systems, which must be sensitive to costs and cannot apportion health care in proportion to its effectiveness alone. Coverage limits within health insurance mean that among some health conditions that are equally debilitating or risky, some will be treated and some will not be treated.

On the other hand, if cost is one of the determinants of the strength of claims, then perhaps in practice c-e allocation is as fair a criterion for the allocation of health-related resources as one can reasonably expect. In suggesting this, I am not saying that c-e allocation conforms to Broome's account of fairness. It certainly does not. By the standards of Broome's theory or indeed any other, the allocation of health care resulting from a consideration of cost-effectiveness will not be fair, but neither will the result of any other criterion for the distribution of health care, apart from providing no health care at all. There is no sensible way to implement a policy of satisfying claims to health care in proportion to their strength. For example, suppose (plausibly) that claims to setting a broken leg are stronger than claims to an expensive drug for psoriasis, and the health care budget will not cover both. One might think that if there is a less effective but cheaper medication available for psoriasis, then there is a way to apportion the treatments to the strength of claims. But that is not the case, because the claim to treatment of a broken leg is satisfied completely and hence not in proportion to its greater strength compared to the claim to the expensive psoriasis treatment. Because the setting of a broken leg might be better regarded as an indivisible good, one might try to implement Broome's view of fairness by means of a weighted lottery between setting broken legs and treating psoriasis. But would this way of distributing treatments be tolerable or feasible?

10.6 Concluding Words

In casual remarks on February 28, 2017, then President Donald J. Trump stated, "Nobody knew health care could be so complicated." Perhaps by now readers feel

---

[10] It might be possible to make the distribution of health fairer by diminishing the health of the healthy, but I shall suppose that such leveling down is ruled out by efficiency, compassion, and solidarity.

this way (they should!). The complications are ethical, economic, and practical. Both philosophical reflection on moral notions such as fairness and freedom and appreciation of the distinctive economic issues involved in the distribution of health care are essential to understanding and addressing the complications in assessing and improving the allocation of health care. At least five different values are relevant: efficiency (at making people better off), fairness, freedom, compassion, and solidarity. Each of these is in turn a complicated notion in need of further elaboration. Markets for health care face special difficulties because needs for health care services are intermittent, often unpredictable, and sometimes both urgent and extremely expensive. Insurance is necessary to cope, but given asymmetric information, it brings in its wake a host of further complications.

A universal health care system, whether implemented by means of a heavily regulated market or via centralized control, will be efficient if it is guided by something like cost-effectiveness. Although UHC limits negative liberty, its efficiency is itself liberating in making possible wider opportunities and making available more resources for activities other than health care. Cost-effective UHC will not satisfy our compassion, but it is one powerful way to express our solidarity and to move toward a society of equals. To meet our concerns for fairness, care needs to be taken to avoid cost-effective policies that result in oppression or that stigmatize those who are disadvantaged, but there is nothing unfair about withholding cost-ineffective treatment, in aggregating small benefits or costs, or in not giving any additional priority to severity, provided that the value of health is measured properly in the first place. What is cost-effective is unjustly discriminatory when it places a lesser value on the lives of the disabled and when it contributes to stigmatizing, excluding, demeaning, or oppressing people. In such cases, rare as they may be in practice, constraints are called for, which are sensitive to the details of the circumstances.

I have not argued that cost-effective UHC, with modifications when needed to avoid discrimination, is entirely fair. To the contrary, I suggest that there is no satisfactory characterization of a fair health care system. With further formal developments, there may be other ways of balancing the benefits and costs of health care, such as equity-weighted cost–benefit analysis (Frankhauser et al. 1997) and other alternatives such as Fleurbaey et al. (2013). Currently, there is nothing fairer or all-things-considered better than cost-effectiveness, and with significant improvements to correct its measurements of the values of health states, it should be one of the central considerations guiding the allocation of health care.

Acknowledgments and Sources

I have been working on issues related to this book for such a long time that it is difficult to recall all the help I have had, and I apologize to those who have offered criticisms and suggestions that I fail to mention here. Without the criticism of others, this book would contain many more flaws. Most of what is correct and useful in this book has many co-authors.

My interests in the measurement of health, health inequalities, and the allocation of health care resources were stimulated by Dan Wikler, who remains a valued friend and inspiration. Dan was a colleague at the University of Wisconsin–Madison, who, while on leave working at the World Health Organization, invited me to join a stellar ethics consulting group advising the Global Burden of Disease project, which was led by Chris Murray. Murray and Joshua Salomon have taught me a great deal during the past two decades. Members of the ethics consulting group to whom I owe large intellectual debts are Dan Brock (sadly now deceased), John Broome, Norman Daniels, Marc Fleurbaey, Robert Goodin, James Griffin, Frances Kamm, Serge Kolm, Erik Nord, Fabienne Peter, Larry Temkin, and Aki Tsuchiya.

Through meetings with this group and a gathering of ethicists, health economists, and epidemiologists in 1999 in Marrakesh, Morocco, attended by virtually all the leading figures concerned with measures of population health, I received an amazing crash course in health measures. In addition, some of the individuals whom I met in Marrakesh have given me substantial help for many years. Although constantly disagreeing with me, Paul Dolan has been amazingly patient with my questions and criticisms, and his expertise has been irreplaceable. What I learned about measures of population health from the Global Burden of Disease project and the Marrakesh meeting presented me with fascinating questions, which led to a major reorientation of my research, culminating in two books: *Preference, Value, Choice and Welfare* (2012c) and *Valuing Health: Well-Being, Freedom, and Suffering* (2015).

In June 2020, I retired from the University of Wisconsin–Madison after 32 years, and in July I started my current position at the Center for Population-Level Bioethics at Rutgers University. During my decades in Madison, I had terrific colleagues in the Department of Philosophy, the Department of Medical History and Bioethics, the Department of Population Health, and scattered through the university. I am indebted to Dave Kindig, John Mullahy, and especially Denny Fryback from Population Health. Without their instruction, my remedial course in Marrakesh would have been totally inadequate. While helping to supervise Yukiko Asada's dissertation in population health, I learned at least as much from her as I ever taught her.

In Medical History and Bioethics, Norm Fost has been a supportive friend and an inexhaustible source of knowledge concerning medicine and health care. Rob Streiffer and Paul Kelleher, who are also in the philosophy department, have read and commented on my work, and I have learned a great deal from conversations and reading groups with them. Also in the philosophy department, Russ Shafer-Landau has helped me clarify my thinking concerning metaethics, and Harry Brighouse has helped clarify my thinking about fairness, especially concerning opportunity. Although he does not work on the issues this book is concerned with, Elliott Sober has been a great sounding board. Always sensible and incisive, I value my many conversations with Elliott deeply. I co-taught with Erik Wright in the Department of Sociology; he was a unique intellectual resource, and his death and the more recent passing of my former colleague, Andy Levine, have been great losses to me and to many others.

This book arose from the criticisms of cost-effectiveness summarized and synthesized in a superb essay by the late Dan Brock (2003a). I discussed Brock's criticisms superficially in Chapters 15 and 16 of *Valuing Health*, but I knew that I wanted to treat them much more carefully. I began work in the fall of 2017 on an essay questioning the fair chances objection to cost–effectiveness analysis, which became a predecessor of Chapter 6 of this book. I had the leisure to do so in virtue of a sabbatical from the University of Wisconsin–Madison and with support from the Centre for Philosophy of Natural and Social Science at the London School of Economics and Political Science (LSE) as a Ludwig Lachmann Fellow. I am much indebted to both these institutions. While at the LSE, I profited especially from conversations with Alex Voorhoeve.

With the help of far-reaching criticisms of my fair chances essay from John Broome, I decided that I could not condense everything I needed to say about the fair chances objection into a stand-alone essay. Rather than addressing Brock's concerns in a series of essays, I began working on this book. Along the way, I published one essay addressing Brock's concerns about cost-effectiveness, "The Significance of 'Severity'" (2019), a revision of which constitutes Chapter 7 of this book. Erik Nord provided helpful criticism of that essay, and he has been an extremely generous and perceptive critic of my work during the past two decades.

In the fall of 2019, I explored issues concerning fairness further in a graduate seminar at Wisconsin on fairness and equality, and I profited from the perceptive comments and criticisms of the participants: Joel Ballivian, Katie Deaven, Liz Fansler, Megan Fritts, Stephanie Hoffmann, Alex Pho, Marcos Picchio, Glenn Poole, and Emma Prendergast. More recently, I had the opportunity to teach an advanced undergraduate seminar at Rutgers University with Frances Kamm, in which the students read a complete early draft of this book. I am extremely indebted to them and especially to Frances, whose comments were consistently insightful and helpful. The participants in the seminar were Kayla Jackson, Jürgen Lipps, Alpheus Llantero, Harisan Nazir, Audrey Powers, Nathaniel Serio, Deven Singh, and Audrey Xu. Kristi Olson visited one meeting of the seminar remotely and had very helpful things to say about Chapter 5. I am also grateful for Harisan Nasir's help with the index.

My colleagues at the Center for Population-Level Bioethics have been wonderfully supportive. Bastian Steuwer guided me into the complexities concerning partial aggregation, which are discussed in Chapter 8, and he gave me detailed and perceptive criticisms of that chapter and Chapter 7. Nir Eyal, the head of the Center, and I have had many fruitful exchanges, especially concerning risk and the fair distribution of chances. David O'Brien at Tulane University gave me pages and pages of penetrating comments that greatly improved the book. The Center also arranged seminars devoted to two chapters of the manuscript and then, in September 2021, a day-long workshop on the central four chapters. I am deeply indebted to the speakers, Anders Herlitz, Leah McClimans, Debra Satz, and Alex Voorhoeve; the designated commentators, Richard Cookson and James Hammitt; and the other attendees, Mark Budolfson, Nir Eyal, Monica Magalhaes, Bastian Steuwer, Bridget Williams, Dan Wikler, Drew Schroeder, David O'Brien, Yukiko Asada, Erik Zhang, Paul Kelleher, Norm Fost, Gerard Vong, Aki Tsuchiya, Thierry Ngosso, and Lisa Robinson. In December 2021, I presented a lecture drawing from Chapters 5–7 of this book to a seminar jointly organized by the Center for Population-Level Bioethics and the Stockholm Institute for Future Studies, and I am indebted to the comments and criticisms of the participants, including especially Anders Herlitz and Michael Otsuka. I am also indebted to two anonymous referees for Oxford University Press, who provided a great many specific criticisms and suggestions.

While thinking through the issues in this book, I have called upon Richard Cookson several times for help, and he has been generous with his time and expertise. I have also had the good fortune to have supervised David Obrien's remarkable dissertation, which attempts to provide a grounding for distributional egalitarianism in an account of fairness. Although I am not convinced by his arguments and believe that egalitarianism should be concerned with relations among people rather than distribution, David (who now teaches at Tulane University) has been a superb critic and important resource.

The Introduction and Chapter 1 summarize conclusions that I argue for at length in *Valuing Health*, and there are some echoes of *Valuing Health* elsewhere, mainly in Chapter 3. Portions of Chapter 7 derive from "Cost Effectiveness: Finding Our Way Through the Ethical Morass" (2017) and "The Significance of Severity" (2019a), and parts of Chapter 10 derive from my essay

"Economics, Ethics, and Health Insurance" (2019b). Otherwise, the content of this book is new.

With so much help, this book ought to be great, but I'd be pleased if readers find it at least sensible and thought-provoking. Despite all this help, it is ultimately my book, and its blemishes are my doing.

References

Adler, Matthew. 2012. *Well-Being and Fair Distribution: Beyond Cost–Benefit Analysis*. New York: Oxford University Press.

Adler, Matthew. 2019. *Measuring Social Welfare: An Introduction*. New York: Oxford University Press.

Adler, Matthew and Marc Fleurbaey, eds. 2016. *The Oxford Handbook of Well-Being and Public Policy*. New York: Oxford University Press.

Akerlof, George. 1970. "The Market for 'Lemons': Quality Uncertainty and the Market Mechanism." *Quarterly Journal of Economics* 84: 488–500.

Aldrich, Melinda, Eric Grogan, Heather Munro, Lisa Signorello, and William Blot. 2013. "Stage-Adjusted Lung Cancer Survival Does Not Differ Between Low-Income Blacks and Whites." *Journal of Thoracic Oncology* 8: 1248–1254.

Alexander, Shana. 1962. "They Decide Who Lives, Who Dies." *Life Magazine*, November 9.

Allais, Maurice. 1979 [1953]. "The Foundations of a Positive Theory of Choice Involving Risk and a Criticism of the Postulates and Axioms of the American School." In *Expected Utility Hypotheses and the Allais Paradox*, edited by Maurice Allais and Otto Hagen, 27–145. Dordrecht, the Netherlands: Reidel.

American Psychiatric Association. 2000. *Diagnostic and Statistical Manual of Mental Disorders*. 4th ed., text rev. Arlington, VA: American Psychiatric Association.

Anand, Sudhir and Kara Hanson. 1997. "Disability-Adjusted Life Years: A Critical Review." *Journal of Health Economics* 16: 685–702.

Anderson, Elizabeth. 1999. "What Is the Point of Equality?" *Ethics* 109: 287–337.

Ariew, A., R. Cummins, and M. Perlman, eds. 2002. *Functions: New Essays in the Philosophy of Psychology and Biology*. New York: Oxford University Press.

Arneson, R. 2000. "Luck Egalitarianism and Prioritarianism." *Ethics* 110: 339–349.

Arrow, Kenneth. 1963. "Uncertainty and the Welfare Economics of Health Care." *American Economic Review* 53: 941–973.

Aumann, Robert, and Michael Maschler. 1985. "Game Theoretic Analysis of a Bankruptcy Problem from the Talmud." *Journal of Economic Theory* 36: 195–213.

Balaban D., P. Sagi, N. Goldfarb, and S. Nettler. 1986. "Weights for Scoring the Quality of Well-Being Instrument Among Rheumatoid Arthritics: A Comparison to General Population Weights." *Medical Care* 24: 973–980.

Basu, Anirban, Josh Carlson, and David Veenstra. 2020. "Health Years in Total: A New Health Objective Function for Cost-Effectiveness Analysis." *Value in Health* 23: 96–103.

Bennett C., G. Chapman, A. Elstein, et al. 1997. "A Comparison of Perspectives on Prostate Cancer: Analysis of Utility Assessments of Patients and Physicians." *European Urology* 32(S3): 86–88.

Berlin, Isaiah. 1969. "Two Concepts of Liberty." In *Four Essays on Liberty*, 118–172. Oxford: Oxford University Press.

Bhargava, Saurabh, George Loewenstein, and Justin Sydnor. 2017. "Choose to Lose: Health Plan Choices from a Menu with Dominated Options." *Quarterly Journal of Economics* 135: 1319–1372.

Black, William, Ilana Gareen, Samir Soneji, JoRean Sicks, Emmett Keeler, Denise Aberle, Arash Naeim, et al. 2014a. "Cost-Effectiveness of CT Screening in the National Lung Screening Trial." *New England Journal of Medicine* 371: 1793–1802. doi:10.1056/NEJMoa1312547

Black, William, Ilana Gareen, Samir Soneji, JoRean Sicks, Emmett Keeler, Denise Aberle, Arash Naeim, et al. 2014b. "Supplementary Appendix to 'Cost-Effectiveness of CT Screening in the National Lung Screening Trial.'" https://www.nejm.org/doi/suppl/10.1056/NEJMoa1312547/suppl_file/nejmoa1312547_appendix.pdf

Boadway, Robin. 2016. "Cost-Benefit Analysis." In Adler and Fleurbaey, eds. (2016), pp. 47–81.

Bognar, Greg, and Iwao Hirose. 2014. *The Ethics of Health Care Rationing: An Introduction*. London: Routledge.

Boorse, Christopher. 1977. "Health as a Theoretical Concept." *Philosophy of Science* 44: 542–573.

Boorse, Christopher. 1987. "Concepts of Health." In *Health Care Ethics: An Introduction*, edited by D. VanDeVeer and T. Regan, 359–393. Philadelphia, PA: Temple University Press.

Boorse, Christopher. 1997. "A Rebuttal on Health." In *What Is Disease?* edited by J. M. Humber and R. F. Almeder, 1–134. Totowa, NJ: Humana Press.

Boyd, N., H. Sutherland, K. Heasman, D. Tritchler, and B. Cummings. 1990. "Whose Utilities for Decision Analysis?" *Medical Decision Making* 10: 58–67.

Brazier, John, Julie Ratcliffe, Aki Tsuchiya, and Joshua Salomon. 2007. *Measuring and Valuing Health Benefits for Economic Evaluation*. New York: Oxford University Press.

Brazier, John, Jennifer Roberts, and Mark Deverill. 2002. "The Estimation of a Preference-Based Measure of Health from the SF-36." *Journal of Health Economics* 21: 271–292.

Brazier, John, Jennifer Roberts, Aki Tsuchiya, and Jan Busschbach. 2004. "A Comparison of the EQ-5D and SF-6D Across Seven Patient Groups." *Health Economics* 13: 873–884.

Brock, Dan. 1995. "Justice and the ADA: Does Prioritizing and Rationing Health Care Discriminate Against the Disabled?" *Social Philosophy and Policy* 12: 159–185.

Brock, Dan. 1998. "Ethical Issues in the Development of Summary Measures of Population Health Status." In edited by Field and Gold, 73–81.

Brock, Dan. 2002. "The Separability of Health and Well-being." In *Summary Measures of Population Health: Concepts, Ethics, Measurement and Applications*, edited by Christopher Murray, Joshua Salomon, Colin Mathers, and Alan Lopez, 115–120. Geneva, Switzerland: World Health Organization.

Brock, Dan. 2003a. "Ethical Issues in the Use of Cost-Effectiveness Analysis for the Prioritization of Health Care Resources." In *WHO Guide to Cost-Effectiveness Analysis*, edited by T. Edejer, R. Baltussen, T. Adam, R. Hutubessy, A. Acharya, D. Evans, and C. Murray, 289–311. Geneva, Switzerland: World Health Organization.

Brock, Dan. 2003b. "Separate Spheres and Indirect Benefits." *Cost Effectiveness and Resource Allocation* 1: article No. 4. http://www.resource-allocation.com/content/1/1/4

Brock, Dan. 2009. "Cost-Effectiveness and Disability Discrimination." *Economics and Philosophy* 25: 27–47.

Brock, Dan. 2012. "Priority to the Worse Off in Health-Care Resource Prioritization." In *Medicine and Social Justice: Essays on the Distribution of Health Care*, edited by Rosamond Rhodes, Margaret P. Battin, and Anita Silvers, 362–372. New York: Oxford University Press.

Broome, John. 1990. "Fairness." *Proceedings of the Aristotelian Society* 91: 87–101.

Broome, John. 1991. *Weighing Goods*. Oxford, UK: Blackwell.

Broome, John. 2002a. "All Goods Are Relevant." In *Summary Measures of Population Health: Concepts, Ethics, Measurement and Applications*, edited by Christopher Murray,

Joshua Salomon, Colin Mathers, and Alan Lopez, 727–729. Geneva, Switzerland: World Health Organization.

Broome, John. 2002b. "Measuring the Burden of Disease by Aggregating Well-Being." In *Summary Measures of Population Health: Concepts, Ethics, Measurement and Applications*, edited by Christopher Murray, Joshua Salomon, Colin Mathers, and Alan Lopez, 91–113. Geneva, Switzerland: World Health Organization.

Bryan, Stirling, Lestyn Williams, and Shirley McIver. 2007. "Seeing the NICE Side of Cost-Effectiveness Analysis: A Qualitative Investigation of the Use of CEA in NICE Technology Appraisals." *Health Economics* 16: 179–193.

Callahan, Daniel. 1994. "Setting Mental Health Priorities: Problems and Possibilities." *The Milbank Quarterly* 72: 451–470.

Cannon, Michael, and Michael Tanner. 2007. *Healthy Competition: What's Holding Back Health Care and How to Free It*. Washington, DC: Cato Institute.

Chang, Ruth. 2002. "The Possibility of Parity." *Ethics* 112: 659–688.

Chatterji, Somnath, Bedirhan Ustün, Ritu Sadana, Joshua Salomon, Colin Mathers, and Christopher Murray. 2002. "The Conceptual Basis for Measuring and Reporting on Health." Global Programme on Evidence for Health Policy Discussion Paper No. 45. Geneva, Switzerland: World Health Organization.

Claxton, K., M. Paulden, H. Gravelle, W. B. F. Brouwer, and A. J. Culyer. 2011. "Discounting and Decision Making in the Economic Evaluation of Health Care Technologies." *Health Economics* 20: 2–15.

Claxton, K., M. Sculpher, A. J. Culyer, C. McCabe, A. Briggs, R. Akehurst, M. Buxton, and J. Brazier. 2006. "Discounting and Cost-Effectiveness in NICE—Stepping Back to Sort out a Confusion." *Health Economics* 15: 1–4.

Claxton, Karl, Mark Sculpher, Stephen Palmer and Anthony J Culyer. 2015a. "Causes for Concern: Is Nice Failing to Uphold its Responsibilities to All NHS Patients? Comment." *Health Economics* 24: 1–7. doi:10.1002/hec.3130

Claxton, Karl, Steve Martin, Marta Soares, Nigel Rice, Eldon Spackman, Sebastian Hinde, Nancy Devlin, Peter C Smith and Mark Sculpher. 2015b. "Methods for the Estimation of the National Institute for Health and Care Excellence Cost-effectiveness Threshold." *Health Technology Assessment* 19. doi:10.3310/hta19140

Cohen, I. Glenn, Norman Daniels, and Nir Eyal, eds. 2015. *Identified Versus Statistical Lives: An Interdisciplinary Perspective*. New York: Oxford University Press.

Cookson, Richard. 2003. "Willingness to Pay Methods in Health Care: A Sceptical View." *Health Economics* 12: 891–894.

Cookson, Richard, and Anthony Culyer. 2010. "Measuring Overall Population Health: The Use and Abuse of QALYs." In *Evidence-Based Public Health: Effectiveness and Efficiency*, edited by Amanda Killoran and Mike P. Kelly, 148–168. New York: Oxford University Press.

Cookson, Richard, and Paul Dolan. 2000. "Principles of Justice in Health Care Rationing." *Journal of Medical Ethics* 26: 323–329.

Cookson, Richard, Susan Griffin, and Erik Nord. 2014. "Incorporation of Concerns for Fairness in Economic Evaluation of Health Programs: Overview." In *Encyclopedia of Health Economics*, edited by Anthony Culyer, 27–34. Amsterdam, the Netherlands: Elsevier.

Cookson, Richard, Susan Griffin, Ole Norheim, and Anthony Culyer, eds. 2021. *Distributional Cost-Effectiveness Analysis: Quantifying Health Equity Impacts and Trade-Offs*. Oxford, UK: Oxford University Press.

Cooper, R. 2002. "Disease." *Studies in History and Philosophy of Biological and Biomedical Science* 33: 263–282.

Cotton-Barratt, Owen. 2020. "Discounting for Uncertainty in Health." In *Measuring the Global Burden of Disease: Philosophical Dimensions*, edited by Nir Eyal, Samia Hurst, Christopher Murray, Andrew Schroeder, and Daniel Wikler, 243–256. New York: Oxford University Press.

Culyer, Anthony. 2001. "Equity - Some Theory and its Policy Implications." *Journal of Medical Ethics* 27: 275–283.

Culyer, Anthony, ed. 2014. *Encyclopedia of Health Economics*. Amsterdam, the Netherlands: Elsevier.

Culyer, Anthony. 2016. "Cost-Effectiveness Thresholds in Health Care: A Bookshelf Guide to Their Meaning and Use." *Health Economics, Policy and Law* 11: 415–432.

Curtis, Benjamin. 2014. "To Be Fair." *Analysis* 74: 47–57.

Daley, Claire, and James Gubb (Updated 2011 by Emily Clark and 2013 by Elliott Bidgood). 2013. *Healthcare Systems: The Netherlands*. London: Civitas—The Institute for the Study of Civil Society.

Dalton, Susanne, Marianne Steding-Jessen, Erik Jakobsen, Anders Mellemgaard, Kell Vòsterlind Joachim Schurtz, and Christoffer Johansen. 2015. "Socioeconomic Position and Survival After Lung Cancer: Influence of Stage, Treatment and Comorbidity Among Danish Patients with Lung Cancer Diagnosed in 2004–2010." *Acta Oncologica* 54: 797–804.

Daniels, Norman. 1985. *Just Health Care*. Cambridge, UK: Cambridge University Press.

Daniels, Norman. 1993. "Rationing Fairly: Programmatic Considerations." *Bioethics* 7: 224–233.

Daniels, Norman. 1994. "Four Unsolved Rationing Problems." *Hastings Center Report* 24(4): 27–29.

Daniels, Norman. 2007. *Just Health*. Cambridge, UK: Cambridge University Press.

Daniels, Norman, and James Sabin. 2002. *Setting Limits Fairly: Can We Learn to Share Medical Resources?* New York: Oxford University Press.

Darwall, Stephen. 1977. "Two Kinds of Respect." *Ethics* 88: 36–49.

Darwall, Stephen. 2004. "Respect and the Second-Person Standpoint." *Proceedings and Addresses of the American Philosophical Association* 78(2): 43–59.

Dawson, Angus. 2011. *Public Health Ethics: Key Concepts and Issues in Policy and Practice*. Cambridge: Cambridge University Press.

Deaton, Angus. 2013. "What Does the Empirical Evidence Tell Us about the Injustice of Health Inequalities?" In Eyal, et al., edited by 263–281.

Diamond, Peter. 1967. "Cardinal Welfare, Individualistic Ethics, and Interpersonal Comparisons of Utility: Comment." *Journal of Political Economy* 75: 765–766.

Dolan, Paul. 1997. "Modeling Valuations for Euroqol Health States." *Medical Care* 35: 1095–1108.

Dolan, Paul. 1998. "The Measurement of Individual Utility and Social Welfare." *Journal of Health Economics* 17: 39–52.

Dolan, Paul. 1999. "Whose Preferences Count?" *Medical Decision Making* 19: 482–486.

Dolan, Paul. 2011. *Using Happiness to Value Health*. London: Office of Health Economics.

Dolan, Paul, Richard Cookson, and Brian Ferguson. 1999. "Effect of Discussion and Deliberation on the Public's Views of Priority Setting in Health Care: Focus Group Study." *British Medical Journal* 318: 916–919.

Drummond, M., B. O'Brien, G. Stoddart, and G. Torrance. 1997. *Methods for the Economics Evaluation of Health Care Programmes*. 2nd ed. Oxford, UK: Oxford University Press.

Dworkin R. 1981. "What Is Equality? Part II: Equality of Resources." *Philosophy & Public Affairs* 10: 283–345.

Dworkin, R. 1985. "Liberalism." In *A Matter of Principle*, 185–204. Cambridge, MA: Harvard University Press.

Dworkin, R. 1994. "Will Clinton's Plan Be Fair?" *The New York Review*, January 13. https://www.nybooks.com/articles/1994/01/13/will-clintons-plan-be-fair

Edejer, T., R. Baltussen, T. Adam, R. Hutubessy, A. Acharya, D. Evans, and C. Murray, eds. 2003. *WHO Guide to Cost-Effectiveness Analysis*. Geneva, Switzerland: World Health Organization.

Ellsberg, Daniel. 1961. "Risk, Ambiguity, and the Savage Axioms." *Quarterly Journal of Economics* 75: 643–669.

Elster, Jon. 1987. "Taming Chance: Randomization in Individual and Social Decisions." The Tanner Lectures on Human Values, University of Utah.

Engelhardt, H. T., Jr. 1997. "Freedom and Moral Diversity: The Moral Failures of Health Care in the Welfare State." *Social Philosophy and Policy* 24: 180–196.

Eyal, Nir. n.d. "Fair Chances: The Very Notion." Unpublished manuscript.

Eyal, Nir, Samia Hurst, Christopher Murray, Andrew Schroeder, and Daniel Wikler, eds. 2020. *Measuring the Global Burden of Disease: Philosophical Dimensions*. New York: Oxford University Press.

Eyal, Nir, Samia Hurst, Ole Norheim, and Daniel Wikler, eds. 2013. *Inequalities in Health: Concepts, Measures and Ethics*. New York: Oxford University Press.

Fankhauser, Samuel, Richard Tol, and David Pearce. 1997. "The Aggregation of Climate Change Damages: A Welfare Theoretic Approach." *Environmental and Resource Economics* 10: 249–266.

Feeny, David. 2002. "The Utility Approach to Assessing Population Health." In *Summary Measures of Population Health: Concepts, Ethics, Measurement and Applications*, edited by Christopher Murray, Joshua Salomon, Colin Mathers, and Alan Lopez, 515–528. Geneva, Switzerland: World Health Organization.

Feinberg, Joel. 1974. "Noncomparative Justice." *Philosophical Review* 83: 297–338.

Field, Marilyn, and Marthe Gold, eds. 1998. *Summarizing Population Health: Directions for the Development and Application of Population Metrics*. Washington, DC: National Academies Press.

Finkelstein A., K. J. Arrow, J. Gruber, J. P. Newhouse, and J. E. Stiglitz. 2015. *Moral Hazard in Health Insurance*. New York: Columbia University Press.

Fleurbaey, Marc, and Erik Schokkaert. 2012. "Equity in Health and Health Care." In *Handbook of Health Economics*, edited by Mark Pauly, Thomas Mcguire, and Pedro Barros, vol. 2, 1003–1092. Amsterdam: Elsevier.

Fleurbaey, Marc, Erik Schokkaert, Stéphane Luchini, Christophe Muller. 2013. "Equivalent Incomes and the Economic Evaluation of Health Care." *Health Economics* 22: 711–729.

Fleurbaey, Marc, and Stéphane Zuber. 2020. "To Discount or Not to Discount." In *Measuring the Global Burden of Disease: Philosophical Dimensions*, edited by Nir Eyal, Samia Hurst, Christopher Murray, Andrew Schroeder, and Daniel Wikler, 227–242. New York: Oxford University Press.

Frick, Johann. 2015a. "Contractualism and Social Risk." *Philosophy & Public Affairs* 43: 175–223.

Frick, Johann. 2015b. "Treatment Versus Prevention in the Fight Against HIV/AIDS and the Problem of Identified Versus Statistical Lives." In *Identified Versus Statistical Lives: An Interdisciplinary Perspective*, edited by I. Glenn Cohen, Norman Daniels, and Nir Eyal, 182–202. New York: Oxford University Press.

Fryback, Denis. 1998. "Methodological Issues in Measuring Health Status and Health-Related Quality of Life for Population Health Measures: A Brief Overview of the 'HALY' Family of Measures." In *Summarizing Population Health: Directions for the Development and Application of Population Metrics*, edited by Marilyn J. Field and Marthe R. Gold, 39–57. Washington, DC: National Academies Press.

Gamlund, Espen. 2019. "Age, Death, and the Allocation of Life-Saving Resources." In *Saving People from the Harm of Death*, edited by Espen Gamlund and Carl Solberg, 76–88. New York: Oxford University Press.

Gamlund, Espen, and Carl Solberg, eds. 2019. *Saving People from the Harm of Death*. New York: Oxford University Press.

Global Burden of Disease Collaborative Network. *Global Burden of Disease Study 2016 (GBD 2016) Disability Weights*. Seattle, WA: Institute for Health Metrics and Evaluation. http://ghdx.healthdata.org/record/ihme-data/gbd-2016-disability-weights

Gold, Marthe, Donald Patrick, George Torrance, Dennis Fryback, David Hadorn, Mark Kamlet, Norman Daniels, and Milton Weinstein. 1996. "Identifying and Valuing Outcomes." In *Cost-Effectiveness in Health and Medicine: Report to the U.S. Public Health Service, Panel on Cost-Effectiveness in Health and Medicine*, 82–134. New York: Oxford University Press.

Greaves, Hilary. 2020. "Discounting Future Health." In *Global Health Priority Setting: Beyond Cost-Effectiveness*, edited by Ole Norheim, Ezekiel Emanuel, and Joseph Millum, 223–238. New York: Oxford University Press.

Gu, Y., E. Lancsar, P. Ghijben, J. R. G. Butler, and C. Donaldson. 2015. "Attributes and Weights in Health Care Priority Setting: A Systematic Review of What Counts and to What Extent." *Social Science and Medicine* 146: 41–52.

Handel, Benjamin, Jonathan Kolstad, Thomas Minten, and Johannes Spinnewijn. 2020. "The Social Determinants of Choice Quality: Evidence from Health Insurance in the Netherlands." NBER Working Paper No. 27785, September.

Harris, J. 1987 "QALYfiying the value of human life." *Journal of Medical Ethics* 13(3): 117–123.

Harsanyi, John. 1955. "Cardinal Welfare, Individualistic Ethics, and Interpersonal Comparisons of Utility." *Journal of Political Economy* 63: 309–321.

Harsanyi, John. 1977. *Rational Behavior and Bargaining Equilibrium in Games and Social Situations*. Cambridge, UK: Cambridge University Press.

Hausman, Daniel. 1987. "Health Care: Efficiency and Equity." In *Ethical Dimensions of Geriatric Care: Value Conflicts for the 21st Century*, edited by S. Spicker, S. Ingman, and I. Lawson, 67–78. Dordrecht, the Netherlands: Reidel.

Hausman, Daniel. 2006. "Valuing Health." *Philosophy & Public Affairs* 34: 246–274.

Hausman, Daniel. 2007. "What's Wrong with Health Inequalities?" *Journal of Political Philosophy* 15: 46–66.

Hausman, Daniel. 2011. "Is an Overdose of Paracetamol Bad for One's Health?" *British Journal for Philosophy of Science* 62(3). doi:10.1093/bjps/axr008

Hausman, Daniel. 2012a. "Evaluating Social Policy." In *Oxford Handbook of the Philosophy of the Social Sciences*, edited by Harold Kincaid, 607–624. Oxford, UK: Oxford University Press.

Hausman, Daniel. 2012b. "Health, Naturalism, and Functional Efficiency." *Philosophy of Science* 74: 519–541.

Hausman, Daniel. 2012c. *Preference, Value, Choice and Welfare*. Cambridge, UK: Cambridge University Press.

Hausman, Daniel. 2012d. "What's Wrong with Global Health Inequalities?" In *Health Inequality and Global Justice*, edited by Patti Lenard and Christine Straehle, 34–51. Edinburgh, UK: Edinburgh University Press.

Hausman, Daniel. 2013. "Injustice and Inequality in Health and Health Care." In *Justice, Luck and Responsibility in Health Care*, edited by Y. Dernier, C. Gastmans, and A. Vandevelde, 29–42. Dordrecht, the Netherlands: Springer.

Hausman, Daniel. 2014. "Health and Functional Efficiency." *Journal of Medicine and Philosophy* 39: 634–647.

Hausman, Daniel. 2015. *Valuing Health: Well-Being, Freedom, and Suffering*. New York: Cambridge University Press.

Hausman, Daniel. 2017a. "Cost Effectiveness: Finding Our Way Through the Ethical Morass." In *Measurement in Medicine: Philosophical Essays on Assessment and Evaluation*, edited by Leah Mcclimans, 169–186. Lanham, MD: Rowman & Littlefield.

Hausman, Daniel. 2017b. "Responses to My Critics." *Public Health Ethics* 10: 164–175.

Hausman, Daniel. 2019a. "The Significance of 'Severity.'" *Journal of Medical Ethics* 45: 5.

Hausman, Daniel. 2019b. "Ethics, Economics, and Health Insurance." In *The Oxford Handbook of Ethics and Economics*, edited by Mark D. White. New York: Oxford University Press. https://doi.org/10.1093/oxfordhb/9780198793991.013.24

Hausman, Daniel. 2022. "Constrained Fairness in Distribution." *Journal of Ethics and Social Philosophy* 22. https://doi.org/10.26556/jesp.v22i1.1647

Hausman, Daniel, Michael McPherson, and Debra Satz. 2017. *Economic Analysis, Moral Philosophy, and Public Policy*. New York: Cambridge University Press.

Hausman, Daniel and Matt Sensat Waldren. 2011. "Egalitarianism Reconsidered." *Journal of Moral Philosophy* 8(2011): 567–586.

Heilmann, Conrad, and Stefan Wintein. 2017. "How to Be Fairer." *Synthese* 194: 3475–3499. doi:10.1007/s11229-015-0967-y

Heisler, Michele, Dylan Smith, Rodney Hayward, Sarah Krein, and Eve Kerr. 2003. "Racial Disparities in Diabetes Care Processes, Outcomes, and Treatment Intensity." *Medical Care* 41(11): 1221–1232.

Hellman, Deborah. 2008. *When Is Discrimination Wrong?* Cambridge, MA: Harvard University Press.

Hellman, Deborah. 2018. "Indirect Discrimination and the Duty to Avoid Compounding Injustice." In *Foundations of Indirect Discrimination Law*, edited by Hugh Collins and Tarunabh Khaitan, 105–121. London: Bloomsbury.

Henning, Tim. 2015. "From Choice to Chance? Saving People, Fairness, and Lotteries." *Philosophical Review* 124: 169–206.

Hooker, Brad. 2005. "Fairness." *Ethical Theory and Moral Practice* 8: 329–352.

Hutubessy, Raymond, Rob Baltussen, Tess Tan-Torres Edejer, and David Evans. 2002. "Generalised Cost-Effectiveness Analysis: An Aid to Decision-Making in Health." *Applied Health Economics and Health Policy* 1(2): 89–95.

Ismael, Jenan. 2009. "Probability in Deterministic Physics." *Journal of Philosophy* 106: 89–108.

Jacobs, L., T. Marmor, and J. Oberlander. 1999. "The Oregon Health Plan and the Political Paradox of Rationing: What Advocates and Critics Have Claimed and What Oregon Did." *Journal of Health Politics, Policy, and Law* 24(1): 161–180.

John, T., J. Millum, and D. Wasserman. 2017. "How to Allocate Scarce Health Resources Without Discriminating Against People with Disabilities." *Economics and Philosophy* 33: 161–184.

Johnson R. 2017. "Where the Senate Health Care Bill Fails." *The New York Times*, June 26.

Kahneman, Daniel. 1999. "Objective Happiness." In *Well-Being: Foundations of Hedonic Psychology*, edited by D. Kahneman, E. Diener, and N. Schwarz, 3–27. New York: Russell Sage Foundation.

Kahneman, Daniel. 2000a. "Evaluation by Moments: Past and Future." In *Choices, Values and Frames*, edited by D. Kahneman and A. Tversky, 693–708. New York: Cambridge University Press and Russell Sage Foundation.

Kahneman, Daniel. 2000b. "Experienced Utility and Objective Happiness: A Moment-Based Approach." In *Choices, Values and Frames*, edited by D. Kahneman and A. Tversky, 673–692. New York: Cambridge University Press and Russell Sage Foundation.

Kamm, Frances. 1993. *Morality, Mortality, Volume 1: Death and Whom to Save from It*. New York: Oxford University Press.

Kamm, Frances. 2002a. Health and equity. In *Summary Measures of Population Health: Concepts, Ethics, Measurement and Applications*, edited by C. Murray, J. Salomon, C. Mathers, and A. Lopez, 685–706. Geneva, Switzerland: World Health Organization.

Kamm, Frances. 2002b. "Owing, Justifying, and Rejecting." *Mind* 111: 323–354.

Kamm, Frances. 2004. "Deciding Whom to Help, Health-Adjusted Life Years and Disabilities." In *Public Health, Ethics, and Equity*, edited by Sudhir Anand, Fabienne Peter, and Amartya Sen, 225–242. Oxford, UK: Oxford University Press.

Kamm, Frances. 2013a. *Bioethical Prescriptions: To Create, End, Choose, and Improve Lives*. New York: Oxford University Press.

Kamm, Frances. 2013b. "Rationing and the Disabled." In *Bioethical Prescriptions: To Create, End, Choose, and Improve Lives*, 486–505. New York: Oxford University Press.

Kamm, Frances. 2013c. "Aggregation, Allocating Scarce Resources, and Discrimination Against the Disabled." In *Bioethical Prescriptions: To Create, End, Choose, and Improve Lives*, 424–485. New York: Oxford University Press.

Kamm, Frances. 2013d. "Rationing and the Disabled: Several Proposals." In *Inequalities in Health: Concepts, Measures and Ethics*, edited by Nir Eyal, Samia Hurst, Ole Norheim, and Daniel Wikler, 240–259. New York: Oxford University Press.

Kamm, Frances. 2020a. *Almost Over: Aging, Dying, Dead*. New York: Oxford University Press.

Kamm, Frances. 2020b. "The Badness of Death and What to Do About It (if Anything)." In *Almost Over: Aging, Dying, Dead*, 1–30. New York: Oxford University Press.

Kamm, Frances. 2020c. "Moral Reasoning in a Pandemic: Three Things We Need to Get Right." *Boston Review*, July 6.

Keeler, Emmett, and Shan Cretin. 1983. "Discounting of Life-Saving and Other Nonmonetary Effects." *Management Science* 29: 300–306.

Kelleher, J. Paul. 2014. "Relevance and Non-Consequentialist Aggregation." *Utilitas* 26: 385–408.

Kind, Paul, Kristina Klose, Narcis Gusi, Pedro Olivares, and Wolfgang Greiner. 2015. "Can Adult Weights Be Used to Value Child Health States? Testing the Influence of Perspective in Valuing EQ-5D-Y." *Quality of Life Research* 24: 2519–2539.

Kirkpatrick, James, and Nick Eastwood. 2015. "Broome's Theory of Fairness and the Problem of Quantifying the Strengths of Claims." *Utilitas* 27: 82–91.

Klonschinski Andrea. 2014. "'Economic Imperialism' in Health Care Resource Allocation—How Can Equity Considerations Be Incorporated into Economic Evaluation?" *Journal of Economic Methodology* 14: 158–174.

Kornhauser, Lewis, and Lawrence Sager. 1988. "Just Lotteries." *Rationality and Society* 27: 483–516.

Lauer, Jeremy, Alec Morton, and Melanie Bertram. 2020. "Cost-Effectiveness Analysis." In *Global Health Priority Setting: Beyond Cost-Effectiveness*, edited by Ole Norheim, Ezekiel Emanuel, and Joseph Millum, 69–86. New York: Oxford University Press.

Layard, Richard, and Stephen Glaister, eds. 1994. *Cost–Benefit Analysis*. 2nd ed. Cambridge, UK: Cambridge University Press.

Lazar, Seth. 2018. "Limited Aggregation and Risk." *Philosophy & Public Affairs* 46: 117–159.

Lazenby, Hugh. 2014. "Broome on Fairness and Lotteries." *Utilitas* 26: 331–345.

Lefkowitz, David. 2008. "On the Concept of a Morally Relevant Harm." *Utilitas* 20: 409–423.

Le Grand, Julian. 1987. "Equity, Health and Health Care." *Social Justice Research* 1: 257–274.

Li, David, Gordon Wong, David Martin, David Tybor, Jennifer Kim, Jeffrey Lasker, Roger Mitty, and Deeb Salem. 2017. "Attitudes on cost-effectiveness and equity: A cross-sectional study examining the viewpoints of medical professionals." *British Medical Journal* 7(7): e01725.

Li, Jinshuo, Steve Parrott, Michael Sweeting, Andrew Farmer, Jamie Ross, Charlotte Dack, Kingshuk Pal, Lucy Yardley, and Maria Barnard. 2018. "Cost-Effectiveness of Facilitated Access to a Self-Management Website, Compared to Usual Care, for Patients with Type 2 Diabetes (HeLP-Diabetes): Randomized Controlled Trial." *Journal of Medical Internet Research* 20(6): e201.

Lipman, Stephan, Vivian Reckers-Droog, and Simone Kreimeier. 2021. "Think of the Children: A Discussion of the Rationale for and Implications of the Perspective Used for EQ-5D-Y Health State Valuation." *Value in Health* 24(7): 976–982. https://www.valueinhealthjournal.com/article/S1098-3015(21)00141-8/fulltext?_returnURL=https%3A%2F%2Flinkinghub.elsevier.com%2Fretrieve%2Fpii%2FS1098301521001418%3Fshowall%3Dtrue

Lomasky, Loren. 1981. "Medical Progress and National Health Care." *Philosophy & Public Affairs* 10: 65–88.

MacCallum, Gerald. 1967. "Negative and Positive Freedom." *Philosophical Review* 76: 312–34.

Marmot, Michael. 2004. *Status Syndrome: How Your Social Standing Directly Affects Your Health and Life Expectancy*. London: Bloomsbury.

Martin, Danielle, Ashley Miller, Amélie Quesnel-Vallée, Nadine Caron, Bilkis Vissandjée, and Gregory Marchildon. 2018. "Canada's Universal Health-Care System: Achieving Its Potential." *Lancet* 391: 1718–1735.

McWilliams, J. Michael, Christopher Afendulis, Thomas McGuire, and Bruce Landon. 2011. "Complex Medicare Advantage Choices May Overwhelm Seniors—Especially

Those with Impaired Decision Making." *Health Affairs* 30(9). https://doi.org/10.1377/hlthaff.2011.0132

Mehrez, A., and A. Gafni. 1989. "Quality-Adjusted Life Years, Utility Theory, and Healthy-Years Equivalents." *Medical Decision Making* 9: 142–149.

Mehrez, A., and A. Gafni. 1993. "Healthy-Years Equivalents Versus Quality-Adjusted Life Years: In Pursuit of Progress." *Medical Decision Making* 13: 287–292.

Menzel, Paul. 1999. "How Should What Economists Call 'Social Values' Be Measured?" *Journal of Ethics* 3: 249–273.

Menzel, Paul. 2011. "Should the Value of Future Health Benefits Be Time-Discounted?" In *Prevention vs. Treatment: What's the Right Balance?* edited by Halley Faust and Paul Menzel, 245–275. New York: Oxford University Press.

Menzel, Paul. 2014. "Utilities for Health States: Whom to Ask." In *Encyclopedia of Health Economics*, edited by Anthony Culyer, 417–424. Amsterdam, the Netherlands: Elsevier.

Mill, John Stuart. 1859. *On Liberty*. Rpt. Indianapolis: Hackett, 1978.

Mishan, Ezra J. 1971. *Cost Benefit Analysis: An Introduction*. New York: Praeger.

Mishan, Ezra J. 1981. *An Introduction to Normative Economics*. Oxford, UK: Oxford University Press.

Murray, Christopher. 1996. "Rethinking DALYs." In *The Global Burden of Disease: A Comprehensive Assessment of Mortality and Disability from Diseases, Injuries, and Risk Factors in 1990 and Projected to 2020*, edited by Christopher Murray and Alan Lopez, 1–98. Boston, MA: Harvard School of Public Health.

Murray, Christopher, and David Evans, eds. 2003. *Health Systems Performance Assessment Debates, Methods and Empiricism*. Geneva, Switzerland: World Health Organization.

Murray, Christopher, Joshua Salomon, Colin Mathers, and Alan Lopez, eds. 2002. *Summary Measures of Population Health: Concepts, Ethics, Measurement and Applications*. Geneva, Switzerland: World Health Organization.

Murray, Christopher, and Andrew Schroeder. 2020. "Ethical Dimensions of the Global Burden of Disease." In *Measuring the Global Burden of Disease: Philosophical Dimensions*, edited by Nir Eyal, Samia Hurst, Christopher Murray, Andrew Schroeder, and Daniel Wikler, 24–47. New York: Oxford University Press.

Nagel, Thomas. 1979. "Equality." In *Mortal Questions*, 106–127. Cambridge, UK: Cambridge University Press.

Nagel, Thomas. 1991. *Equality and Partiality*. New York: Oxford University Press.

National Institute for Health and Clinical Excellence. 2009. *Guidelines Manual*. London: National Institute for Health and Clinical Excellence.

Neumann, Peter, Gillian Sanders, Louise Russell, Joanna Siegel, and Theodore Ganiats, eds. 2017. *Cost-Effectiveness in Health and Medicine*. 2nd ed. New York: Oxford University Press.

Nord, Erik. 1999. *Cost-Value Analysis in Health Care: Making Sense Out of QALYs*. Cambridge, UK: Cambridge University Press.

Nord, Erik. 2001a. "The Desirability of a Condition Versus the Well-being and Worth of a Person." *Health Economics* 10: 579–581.

Nord, Erik. 2001b. Severity of illness versus expected benefit in societal evaluation of healthcare interventions. *Expert Review of Pharmacoeconomics & Outcomes Research* 1: 85–92.

Nord, Erik. 2011. "Discounting Future Health Benefits: The Poverty of Consistency Arguments." *Health Economics* 20: 16–26.

Nord, Erik. 2012. "Measuring Concerns for Severity: Re-examination of a Health Scale with Purported Equal Interval Properties." *Health Policy* 105: 312–316.

Nord, Erik. 2013. "Priority to the Worse Off: Severity of Current and Future Illnesses Versus Shortfall in Lifetime Health." In *Inequalities in Health: Concepts, Measures and Ethics*, edited by N. Eyal, S. Hurst, and O. Norheim, 66–73. New York: Oxford University Press.

Nord, Erik. 2017. "Public Values for Health States Versus Societal Valuations of Health Improvements: A Critique of Dan Hausman's 'Valuing Health.'" *Public Health Ethics* 10(2). doi:10.1093/phe/phw008

Nord, Erik. 2018. "Beyond QALYs: Multi-criteria Based Estimation of Maximum Willingness to Pay for Health Technologies." *European Journal of Health Economics* 19: 267–275.

Nord, Erik, Norman Daniels, and Mark Kamlet. 2009. "QALYs: Some Challenges." *Value in Health* 12(Suppl 1): S10–S15.

Nord, Erik, and Rune Johansen. 2014. "Concerns for Severity in Priority Setting in Health Care: A Review of Trade-Off Data in Preference Studies and Implications for Societal Willingness to Pay for a QALY." *Health Policy* 116: 281–298.

Nord, Erik, José-Luis Pinto, Jeff Richardson, Paul Menzel, and Peter Ubel. 1999. "Incorporating Societal Concerns for Fairness in Numerical Evaluations of Health Programs." *Health Economics* 8: 25–39.

Norheim, Ole, Ezekiel Emanuel, and Joseph Millum, eds. 2020. *Global Health Priority Setting: Beyond Cost-Effectiveness*. New York: Oxford University Press.

Nozick, Robert. 1974. *Anarchy, State, and Utopia*. New York: Basic Books.

Nussbaum, Martha and Amartya Sen, eds. 1993. *The Quality of Life*. Oxford: Clarendon Press.

Nussbaum, Martha. 2000. *Women and Human Development: The Capabilities Approach*. New York: Cambridge University Press.

Olsen, J. A. 2013. "Priority Preferences: 'End of Life' Does Not Matter, But Total Life Does." *Value in Health* 16: 1063–1066.

Olson, Kristi. 2019. "Impersonal Envy and the Fair Division of Resources." *Philosophy & Public Affairs* 46: 269–292.

Olson, Kristi. 2020. *The Solidarity Solution: Principles for a Fair Income Distribution*. New York: Oxford University Press.

Organisation for Economic Co-operation and Development. 2013. "Health at a Glance 2013: OECD Indicators." OECD Publishing. http://dx.doi.org/10.1787/health_glance-2013-en

Otsuka, Michael. n.d. "Determinism and the Value and Fairness of Equal Chances." Unpublished manuscript.

Ottersen, T., F. Reidun, K. Meetali, A. Kjellevold, H. O. Melberg, A. Moen, et al. 2016. A new proposal for priority setting in Norway: Open and fair. *Health Policy* 120: 246–251.

Parfit, Derek. 1978. "Innumerate Ethics." *Philosophy & Public Affairs* 7: 285–301.

Parfit, Derek. 1991. *Equality or Priority: The Lindley Lecture*. Lawrence, KS: University of Kansas.

Paseau, A. C., and Ben Saunders. 2015. "Fairness and Aggregation." *Utilitas* 27: 460–469.

Patrick, D. L., H. Peach, and I. Gregg. 1982. "Disablement and Care: A Comparison of Patient Views and General Practitioner Knowledge." Journal of the Royal College of General Practitioners 32: 429–434.

Paulden, M. 2014. "Time Preference and Discounting." In *Encyclopedia of Health Economics*, edited by Anthony Culyer, 395–403. Amsterdam, the Netherlands: Elsevier.

Pereira, Joao. 1993. "What Does Equity in Health Mean?" *Journal of Social Policy* 22: 19–48.

Persad, Govind, and Jessica du Toit. 2020. "The Case for Valuing Non-Health and Indirect Benefits." In *Global Health Priority Setting: Beyond Cost-Effectiveness*, edited by Ole Norheim, Ezekiel Emanuel, and Joseph Millum, 207–222. New York: Oxford University Press.

Piller, C. 2016. "Treating Broome Fairly." *Utilitas* 29: 214–238.

Pinkerton, Steven, Ana Johnson-Masotti, Arthur Derse, and Peter M. Layde. 2002. "Ethical Issues in Cost-Effectiveness Analysis." *Evaluation and Program Planning* 25: 71–83.

Prainsack, Barbara, and Alena Buyx. 2011. *Solidarity: Reflections on an Emerging Concept in Bioethics*. Swindon, UK: Nuffield Foundation.

Rawls, John. 1970. *A Theory of Justice*. Cambridge, MA: Harvard University Press.

Rawls, John. 1993. *Justice as Fairness: A Restatement*. Cambridge, MA: Harvard University Press.

Reiff, Mark. 2009. "Proportionality, Winner-Take-All and Distributive Justice." *Politics, Philosophy & Economics* 8: 5–42.

Revicki, D. A., A. Shakespeare, and P. Kind. 1996. "Preferences for Schizophrenia-Related Health States: A Comparison of Patients, Caregivers, and Psychiatrists." *International Clinical Psychopharmacology* 11: 101–108.

Reznek, Lawrie. 1987. *The Nature of Disease*. London: Routledge & Kegan Paul.

Richardson, Jeff. 2002a. "Age Weighting and Time Discounting: Technical Imperative Versus Social Choice." In *Summary Measures of Population Health: Concepts, Ethics, Measurement and Applications*, edited by Christopher Murray, Joshua Salomon, Colin Mathers, and Alan Lopez, 663–676. Geneva, Switzerland: World Health Organization.

Richardson, Jeff. 2002b. "The Poverty of Ethical Analyses in Economics and the Unwarranted Disregard of Evidence." In *Summary Measures of Population Health: Concepts, Ethics, Measurement and Applications*, edited by Christopher Murray, Joshua Salomon, Colin Mathers, and Alan Lopez, 627–640. Geneva, Switzerland: World Health Organization.

Robberstad, B. 2015. Age and severity. *Tidsskr nor legeforen* 135: 1376–1378.

Robeyns, Ingrid. 2017. *Wellbeing, Freedom and Social Justice: The Capability Approach Re-Examined*. Cambridge, UK: Open Book.

Robinson, Lisa, and James Hammitt. 2020. "Benefit–Cost Analysis." In *Global Health Priority Setting: Beyond Cost-Effectiveness*, edited by Ole Norheim, Ezekiel Emanuel, and Joseph Millum, 103–122. New York: Oxford University Press.

Roemer, John. 1985. "Equality of Talent." *Economics and Philosophy* 1: 151–188.

Rowe, Thomas. 2019. "Risk and the Unfairness of Some Being Better Off at the Expense of Others." *Journal of Ethics and Social Philosophy* 16: 44–66.

Rüger, Korbinian. 2018. "On *Ex Ante* Contractualism." *Journal of Ethics and Social Philosophy* 13: 240–258.

Sackett, D. L., and G. W. Torrance. 1978. "The Utility of Different Health States as Perceived by the General Public." *Journal of Chronic Diseases* 31: 697–704.

Salomon, Joshua. 2014. "Techniques for Valuing Health States." In *Encyclopedia of Health Economics*, edited by Anthony Culyer, 454–458. Amsterdam, the Netherlands: Elsevier.

Salomon, Joshua, Colin Mathers, Somnath Chatterji, Ritu Sadana, T. Bedirhan Üstün, and Christopher Murray. 2003. "Quantifying Individual Levels of Health: Definitions, Concepts, and Measurement Issues." In *Health Systems Performance Assessment Debates, Methods and Empiricism*, edited by Christopher Murray and David Evans, 301–318. Geneva, Switzerland: World Health Organization.

Salomon, Joshua, Christopher Murray, T. Bedirhan Üstün, and Somnath Chatterji. 2003. "Health State Valuations in Summary Measures of Population Health." In

Health Systems Performance Assessment Debates, Methods and Empiricism, edited by Christopher Murray and David Evans, 409–436. Geneva, Switzerland: World Health Organization.

Salomon, Joshua, T. Vos, D. Hogan, et al. 2012. "Common Values in Assessing Health Outcomes from Disease and Injury: Disability Weights Measurement Study for the Global Burden of Disease Study 2010." *Lancet* 380: 2129–2143.

Scanlon, Thomas. 1975. "Preference and Urgency." *Journal of Philosophy* 72: 655–669.

Scanlon, Thomas. 1982. "Contractualism and Utilitarianism." In *Utilitarianism and Beyond*, edited by Amartya Sen and Bernard Williams, 103–128. Cambridge, UK: Cambridge University Press.

Scanlon, Thomas. 1998. *What We Owe to Each Other*. Cambridge, MA: Harvard University Press.

Scanlon, Thomas. 2003. "Value, Desire, and the Quality of Life." In *The Difficulty of Tolerance: Essays in Political Philosophy*, 169–186. Cambridge, UK: Cambridge University Press.

Schabath, M. B, D. Cress, and T. Munoz-Antonia. 2016. "Racial and Ethnic Differences in the Epidemiology and Genomics of Lung Cancer." *Cancer Control* 23(4): 338–346. doi:10.1177/107327481602300405

Scheffler, Samuel. 2003. "What Is Egalitarianism?" *Philosophy & Public Affairs* 31: 5–39.

Schokkaert, Erik. 2020. "Equivalent Income and the Well-Being Burden of Disease." In *Inequalities in Health: Concepts, Measures and Ethics*, edited by N. Eyal, S. Hurst, and O. Norheim, 107–125. New York: Oxford University Press.

Schroeder, S. Andrew. 2013. "Rethinking Health: Healthy, or Healthier Than?" *British Journal for Philosophy of Science* 64(1).

Segall, Shlomi. 2016. *Equality and Opportunity*. New York: Oxford University Press.

Sen, Amartya. 1985. "Well-being, Agency and Freedom: The Dewey lectures 1984." *Journal of Philosophy* 82: 169–221.

Sen, Amartya. 1993. "Capability and Well-Being." In Nussbaum and Sen, eds., 30–53.

Shah, K. 2009. "Severity of Illness and Priority Setting in Health Care: A Review of the Literature." *Health Policy* 93: 77–84.

Sharadin, Nathaniel. 2016 "Fairness and the Strengths of Agents' Claims." *Utilitas* 28: 347–360.

Sher, George. 1980. "What Makes a Lottery Fair?" *Noûs* 14: 203–216.

Sidorchuk, Anna, Emilie Agardh, Olatunde Aremu, Johan Hallqvist, Peter Allebeck, and Tahereh Moradi. 2009. "Socioeconomic Differences in Lung Cancer Incidence: A Systematic Review and Meta-Analysis." *Cancer Causes & Control* 20: 459–471.

Singer, Peter, John McKie, Helga Kuhse, and Jeff Richardson. 1995. "Double Jeopardy and the Use of QALYs in Healthcare Allocation." *Journal of Medical Ethics* 21: 144–150.

Slevin, M., L. Stubbs, H. Plaant, P. Wilson, and W. Gregory. 1990. "Attitude to Chemotherapy: Comparing Views of Patients with Cancer with Those of Doctors, Nurses, and General Public." *British Medical Journal* 300: 1458–1460.

Smith, Dylan, Ryan Sherriff, Laura Damschroder, George Lowewenstein, and Peter Ubel. 2006. "Misremembering Colostomies? Former Patients Give Lower Utility Ratings Than Do Current Patients." *Health Psychology* 25: 688–695.

Sober, Elliott. 1980. "Evolution, Population Thinking, and Essentialism." *Philosophy of Science* 47: 350–383.

Spiekermann, Kai. 2021. "Good Reasons for Losers: Lottery Justification and Social Risk." *Economics and Philosophy* 38(1): 108–131. doi:10.1017/S0266267121000043

Steuwer, Basian. 2021a. "Aggregation, Balancing, and Respect for the Claims of Individuals." *Utilitas* 33: 17–34.

Steuwer, Bastian. 2021b. "Contractualism, Complaints, and Risks." *Journal of Ethics and Social Philosophy* 19: 111–147.

Stone, Peter. 2007. "When Lotteries Are Just." *Journal of Political Philosophy* 15: 276–295.

Stuart, Neil. 2001. "Our Changing Social Value and Healthcare: From Social Solidarity to Consumerism?" *Healthcare Management Forum.* https://journals.sagepub.com/doi/pdf/10.1016/S0840-4704%2810%2960418-8

Sumriddetchkajorn, Kanitsorn, Kenji Shimazaki, Taichi Ono, Tesshu Kusaba, Kotaro Sato, and Naoyuki Kobayashi. 2019. "Universal Health Coverage and Primary Care, Thailand." *Bulletin of the World Health Organization* 97(6): 415–422.

Tadros, Victor. 2019. "Localized Restricted Aggregation." *Oxford Studies in Political Philosophy*, vol. 5, ed. David Sobel, Peter Vallentyne, and Steven Wall. Oxford: Oxford University Press, pp. 171–204.

Taurek, John. 1977. "Should the Numbers Count?" *Philosophy & Public Affairs* 6: 293–316.

Temkin Larry. 1993. *Inequality.* New York: Oxford University Press.

Temkin, Larry. 2003. "Egalitarianism Defended." *Ethics* 113: 764–782.

Temkin, Larry. 2011. "Justice, Equality, Fairness, Desert, Rights, Free Will, Responsibility, and Luck." In *Responsibility and Distributive Justice*, edited by Carl Knight and Zofia Stemmplowka, 51–76. New York: Oxford University Press.

Temkin, Larry. 2016. "A Few Concerns About Bioethics." *Ethics, Medicine, and Public Health* 13: 272–287.

Temkin, Larry. 2017. "Equality as Comparative Fairness." *Journal of Applied Philosophy* 34: 43–60.

Tomlin, Patrick. 2012. "On Fairness and Claims." *Utilitas* 24: 200–213.

Tomlin, Patrick. 2017. "On Limited Aggregation." *Philosophy & Public Affairs* 45: 232–260.

Turner, Grace-Marie, James Capretta, Thomas Miller, and Robert Moffit. 2011. *Why ObamaCare Is Wrong for America: How the New Health Care Law Drives up Costs, Puts Government in Charge of Your Decisions, and Threatens Your Constitutional Rights.* New York: Broadside Books.

Ubel, Peter. 1999. "How Stable Are People's Preferences for Giving Priority to Severely Ill Patients?" *Social Science and Medicine* 49: 895–903.

Ubel, Peter. 2000. *Pricing Life: Why It's Time for Health Care Rationing.* Cambridge, MA: MIT Press.

Ubel, Peter, Michael Dekay, Jonathan Baron, and David Asch. 1996. "Cost-Effectiveness Analysis in a Setting of Budget Constraints Is It Equitable?" *New England Journal of Medicine* 334: 1174–1177.

Ubel, Peter, Jonathan Baron, Beth Nash, and David Asch. 2000a. "Are Preferences for Equity over Efficiency in Health Care Allocation 'All or Nothing'?" *Medical Care* 38: 366–373.

Ubel, Peter, Erik Nord, Marthe Gold, Paul Menzel, Jose-Luis Pinto-Prades, and Jeff Richardson. 2000b. "Improving Value Measurement in Cost-Effectiveness Analysis." *Medical Care* 38: 892–901.

Ubel, Peter, George Loewenstein, and Christopher Jepson. 2003. "Whose Quality of Life? A Commentary Exploring Discrepancies Between Health State Evaluations of Patients and the General Public." *Quality of Life Research* 12: 599–607.

Üstün, Bedirhan, Juergen Rehm, and Somnath Chatterji. 2002. "Are Disability Weights Universal? Ranking of the Disabling Effects of Different Health Conditions in 14 Countries by Different Informants." In *Summary Measures of Population Health: Concepts, Ethics, Measurement and Applications*, edited by Christopher Murray, Joshua Salomon, Colin Mathers, and Alan Lopez, 581–592. Geneva, Switzerland: World Health Organization.

Van de Wetering, E. J., N. J. A. van Exel, J. M. Rose, R. J. Hoefman, and W. B. F. Brouwer. 2016. "Are Some QALYs More Equal Than Others?" *European Journal of Health Economics* 17: 117–127.

van Gils, Aart and Patrick Tomlin. 2020. "Relevance Rides Again? Aggregation and Local Relevance. In David Sobel, Peter Vallentyne & Steven Wall, eds. *Oxford Studies in Political Philosophy*. Series, 6. Oxford: Oxford University Press. Doi 10.1093/oso/9780198852636.003.0008

Varian, Hal. 1974. "Two Problems in the Theory of Fairness." *Journal of Public Economics* 5: 249–260.

Varian, Hal. 1975. "Distributive Justice, Welfare Economics, and the Theory of Fairness." *Philosophy & Public Affairs* 4: 223–247.

Venkatapuram, Sridhar. 2011. *Health Justice: An Argument from the Capabilities Approach*. London: Polity.

Vong, Gerard. 2015. "Fairness, Benefiting by Lottery and the Chancy Satisfaction of Moral Claims." *Utilitas* 27: 470–486.

Vong, Gerard. 2020. "Weighing up Weighted Lotteries: Scarcity, Overlap Cases, and Fair Inequalities of Chance." *Ethics* 130: 320–348.

Voorhoeve, Alex. 2014. "How Should We Aggregate Competing Claims?" *Ethics* 125: 64–87.

Voorhoeve, Alex. 2017. "Why One Should Count Only Claims with Which One Can Sympathize." *Public Health Ethics* 10: 148–156.

Voorhoeve, Alex. 2020a. "Healthy Nails Versus Long Lives: An Analysis of a Dutch Priority-Setting Proposal." In *Measuring the Global Burden of Disease: Philosophical Dimensions*, edited by Nir Eyal, Samia Hurst, Christopher Murray, Andrew Schroeder, and Daniel Wikler, 273–292. New York: Oxford University Press.

Voorhoeve, Alex. 2020b. "Why Health-Related Inequalities Matter and Which Ones Do." In *Global Health Priority Setting: Beyond Cost-Effectiveness*, edited by Ole Norheim, Ezekiel Emanuel, and Joseph Millum, 145–162. New York: Oxford University Press.

Voorhoeve, Alex and Marc Fleurbaey. 2012. "Egalitarianism and the Separateness of Persons." *Utilitas* 24: 381–398.

Walen, Alec. 2020. "Risks and Weak Aggregation: Why Different Models of Risk Suit Different Types of Cases." *Ethics* 131: 62–86.

Wasserman, David. 1996. "Let Them Eat Chances: Probability and Distributive Justice." *Economics and Philosophy* 12: 29–49.

Wikler, Dan. 2013. "Reasoning About Rationing." Lecture at Koç University, Istanbul.

Williams, Alan. 1997. "Intergenerational Equity: An Exploration of the 'Fair Innings' Argument." *Health Economics* 6: 117–132.

Wintein, Stefan, and Conrad Heilmann. 2018a. "Dividing the Indivisible: Apportionment and Philosophical Theories of Fairness." *Politics, Philosophy, & Economics* 15: 51–74.

Wintein, Stefan, and Conrad Heilmann. 2018b. "Theories of Fairness and Aggregation." *Erkenntnis* 85: 715–738.

World Health Organization. 1980. *International Classification of Impairments, Disabilities, and Handicaps*. Geneva, Switzerland: World Health Organization.

Wright, Larry. 1973. "Functions." Philosophical Review 82: 139–168.

Wu, S. 2001. "Adapting to Heart Conditions: A Test of the Hedonic Treadmill." Journal of Health Economics 20: 495–508.

Zhao, Michael. 2019. "Solidarity, Fate-Sharing, and Community." *Philosopher's Imprint* 19.

Index

Adler, M., 93–97, 145, 148, 213
administrative ethics, 1, 161
adverse selection, 10, 198–201
age weighting, 50–51
aggregation, 154–177
    partial, 159–177, 210
    weak, 166
Akerlof, G., 199
Aldrich, M.,
Alexander, S.,
Allais, M., 122
Allais paradox, 122
Ambiguity aversion, 124
Anand, S., 43
Anderson, E., 145
Appendectomies, 176
Ariew, A., 14
Aristotle, 66
Arneson, R.,
Arrow, K., 197
Asada, Y.,
Asymmetries in information, 199
Aumann, R., 71

Bankruptcy, 69–75
baseline respect. *See* respect, baseline
basic health-care package,
Basu, A., 185
bedside ethics,
benefit-cost analysis, 24, 25, 205, 216
Berlin, I., 203
bookshelf analogy, 26–33
Boorse, C., 12–14
Brazier, J., 208
Brock, D., 42, 52–54, 61, 111–112, 125, 131, 139, 146, 148–149, 180
Broome, J., 11, 67, 68, 75–89, 92, 96–99, 101, 103, 106, 108, 110, 113, 115–116, 121, 125, 127–130, 142, 162, 175, 209
    on claims, 75–76, 113–114
Bryan, S., 30
Buyx, A., 150

c-e allocation, 23
Callahan, D., 38, 56
Canadian health system, 151
Cannon, M., 194

can openers, 118
capitation fees, 196
capping teeth, 176
Carlson, J., 185
chances, objective, 81–84, 121
Chang, R., 54
citizenship, 59
claims, 67, 92
    to health care, 99–101
    procedural vs. benefit, 81
    voluntary and non-voluntary, 68
    weighing, 79
claims problems, 88, 90
    corrected, 90
Claxton, K., 29, 49
co-pays, 198
coalitions, 71, 75
colon cancer screening, 119–122
compassion, 150–151, 176, 205, 206
consensual gambles, 81, 117, 124
consequentialism, 142
contractualism, 66
convolution, 83
Cookson, R., 44, 146, 205
Cooper, R., 15
cooperative game theory, 70–75, 96
cost benefit analysis. *See* benefit-cost analysis
cost-effectiveness,
    Brock's objections, 53–61
    cost effectiveness ratio, 26
    incremental, 30–32,
    threshold, 27–33
cost-utility analysis, 9
cost-value analysis, 9
Cotton-Barratt, O., 48
coupons, 128
coverage limits, 198
covid-19, 202
Cretin, S., 49, 50
Culyer, A., 7, 26, 28
Curtis, B., 77, 88

Daniels, N., 3, 46, 53–56, 59, 60, 99, 101, 111–112, 122, 195
    fair-chances objection, 53–54, 112
    on universal health care, 195
Darwall, S., 64

deafness, 39
Deaton, A., 201
deductibles, 198
deferral paradox, 49–50
deliberative groups, 10
desert, 67, 91–93
   duty-defined, 67
   intrinsic or rule-determining, 67
   Kantian, 67
   rule-determined, 67
diabetes, 206, 207
dialysis, 2, 93, 159, 168–172
Diamond, P., 54, 55, 122
difference principle, 66
dignity, 65
diminishing marginal utility, 48, 146
disability discrimination. See discrimination: disability
discounting, 46–50
discrimination, 178–192, 210–212
   cost, 180
   disability, 179, 182, 184, 189–191
   effectiveness, 180
   racial, 182
   "reverse," 182
   when wrong, 178, 181–184
distributive weights, 43
Dolan, P., 22, 144, 146
double jeopardy, 180, 182, 184
Drummond, M., 17, 25
Dworkin, R., 104–105, 145

Eastwood, N., 62
efficiency, 3
   vs. fairness, 3
egalitarianism, 93, 119
   distributional, 123, 140, 145–149
   leveling down, 215
   luck, 123
   relational, 119, 128, 145
Ellsberg, D., 124
Elster, J., 62
Engelhardt, H. T., 15, 202
envy-free distribution, 103, 106
epidemic, 114f
epistemic probabilities. See probability
EQ5D, 17, 23
externalities, 37
Eyal, N., 78, 113, 175

fair chances, 111–130, 209
   objection, 53–56
fair equality of opportunity, 195

fair innings, 51
fairness, 213
   comparative and non-comparative, 67, 77
   and equality, 62
   of health-care distribution, 110
   and social values, 44–46
Fankhauser, S., 216
fee for service, 196
Feinberg, J., 77
Finkelstein, A., 198
Fleurbaey, M., 7, 48, 125, 216
freedom, 203
   negative, 203
   self-determination, 203
   choice, 203
free riding, 195
Frick, J., 168, 169, 171
Fugitive Slave Act, 62
functional efficiency, 13, 14
functions, 12–15
   etiological view, 14
   functional ascription vs. functional explanation, 14
   goal contribution view, 14

Gafni, A., 18
Gamlund, E., 51
Global Burden of Disease, 20, 44, 51
Greaves, H., 48
Gu, Y., 134, 137

Hammitt, J., 36
handicap, 100
Hanson, K., 43
Harris, J., 180
Harsanyi, J., 93, 122, 125
health, 4
   of children, 17
   comparisons of, 15–17
   conceptions of, 12–15
   measurement of, 17
   personal or private value of, 22, 35–41, 134–135, 138, 140, 141
   public value of, 22, 37–42, 44, 108, 135
   social value of, 41–45, 138, 140, 141, 187
health care
   access to, 98, 105–106, 108–109
   claims to, 98–101
   goals, 5
   markets, 196–202
   palliative, 175
   universal, 113, 193–196
health claims assumption, 99

health insurance, 10, 194–204. *See also* insurance
health-related quality of life, 18. *See also* HRQoL
    imprecision, 21
health states, 15–23, 34–44, 132–144
health utilitarianism, 36, 43
health years in total, 185–189
Heilmann, C., 71, 88–90, 97
Hellman, D., 180, 181
HeLP-Diabetes, 206, 207, 209–212
Henning, T., 78, 81, 117–118, 123
Herlitz, A., 104
heterogeneity, 102, 108–109, 214
Hooker, B., 63, 77, 78, 89
HRQoL, 18, 35, 36. *See also* health-related quality of life
HUI, 18, 20. *See also* Health Utilities Index

impairment, 100
impartiality, 65–66, 84, 93, 127
imperfect duties, 100, 194
impersonal goods, 158
information asymmetry, 199
Institute for Health Metrics and Evaluation, 20
insurance, 104–105
    community-rated, 199, 203
    high risk pools, 201
    hypothetical, 145
    prudent, 104–105
    risk adjusted, 199, 203
    supplementary, 204
intransitivity, 165, 189
Ismael, J., 83

Jacobs, L., 154
Johansen, R., 137, 140, 144, 145, 150
John, T., 43
Johnson, R., 197, 198
justice, 6
    comparative vs. non-comparative, 6, 92

Kamlet, M., 46
Kamm, F., 51, 55, 57–59, 85–87, 125, 127, 131, 146, 148, 154–156, 160, 162, 167, 180, 188, 195
    on relevance, 57–58
Kant, I., 64–65, 127
Keeler, E., 49, 50
Kelleher, P., 59, 155
Keller, H., 190
Kind, P., 17
Kirkpatrick, J., 62

Klonschinski, A., 142
Kornhauser, L., 83, 123

Lauer, J., 33
Lazar, S., 59
Lazenby, H., 80, 89, 118
lead poisoning, 10
Lefkowitz, D., 166
Le Grand, J., 7, 8
Li, J., 120
liberal state, 38, 39
    neutrality, 40
libertarianism, 5, 195
    and universal health care, 195
licensing, 199
Lipman, S., 17
Lomasky, L., 194, 202
lotteries, 78, 82, 116–122
    explicit, 129
    natural, 122–124

MacCallum, G., 203
markets and health care. *See* health care: markets
Martin, D., 151
Maschler, M., 71
Mehrez, A., 18
Menzel, P., 42
Mill, J.S., 37
Millum, J., 43
moral hazard, 198
Morgenbesser, S., 6
Murray, C., 50, 51
mutual advantage, 66

Nagel, T., 94, 155
National Health Service, 203
National Institute for Health and Care Excellence, 17, 29, 30, 207
National Lung Screening Trial, 207–211
natural lottery. *See* lotteries: natural
negative freedom. *See* freedom: negative
Netherlands, health system, 200, 203
NICE. *See* National Institute for Health and Care Excellence
non-aggregation, 156–159
non-linkage principle, 180
pairwise comparisons, 155, 156, 165, 189
Nord, E., 9, 42–47, 49, 59, 131, 133–134, 136–144, 146, 150, 183, 184, 186, 187, 190
    on severity, 131, 133–134, 136–144
    on social value, 42–47, 49, 184
Nozick, R., 67, 194

nucleolus, 70–72
Nussbaum, M., 213

Obama, B., 15
objective chances. *See* chances, objective
Olsen, J.A., 134
Olson, K., 103
opportunity and health, 99, 195
opportunity cost, 29–33, 107
Oregon rationing plan, 154
Otsuka, M., 82, 118
Ottersen, T., 133

Parfit, D., 57, 146, 158
partial aggregation, 159–177
Paseau, A.C., 62
Patrick, D., 19
person trade-offs, 43, 137, 141
Piller, C., 62
Pinkerton, S., 9
Powers, A., 132
Prainsack, B., 150
preexisting conditions, 10, 199, 201–203
preferences
    elicitation, 19
    and well-being, 19
Prendergast, E., 90
prioritarianism, 57, 94–96, 145–150
probability
    epistemic, 82–84
    objective (*see* chance, objective)
procedural fairness. *See* fairness, procedural
proportional distribution
    of chances, 78–87
    of divisible goods, 75–78
proportional satisfaction of claims, 73–77, 79, 82–84, 87–91, 93, 96, 98, 101, 102, 113, 126–130, 214
public health, 2
punishment and desert, 64

QALY, 18, 19
QALY trap, 184, 190, 191
quality adjusted life year, 18. *See* QALY
Quality of Well-Being Index, 42
Queen Elizabeth, 15

Rawls, J., 65–66, 94, 95, 125, 195
    difference principle, 66
    reciprocity, 65–66, 94, 127
respect, baseline, 64, 65, 82, 113, 124, 156, 163, 179, 181, 213
Reznek, L., 15

risks, 168
    ex ante vs. ex post, 168
    pooling, 203
Robberstad, B., 134
Robeyns, I., 213
Roemer, J., 50, 145
Rowe, T., 148
Rüger, K., 171

Sabin, J., 3
Sackett, D. L., 19
Sager, L., 83, 123
Salomon, J., 20
Satz, D., 105
Saunders, B., 62
Scanlon, T., 37, 66, 86, 146, 154, 155, 160, 161
    on relevance, 154, 160, 161
Schabath, M. B., 211
Scheffler, S., 145
Schokkaert, E., 7, 11
Schroeder, A., 13, 50
scratch cards, 82–83
Segall, S., 123
self-determination, 4, 39, 203, 204
Sen, A., 213
sensitivity testing, 207
separateness of persons, 90, 126
separate spheres, 149
sequential balancing, 163–164
severity, 56–57, 131–153, 209
    acute, 132, 137, 139, 141
    acute vs. chronic, 132–133
    relevant vs. irrelevant, 143, 144
SF36–6D, 208
Shah, K., 137, 140
Shapley value, 72–75
Sharadin, N., 62
Sher, G., 82, 123
Sidorchuk, A., 211
Singer, P., 180
Slevin, M., 19
Smith, D.,
Sober, E., 84
social value. *See* health: social value of
social welfare functions, 93
Solberg, C., 51
solidarity, 150–151, 203, 205, 206
Spiekermann, K., 83, 123
statistical lives, 150
Steuwer, B., 59, 134, 162–165, 167, 169, 171
    on limited aggregation, 162–165, 167
Stone, P., 78, 82, 123
strep throat screening, 159, 168–172

Stuart, N., 151
Sumriddetchkajorn, K., 194
surrogate satisfaction, 78–81, 84

Tadros, V., 165, 167
Talmud, 71
Tanner, M., 194
Taurek, J., 85, 87, 125, 156–158, 160, 165
teleology, 142
Temkin, L., 7, 63, 66, 67, 77, 91–93, 96, 97
time bombs, 135
time preference, 48
time trade offs, 19, 137, 187
Tomlin, P., 59, 68, 69, 99, 166–167
Torrance, G., 19
Trump, D., 215
Turner, G., 194
turn-taking, 113

Ubel, P., 119–122, 136–139, 144, 184
universal health care. *See* health care: universal
utilitarianism, 5, 54–56, 93, 96

vaccination, 37, 202
Van de Wetering, E. J., 135
Van Gils, A., 167
Varian, H., 103
Veenstra D., 185
veil of ignorance, 93, 125, 126
veterinarians, 42
Vong, G., 77, 80–81, 84–85, 92, 118
   on surrogate satisfaction, 80, 81
Voorhoeve, A., 59, 125, 145, 155, 162, 165–166, 175
vouchers, 197

Waldren, M., 93
Walen, A., 166
Wasserman, D., 43, 82, 123
Webster's method, 89
well-being, as preference satisfaction, 19
Wikler, D., 114
Williams, A., 51
Williams, S., 190
Wilson, J., 11
Wintein, M., 71, 88–90, 97
World Cup, 160–161
Wright, L., 14

Xu, A., 133

Zhao, M., 150
Zuber, S., 48